Christianity and Extraterrestrials?

Christianity and Extraterrestrials?

A Catholic Perspective

Marie I. George

iUniverse, Inc.
New York Lincoln Shanghai

Christianity and Extraterrestrials?
A Catholic Perspective

Copyright © 2005 by Marie I. George

All rights reserved. No part of this book may be used or reproduced by any means, graphic, electronic, or mechanical, including photocopying, recording, taping or by any information storage retrieval system without the written permission of the publisher except in the case of brief quotations embodied in critical articles and reviews.

iUniverse books may be ordered through booksellers or by contacting:

iUniverse
2021 Pine Lake Road, Suite 100
Lincoln, NE 68512
www.iuniverse.com
1-800-Authors (1-800-288-4677)

ISBN-13: 978-0-595-35827-4 (pbk)
ISBN-13: 978-0-595-80290-6 (ebk)
ISBN-10: 0-595-35827-6 (pbk)
ISBN-10: 0-595-80290-7 (ebk)

Printed in the United States of America

To my friend Mark

Contents

Introduction	The Purported Conflict between Christianity and ETI	1

Part I
The Possibility of ETI Existence in Light of Christianity

Chapter 1	The Son of Man and ETI	17
Chapter 2	Something Wrong with Being Special?	42
Chapter 3	The Bible's Silence on ETI	59
Chapter 4	What Church Documents and Tradition Say about ETI	61

Part II
The Improbability of ETI Existence in Light of Christianity

Chapter 5	Plenitude or Redundancy?	79
Chapter 6	Probable Arguments that Humans are Unique on the Supposition of One Incarnation: The Case of the Fallen ETIs	90
Chapter 7	Probable Arguments that Humans are Unique on the Supposition of One Incarnation: The Case of the Unfallen ETIs	109
Chapter 8	Probable Arguments that Humans are Unique on the Supposition of More than One Incarnation	116

Part III
Weaknesses in Arguments in Favor of ETI Existence

Chapter 9	Weaknesses of Arguments in Favor of ETI Existence Derived from Science	123
Chapter 10	The Fermi Paradox	137

| Chapter 11 | Philosophical Arguments concerning ETI ....143 |
| Chapter 12 | Fallacious Arguments for ETI Existence ....159 |

Part IV
How Would Church Teaching be Affected if Contact were Made?

Chapter 13	Would Adjustments to Catholic Teaching Have to be Made if ETI was Discovered? 167
Chapter 14	Do ETI Proponents Have an anti-Christian Agenda? ..180
Chapter 15	What Might the Catholic Church Say on the ETI Question? 183

Epilogue 195
Endnotes 197
Bibliography 267
Name Index 279
Scripture Index 283
Subject Index 287

Acknowledgements

I wish to thank those who responded to my email queries, sent me their articles, suggested readings to me, or discussed various ETI issues with me: Mariano Artigas, Robert Augros, Duane Berquist, Sean Collins, Christopher Corbally, S.J., George Coyne, S.J., David Darling, Robert Gahl, Sameh Habiel, Christopher Kaiser, Alfred Karcher, Nino Languilli, Rafael Martinez, Mark Murray, Thomas O'Meara, O.P., Oliver Putz, Gregory Rupp, Martin Schoonen, Cynthia Smith, Glenn Statile, Laura Synder, Allen Tough, and Mark Wyman. Ellen K. George and Wendy Biondi also deserve a thank you for getting me to watch some ETI movies. I would also like to express my appreciation to Jolanta Lisowska for doing the cover design.

Above all, I wish to thank those who so generously read and commented upon the entire manuscript: Michael Augros, Michael Crowe, Christopher DeCaen, and Warren Murray—your help was invaluable to me.

This book is published under the auspices of the Society for Aristotelian Studies as the first volume in the series, *Philosophia Perennis* (general editor: Yvan Pelletier). The Society for Aristotelian Studies is a non-profit, learned society composed of individuals having a strong interest in the Aristotelian philosophical tradition. The SAS accords a privileged place to Thomas Aquinas, for among all the philosophers who embraced Aristotelian principles none carried them to the same heights as he. Conscious of the necessity of a living tradition, the SAS accords considerable importance to applying Aristotelian thought to the problems of the day, especially in the areas of philosophy of science, ethics and politics. For more information, go to the SAS website at www.aristotelian.org/.

Introduction

The Purported Conflict between Christianity and ETI

"In many and various ways God spoke of old to our fathers by the prophets, but in these last days he has spoken to us by a Son." Christ, the Son of God made man, is the Father's one, perfect, and unsurpassable Word. In him he has said everything; there will be no other word than this one. St. John of the Cross, among others, commented strikingly on Hebrews 1:1-2: "In giving us his Son, his only Word (for he possesses no other), he spoke everything to us at once in this sole Word—and he has no more to say...because what he spoke before to the prophets in parts, he has now spoken all at once by giving us the All Who is His Son. Any person questioning God or desiring some vision or revelation would be guilty not only of foolish behavior but also of offending him, by not fixing his eyes entirely upon Christ and by living with the desire for some other novelty."

—*Catechism of the Catholic Church*

It would seem to be common sense that one first determine whether something exists, before one goes on to examine how it relates to something else. Whence one of the more frequent objections to my project has been: Why waste time on speculating about how intelligent extraterrestrials (ETIs)[1] relate to Christianity when we do not even know that they exist? What possible point could there be to making statements such as that Robert Jastrow makes in *God for the 21st Century*: "If and when the communication with advanced life occurs, I believe these implications will have a transforming effect on Western religion, requiring far greater adjustments in theological thought than those prompted by the discovery that the Earth revolves around the Sun or even the evidence in the fossil record that seems to link humans to simpler forms of life."[2] After all, one can contemplate the consequences of hypotheses to no end: if Jupiter is made of cheese, then it will go well with wine.

Historically, however, many have regarded the discovery of ETI as highly probable, if not virtually certain, and people are even more prone to believe that it is the case in our age of telescopes, satellites, space travel, and dramatic advances in biological knowledge. Popular interest in movies such as *Contact*, presentations such as the American Natural History Museum's "The Search for Life: Are We Alone? (2002), the numerous websites concerning UFO's and aliens, and the private and public funding of SETI (Search for Extraterrestrial Intelligence), are all indications of the positive reception the general public nowadays gives to the notion that we are not alone.

Some have used this supposed population of other planets as grounds to discredit Christianity with its belief in one Lord, Jesus Christ, who died to save the members of the race of Adam. Probably the most often cited of past authors who pit Christianity and ETI against each other is Thomas Paine who holds that: "The two beliefs cannot be held together in the same mind; and he who thinks that he believes in both has thought but little of either."[3] Nowadays it appears that an increasing number of authors espouse Paine's point of view. One indication of this is the essays in Steven Dick's *Many Worlds: The New Universe, Extraterrestrial Life & the Theological Implications* (2002). The majority of contributors either are more or less explicitly opposed to organized religion, Christianity included, or advocate some form of pantheism as being most in keeping with ETI existence. It is true that this may be a non-representative sample given that the editor himself is of the view that: "It may be that in learning of alien religions, of alien ways of relating to superior beings, the scope of terrestrial religion will be greatly expanded in ways we cannot foresee…there is no basis for expecting convergence of theistic ideas by intelligences on other planets throughout the universe."[4] Be that as it may, there is no dearth of recent authors espousing like positions. For instance, Paul Davies maintains that "it is hard to see how the world's great religions could continue in anything like their present form should an alien message be received."[5] And Robert Jastrow in *God for the 21st Century* suggests that "some of the older races [of ETI] might be…superior in their moral and ethical values and religious beliefs. Does this not create problems for the traditional Judeo-Christian view of the Deity as being very much concerned with the affairs of the particular race of intelligent beings that exists on our planet?"[6] The Benedictine priest, Stanley Jaki, goes so far as to say that ETI advocates' unspoken agenda is to discredit Christianity.[7] While there are doubtlessly many other reasons that people are interested in ETI, it is plain that ETI is used by quite a few as a justification of their rejection of Christianity.

As premature as a consideration of the relation of the discovery of ETI to Christianity is from the point of view of strict logic, this consideration is being engaged in by growing numbers, in a manner more and more frequently turned to Christianity's detriment. Whence my principal purpose is to show that on the supposition that ETI exists, it is not the case that the Christian faith must be rejected as incompatible with its existence, and those who hold otherwise are using faulty reasoning. I am certainly not the first Catholic author to undertake such a task. However, writings on the subject in the 20th and 21st centuries from a Catholic perspective have been relatively scarce. Steven Dick in *The 20th Century Extraterrestrial Life Debate* names Kenneth Delano's *Many Worlds, One God*[8] as "the most substantial theological discussion of the subject, and the closest the Roman Catholic Church came to an official position."[9] Delano's book, however, while making some important points, is heavier on rhetoric than on substance (as I will show in some detail in chapter twelve). I am unaware of any other book-length treatment of the subject in modern times that approaches the question from a distinctly Catholic perspective.

The Catholic authors who have recently treated certain aspects of the question do so in the form of articles or chapters, where the standard for length limits the scope of their investigations. Although much profit is to be derived from these authors, there are two shortcomings found in quite a few, though not all, of their works. The first is that while the authors give reasons why there is no incompatibility between Catholicism and ETI existence, they do not always make clear why someone would think other, nor do they tend to take up and refute arguments such as those offered by Thomas Paine who dismisses Christianity in favor of ETI. Secondly, they generally do not consider whether the passages of Scripture of a more cosmic bearing may not shed some light on the matter. So one of my goals is to be more exhaustive and explicit in the treatment of adversarial arguments. A second is to look systematically through Scripture to see whether there are not passages relevant to the debate.

Another shortcoming found in some Catholic authors is that they are quite willing to countenance interpretations of doctrines such as original sin which contradict Church teachings that are stated in official Church documents. I intend to address the matter of ETI existence while standing squarely within official Church teachings as found in the papal encyclicals, Conciliar documents, and the *Catechism of the Catholic Church*. In regard to matters not defined by the Church, I use as my guide the traditional teachings found in the writings of the Fathers and Doctors of the Church,[10] and particularly in the works St. Thomas Aquinas. I share the confidence of Thomas Aquinas that there can be no conflict between faith and reason, and thus that the Catholic faith has no need to make concessions as to its teachings in order to withstand attacks from those who claim that ETI existence would spell the end of traditional religion.

Granted that my chief purpose is to clarify what, if any, incompatibility there is between *Catholic* Christian beliefs and the existence of ETIs, still, much of what I have to say will be of interest to non-Catholic Christians. I quote Scriptural passages on numerous occasions. Also, the ETI debate touches upon very fundamental issues such as the Incarnation about which many Christian faith communities share common beliefs. To the extent that there are differences, it may be of interest to some what consequences they might have in regard to the ETI question.

I have another goal in addition to that of showing that Christian belief and ETI existence are not as such mutually exclusive. It is to make a probable case that ETI does not exist. Whether ETI exists is a separate question from whether ETI existence is compatible with Christianity, assuming that it does exist. I choose to also examine the former question mainly because doing so sheds light on a common confusion regarding the ETI-Christianity (in)compatibility question. All too frequently probable arguments against ETI existence are mistaken for arguments that would definitively close the door to the possibility of their existence, with the result that Christianity seems in greater opposition to ETI existence than it perhaps actually is. I am also pursuing the question of ETI existence because of its own intrinsic interest. My arguments regarding this question are admittedly even more speculative than those regarding the compatibility question. However, not only do they help clear up confusion about the compatibility question, they also provide one an opportunity to indulge one's natural curiosity about the nature of the universe, to reflect on human nature and its condition,[11] and for those of us who are Christian, to reflect upon the truths of the faith, as well.

Probable arguments for and against ETI existence can be drawn from a number of disciplines: the sciences, philosophy, and theology. I intend to examine the arguments for and against ETI existence taken from philosophy and Catholic theology (including Sacred Scripture). I do not intend to delve into the science concerning the probability of ETI, as this changes from year to year,[12] with one exception: I do intend to treat fallacies commonly slipped into in scientific discussions of the likelihood of ETI concerning the probability of there being other inhabitable planets, and of life actually originating and complexifying, which treatment requires only some fairly general knowledge of science, along with knowledge of what constitutes fallacious reasoning. I do not intend to investigate particular phenomena such crop circles, UFO abduction stories, etc., which are taken by some to be genuine signs of ETI existence. Skeptical investigators have already debunked some of the purported evidence of this sort, and will doubtlessly continue to do so. Investigating individual reports, however, is an unending task, and even when specific cases are now known to be hoaxes, this does not prove that all such phenomena have causes other than ETIs. One way or the other, my main thesis that Christianity and ETI existence are not incompatible is not affected. Obviously my second thesis that ETIs do not exist would be called into question if sufficient evidence accumulated such that one could rule out natural, human, and demonic/angelic causes for these phenomena.

The ETI-Christianity debate plainly involves questions that are theological. Given that I am a philosopher, and not a theologian, my work will be more circumscribed than it otherwise might be. Certain issues requiring the highest theological expertise come up, such as those concerning the hypostatic union. I will not be able to take these questions so far as I would like, and will offer directions for further inquiry, more than answers. Many questions, however, can be answered without going beyond basic doctrines, and with these I am conversant. Moreover, I intend to rely heavily on Thomas Aquinas, the Angelic Doctor, who holds a place of honor among Catholic theologians.

Philosophers plainly can be of aid in theological pursuits.[13] They can clarify what sorts of questions are rightfully raised by science and religion respectively, and what sort of answers each can give. They have the habit of making distinctions, granted they will not make appropriate distinctions without some familiarity with the subject matter. Philosophers are supposed to be well-studied in logic, and thus ideally have facility in separating good arguments from fallacious ones, and know the importance of distinguishing different meanings of words. In addition, they can sometimes offer arguments based on natural reason concerning the same questions the theologian investigates. These are the tasks I will strive to perform in the best tradition of philosophy as handmaiden to theology.

The historical development of the Christianity-ETI debates has been documented by a number of authors, the most noteworthy of which are Michael J. Crowe and Steven J. Dick. I am grateful to these authors and to other historians of science for their meticulous work in collecting the various arguments that have been offered over the ages. They have provided a very complete list of the arguments pro and con in the Christianity-ETI controversy, accompanied by the historical context without which they are liable to be misunderstood.

The book is divided into four parts:

In Part One, I intend to show what scenarios of ETI existence are excluded by Christianity as impossible, and what scenarios are compatible with Catholic Christian teaching. The two major lines of argument offered to show that Christianity and ETI existence are incompatible will be examined.

After establishing under what conditions ETI life is not excluded by the Catholic faith, I proceed in Part Two to examine a second issue, namely, the probable arguments based on the faith or drawn from philosophy that can be offered against the existence of ETI.

In Part Three, I derive indirect support for my probable position that ETI life does not exist by showing that scientific arguments offered to the opposite conclusion are either inconclusive or sophistical. I also consider philosophical arguments, including those with underlying theistic—atheistic concerns, to show that these arguments do not provide ready answers to the question of ETI existence. Lastly, I point out common fallacies in non-scientific reasoning on the subject.

In Part Four, I face up to the fact that the arguments that I offered against ETI existence are only probable, and consider what, if any, sort of adjustment would have to be made in Catholic teaching and/or worldview if my probable arguments prove to be incorrect. Here I come back to the earlier question of the compatibility of the Catholic faith and ETI, pointing out that probable arguments drawn from the faith may be mistaken without the faith itself being erroneous, a fact generally overlooked by those who want to see ETI existence and the Christian faith as more opposed than they actually are. I also speculate on what position the Church would be likely to take on the matter.

Before I begin it is necessary to first clarify what kind of ETI is of interest in the Christianity-ETI debate. As many authors point out,

Christians do believe that there exist other intelligent beings in the universe, namely, the angels (both the good angels, and the fallen angels, the devils or demons). Thus it is not the existence of these kinds of intelligences that is in putative conflict with Christianity. Some will argue that accounts of UFOs and abductions by aliens can be traced to these beings, who though pure spirits are capable of assuming a physical appearance.[14] Without entering into this debate, it is clear that ETI must have a body of some sort, rather than merely appear in bodily form as Christians believe pure spirits sometimes do.

The ETI's body cannot be just any sort of body. It must have some relation to the being's intelligence. The reason for this can be seen by considering a version of ETI that certain people in antiquity believed in, namely, animate stars. Thomas Aquinas examines this ancient view, and takes the position that if the stars are animate, this is most likely only true in the sense that they are moved by animate things, namely, the angels. Another possibility, one which Aquinas regards as less likely but does not entirely rule out,[15] is that angelic intelligences could be united to these bodies in the manner that a human soul is united to a human body. The simple fact that such beings would have bodies, however, does not make them rational animals. For the human intellect arrives at ideas starting from sense experience, which of course requires a body,[16] unlike the angelic intellect which is naturally endowed with ideas at the time that it is created.[17] A created intelligent being that does not have a body that serves its intellect can only be some sort of angel.

While the modern day vision of ETI is certainly not animate stars, this potential candidate for an intelligent being generically like ourselves still needed to be eliminated, and is no more silly than some contemporary alternatives. Modern technological peoples are more inclined to see matter everywhere rather than spirit everywhere.

This last remark leads us to our next consideration: Some people nowadays propose that ETIs may populate the universe by putting their intelligence into computers or some other sort of physical entity. For instance, Allen Tough in *Crucial Questions about the Future* suggests that: "it may not be pure fiction to imagine intelligent life evolving even further...eventually learn[ing] to transfer their brains and then their thoughts into shiny new homes of metal and plastic."[18] While ETIs are not purely immaterial beings or intelligences, they also cannot be purely material beings. For they could not be intelligent in the strict sense of the word if part of them was not immaterial. They could not form abstract ideas, or grasp the universal principles that are used in science and philosophy, or have a concept of beings that are immaterial, such as the concept of God or moral virtue, if they were purely material beings. Nor could they be free and have self-control if they were purely material beings, for to be free presupposes that one can both reflect on the consequences of one's actions in light of one's ultimate end, and that one is not compelled to fix upon one alternative instead of another. Purely material beings are ultimately passive to causes which they themselves do not determine. ETIs could not be purely material beings, then, if they are to be capable of freely loving God and others.

Of course, many would contest these statements,[19] as do most of those who ascribe intelligence to animals and those who believe that it will be possible someday for computers to think. I do not intend to embark upon discussions of animal intelligence[20] or of artificial intelligence, which would be lengthy ones, although I think that a strong philosophical case can be made for the positions I am adopting. Rather, I am simply going to assume that what I have been saying about intelligent and free natures is so because it is in keeping with the Catholic understanding of what it means to be "created in the image of God"[21] and to be a person. If ETIs are not created in the image of God and thus do not have the dignity of persons as the Church understand these things, none of the putative conflicts between Christianity and ETI existence would have any meaning from the Catholic perspective. Here is what the Catechism of the Catholic Church (*CCC*) has to say:

> Of all visible creatures only man is "able to know and love his creator." He is "the only creature on earth that God has willed for its own sake," and he alone is called to share, by knowledge and love, in God's own life....Being in the image of God the human individual possesses the dignity of a person, who is not just something, but someone. He is capable of self-knowledge, of self-possession and of freely giving himself and entering into communion with other persons.[22]

> "[S]oul" also refers to the innermost aspect of man, that which is of greatest value in him, that by which he is most especially in God's image: soul signifies the spiritual principle[23] in man....The Church teaches that every spiritual soul is created immediately by God—it is not "produced" by the parents—and

also that it is immortal: it does not perish when it separates from the body at death....[24]

The philosophical connections among the various notions spoken of above are elaborated on by Aquinas, among others. But what is essential for our purposes is to recognize that from a Catholic standpoint, ETIs cannot be purely material beings, such as animals or supercomputers, no matter how complex; for such things are neither made in the image of God nor are they worthy of his special care. Only the material beings that have an immaterial and immortal soul are made in God's image and are capable of sharing in the divine life through grace.[25] As pointed out above, ETIs cannot be pure intelligences either—they must have a body, and one that plays a role in the acquisition of intellectual knowledge.

A final question about their nature is whether there are many ways for ETIs' body and soul to be related to one another. There is reason to think that what holds in case of humans will hold in their case as well:

> The unity of soul and body is so profound that one has to consider the soul to be the "form" of the body: i.e., it is because of its spiritual soul that the body made of matter becomes a living, human body; spirit and matter, in man, are not two natures united, but rather their union forms a single nature.[26]

If ETIs of one sort have one nature, and each individual ETI is one substance, not two substances somehow linked together, then the physical and spiritual parts of these beings must be united to form one whole. If these parts are not united, then ETIs will fall into the category of an angelic intelligence, the body being a shell, so to speak, rather than part of ETI nature.

ETIs then possess what we call a "human nature." Regardless of how they diverge from us in physical appearance and features, they are sentient beings whose intellects require experience gained through the senses as their starting point for the formation of ideas. Put more succinctly, ETIs are "rational animals." Any life form that we may discover in space that does not fall into this category, as interesting as it may be, is not relevant to my study here.

There are a number of terms that signify either a group or a kind of being which are best clarified here since we will be speaking throughout about two groups of beings which are in some respect the same, and in other respects different. These terms include: "species," "race," "stock," and "nature."

The word "species" has two senses of interest to us. In the philosophical sense of the word "species" different species have different essential natures, and they do not share the same definition. ETIs are rational animals who differ from us only in an accidental way, i.e., they possess a somewhat different body. Thus they belong to the same species as we do, according to the philosophical definition of species. From a biological perspective, however, since it is a virtual certitude that ETIs could not produce fertile offspring by interbreeding with us, the two groups would constitute two different biological species. (Populations of animals that cannot produce fertile offspring by interbreeding with one another are generally considered separate biological species. There is considerable debate about what defines a biological species, and to try to determine the truth of the matter would take us far from our main purpose.) From a theological perspective, as well, we and the ETIs would have to belong to different biological species. For if we belonged to the same biological species, there would remain nothing to distinguish us from them aside from origin—variations which belong to the same biological species such as differences in skin color do not make one group of human stand as aliens to another. However, that we be distinguished from ETIs merely by origin is ruled out by the Church teaching that there is only one set of first parents for the human race. Pius II, in the encyclical letter *Humani Generis*, states:

> When, however, there is question of another conjectural opinion, namely polygenism, the children of the Church by no means enjoy such liberty. For the faithful cannot embrace that opinion which maintains either that after Adam there existed on this earth true men who did not take their origin through natural generation from him as from the first parent of all, or that Adam represents a certain number of first parents. Now it is in no way apparent how such an opinion can be reconciled with that which the sources of revealed truth and the documents of the Teaching Authority of the Church propose with regard to original sin, which proceeds from a sin actually committed by an individual Adam and which through generation is passed on to all and is in everyone as his own.[27]

This passage adds the qualification that there are no true men *on earth* who are not descended from Adam. This seems to leave the door open to there being true men who are not descendants of Adam on other planets. However, passages in other Church documents equate the human race with the descendants of Adam. The Council of Trent states:

> The holy synod declares first, that, for the correct and sound understanding of the doctrine of justification, it is necessary that each one recognize and confess that…all men had lost their innocence in the prevarication of Adam….[28]

The *CCC* also sets forth the Church's teaching on the unity of the human race:

> How did the sin of Adam become the sin of all his descendants? The whole human race is in Adam "as one body of one man." By this "unity of the human race" all men are implicated in Adam's sin, as all are implicated in Christ's justice….By yielding to the tempter, Adam and Eve committed *a personal sin*, but this sin affected *the human nature* they would then transmit *in a fallen state*. It is a sin which will be transmitted by propagation to all mankind, that is, by the transmission of a human nature deprived of original holiness and justice.[29]

The stated unity of the human race is incompatible with the existence of another human group biologically the same as us that was not affected by Adam's sin.

The reason that *Humani Generis* speaks about there being no true men *on earth* who are not descendants of Adam finds an explanation in the fact Acts 17:24 uses a similar wording: "From one single stock (Gr. "hevos haimatos," literally "one blood") he…created the whole human race so that they could occupy the entire earth." This passage very plainly equates the whole human race (Gr. "pan ethnos anthrôpôn," literally "every people belonging to mankind") with the descendants of Adam.[30] The only reason the earth is mentioned is to indicate that it is the intended (first) home of Adam's progeny—it is not mentioned in order to leave the door open to true human beings not of Adam's lineage having abode elsewhere.

As for the word "race," one of its meanings is close to, but not exactly the same as the meaning of "biological species." Race sometimes refers to members belonging to a biological species (and thus capable of interbreeding) that can be readily distinguished from one another by certain traits, e.g., black skin vs. white skin. However, when we speak of the "human race" or "Adam's race," we are distinguishing ourselves as a group related by descent from other groups related by descent. The reason why race in this sense does not necessarily exactly correspond to biological species is that it is debatable whether all members of a biological species are related by descent; perhaps some species have multiple origins. When I speak of the human race, I mean to indicate a group all the members of which share the same definition *and* a common ancestor, but when I speak of an ETI race, I do not mean to assume the same strict unity of descent, but leave it open as to whether the group has a single set of first parents or some relatively small number of common ancestors. I agree that it is not ideal to use the word "race" in two somewhat different senses, but I do not think that in the context of our discussion the difference in senses is so great as to counter indicate its usage.

Another group word that I will sometimes use is "stock." "Stock" generally refers to an infra-specific group having unity of descent, where infra-specific is taken in the biological sense of "species." I intend to give "stock" a new, albeit related meaning: I will use it to name an infra-specific group having more or less perfect unity of descent, where infra-specific is taken in the philosophical sense of "species." In this sense we and an ETI group belong to the same philosophical species, but to different stocks. I am thus using "race" and "stock" as synonyms.

A final term that needs clarification is "nature." One meaning of "nature" corresponds to essence or to what the substance of a thing is. Once again, in this sense, we humans and ETIs share the same nature: we are both rational animals. Another meaning of "nature" is disposition or temperament. This is something which results from physical make-up. Now the difference in physical composition between a human individual and an ETI individual would have to be greater than that between the most unlike human individuals. Otherwise, the situation would be one where the same biological species had two independent origins—and again Catholic teaching rules out the possibility of two Adams. Thus, sometimes I will use "nature" in the sense of essence, whereas at other time I will use it to indicate a specific range of chemical composition in addition to essence. In other words, sometimes the possessor of a human nature will refer to a rational animal, and other times it will refer to a rational animal possessing the biochemical constitution characteristic of us. I will use "human being" and "man" to name exclusively the latter sort of being. "ETI" and "human-like being" will name a rational animal possessing a biochemical make-up other than ours (such a being, again, would belong to a different biological species than ours). "Human-type being" includes ETI races and us.

I realize that remembering the different meanings of these different terms, and then discerning which is being used in a given passage of this book places mental demands on the reader. However, the alternative of continually reiterating the stipulations recounted here throughout the book would make for tedious reading. I suggest that the reader bookmark this page, and refer back to it, until my usage of the terms in question becomes familiar.

PART I

The Possibility of ETI Existence in Light of Christianity

CHAPTER 1

The Son of Man and ETI

> "For he emptied himself, taking on the form of a slave...." [Ph. 3:7] That "he emptied himself" is beautifully put. For empty is the opposite of full. Divine nature is full, for there lies all perfection of goodness....Human nature and the human soul is not full, but is in potency to fullness, for it is made like a blank slate. Human nature is therefore empty. St. Paul says "he emptied himself" because the Son of God assumed a human nature.
>
> —Thomas Aquinas, *Commentary on Philippians*

The Good News is that the Second Person of the Trinity became man in order to save us from sin,[1] both original sin and personal sin. Christ realized our salvation by his death on the cross and his resurrection from the dead. Since Christ's sacrifice does not save us without cooperation on our part, a substantial amount of Christian doctrine concerns what we must do in order to obtain eternal life. The supposed conflict between Christian belief and belief in ETIs is not principally with the teachings about Christian behavior, but with those concerning the Incarnation and Redemption.

The existence of extraterrestrial life could conflict with the Catholic faith in three ways. First, it could directly conflict with official Church teaching. Second, it could conflict with Scriptural passages. Sometimes the latter conflict coincides with the former, but this is not always the case since Catholicism is not a "religion of the book,"[2] and not all passages of Scripture have an official interpretation. Finally, belief in ETI life could also conflict with traditional beliefs which the faithful are not bound to adhere to (e.g., beliefs such as "Limbo"). The latter two forms of conflict are less acute; such Scriptural passages are subject to reinterpretation, and such traditional beliefs sometimes go out of vogue. I will limit myself here to considering magisterial teachings, and the most relevant and most problematic of the passages of Scripture which do not have an official interpretation. I will first examine the putative conflicts between ETI existence and what is said in Scripture, and then go on from there to look at the conflicts that appear to arise from pronouncements made in official Church documents.

God, of course, has the power to create any number of intelligent races with bodies he wills.[3] However, when God has chosen to do a given thing, those things that are incompatible with this choice are no longer possible, granted that they are not intrinsically impossible. For example, God did not have to create the universe in time. However, once he chose to do so, it is no longer possible that the universe be eternally created. God did not have to create material beings, but once he did so, it can no longer be true that beings naturally subject to change never existed. Now, God has told us in Scripture about some of the things he has chosen to do. For example, Christians believe that the universe had a beginning in time because Genesis opens with: "In the beginning, God created the heavens and the earth,"[4] and the gospel of John (17:5) recounts Christ's prayer: "Now, Father, it is time for you to glorify me with that glory I had with you before the world was." Thus, it is possible that something God has revealed in Scripture concerning his plan for creation might have some bearing on the questions of ETI existence.

I think that there are a couple of reasons why many authors fail to look very carefully at Scripture. First, most of the major points of conflict between Christianity and ETI concern such fundamental and well-known teachings of Christianity, namely, the Incarnation and Redemption, that there seems to be no need to scrutinize Scripture. Secondly, the purpose of Scripture is to lead us humans to God, not to catalog the beings in the universe. It remains the case, however, that there are passages of cosmic significance in Scripture, some of which have bearing on the existence of other intelligent material beings, and others of which at least appear to have bearing thereon. I intend to examine these commonly neglected Scriptural passages, focusing chiefly on the New Testament. The Old Testament is rarely cited in the ETI debate. A couple of exceptions are Ps. 2, 8, 49, and 60,[5] which Montignez uses to make a not particularly strong case for ETI existence.[6] Montignez is right, however, to find Ps. 8 of interest,[7] as it says that God has "set all things under his [man's] feet," and I will address this theme later on. Sir David Brewster (1781-1868) uses Is. 45:12 to make a case that God must populate the planets he has made—

otherwise he would have made them in vain. This general line of argument is not convincing, as I will show in chapter eleven. And then there is the first book of Genesis, from which some formulate an argument of "absence" which I intend to take up in chapter three. I have not myself gone systematically through the Old Testament, as I have through the New, trusting that my theologian predecessors would have discovered Old Testament texts relevant to the Christianity-ETI debate, if any were to be found.

Next to be considered are the principal arguments offered to show that Christianity and ETI existence are mutually exclusive. There appear to be only two main lines of argument, albeit they appear in a number of variations and are accompanied by a certain variety of subsidiary arguments. The first regards the role of Christ, the God-Man, in the Universe. The primary purpose of the Word's Incarnation appears to be human salvation: "God sent into the world his only Son so that we could have life through him…he sent his Son to be the sacrifice that takes our sins away" (1 Jn. 4:9, 10). "We were still helpless when at the appointed moment Christ died for sinful men.…Again, as one man's fall brought condemnation on everyone, so the good act of one man brings everyone life and makes them justified" (Rom. 5: 6, 18). The question then is: If there was another sort of intelligent material creature in the universe, what possible relation could Christ have to individuals of this type? How could Christ be their redeemer, if they were fallen? And if unfallen, what possible relation would he as man have to them? It seems either the only intelligent material species in the universe is the human race, in which case God becoming incarnate as man in order to redeem man makes some kind of sense, or there are also ETI races, in which case God taking on human flesh to redeem the human race, while being essentially foreign to many or most of the intelligent beings in the universe, seems absurd. A second argument purportedly showing the incompatibility of Christian belief with ETI existence assumes that ETI races would have an intimate relationship with God, and concludes that if that is so, then the Bible is mistaken in portraying the human race to be special as the pinnacle of creation and the race to which God has shown particular care.

As to the first issue, I will argue that the role of Christ as stated in Scripture and affirmed by Catholic teaching is compatible with ETI existence, although not with its existence on just any terms (e.g., Scripture excludes the existence of redeemed ETIs who were not redeemed by Christ). As for the second argument, I will show that the specialness of the human race can be understood in a number of ways, and that the scripturally affirmed specialness of man does not exclude the possibility of ETI existence. There is yet a third argument pitting Christianity against ETIs which needs to be addressed. This argument is of secondary importance compared to the other two, for it is less often invoked and is more readily answered. Unlike the others, it proceeds from what Scripture does not say, rather than from what it says, and goes roughly like this: Genesis does not speak of ETI, and thus if ETI proves to exist, the Bible can be nothing other than earthling mythology. In response to this third argument, I will point out that Scripture makes no mention of things that have no bearing on its purpose.

In this chapter I will examine the argument that opposes Christian belief to belief in ETI existence on the grounds that Christ as known through the Catholic faith could not have any relation to such beings. I will take up the other two arguments in the following two chapters.

What possible relations could Our Lord and Savior, the son of David, Jesus Christ have to ETIs?[8] Plainly the relation will differ depending on whether the ETIs are fallen or unfallen. However, there is a prior question about the condition the ETIs are in, namely: Were they made for supernatural happiness or for purely natural happiness? The latter possibility seems to be excluded on the basis of both Scripture and what befits a benevolent God, at least in the case of unfallen ETIs. If unfallen ETIs were made for natural happiness, at the time of the Last Judgment, there would be upright intelligent beings existing in separation from the Church triumphant. This accords poorly, if at all, with Ep. 1:8-10 which says that:

> He has let us know the mystery of his purpose, the hidden plan he so kindly made in Christ from the beginning to act upon when the times had run their course to the end: that he would bring everything together under Christ, as head, everything in the heavens and everything on earth.

The hypothetical unfallen race whose ultimate end was natural happiness would not be part of the mystical body, of which Christ is the head. Though members of this race could know of Christ, they could not know Christ, as this could only be through supernatural faith or through the beatific vision, neither of which are possible to them.

One might object that the position that I am arguing in favor of—namely, that sinless ETIs would be made for supernatural happiness—is precisely that censured by Pope Pius XII in *Humani Generis* when he denounces those who "destroy the gratuity of the supernatural order, since God, they say, cannot create intellectual beings without ordering them and calling them to the beatific vision."[9] However, I do not hold that God does not have the power to create such creatures, nor that elevation of a creature to the supernatural order can be anything other than a free gift of God. My reasoning here is patterned after Aquinas's when he examines the question of whether the angels were created in grace. Aquinas acknowledges that:

> [O]ne cannot discover an efficacious reason for which of the [two opposite] opinions be truer, because the beginning of creatures depends on the simple will of the Creator, which is impossible to investigate by reason....

However, Aquinas goes on to say: "nevertheless according to agreement with other of his [God's] works, one can sustain one side as more probable than the other."[10] Using the latter mode of reasoning, Aquinas then argues that:

> [I]t pertains to divine freedom to infuse grace into all who are capable of grace, unless something resisting is found in them, much more than he gives natural form to any disposed matter. But angels from the beginning of their creation had the motion of free will, and there was nothing in them impeding [the infusion of grace]. Therefore it seems that he immediately infused grace in them.[11]

Nowhere does Aquinas deny the gratuity of the supernatural order, and so it does not seem that the sort of probable reasoning Aquinas uses based on what we know about God's other works is what Pope Pius XII was intending to condemn.

Turning now to the case of the ETIs (unfallen and fallen alike), I will argue that they would be created in grace and thus would be ordered to a supernatural end, patterning my arguments after those of Aquinas. Accordingly, I will look to what God has done with works other than ETIs. Now, not only is it likely that God infused grace in the angels from the beginning of their existence, an even stronger case can be made that Adam was created in grace, albeit this too is only probable as Adam's being created in grace "depends only on the will of God."[12] The case in favor of Adam's being created in grace is based on Qo. 7:30: "God made man upright." The subjection of man's emotion to reason was part of this rectitude. Now, since a creature's natural endowment is not lost as a consequence of sin, but the subjection of man's emotion to reason was lost after the Fall, this subjection must have been a supernatural gift.[13] Adam and Eve were then created in a state of grace.

Judging then from the cases of these two sorts of intelligent beings, the angels and our first parents, it is more probable than not that God would infuse grace in the first ETIs. Again this is not to say that God could not create an ETI species in a state of pure nature. There are many things that God could do, but does not do, e.g., he can annihilate things, but he does not, in keeping with his wisdom.[14] God bestows to creatures the maximal perfection of which they are capable, not from constraint, but out of his infinite goodness.

Of course one might object that God did create rational beings who will only enjoy natural happiness, namely, the babies who die unbaptized. It is certainly true that the Catholic Church urges parents to baptize their child as soon as possible for "unless one is born of water and the spirit, one cannot enter the kingdom of heaven" (Jn. 3:5). Nevertheless, the doctrine that unbaptized children go to a place, "Limbo," where they do not see God as he is, but are in nowise punished, is not a definitive teaching of the Church. Most recently the *CCC* tells us:

> As regards children who have died without Baptism, the Church can only entrust them to the great mercy of God who desires that all men should be saved, and Jesus' tenderness toward children which caused him to say: "Let the children come to me, do not hinder them," allow us to hope that there is a way of salvation for children who have died without Baptism. All the more urgent is the Church's call not to prevent little children coming to Christ through the gift of holy Baptism.[15]

Whether or not deceased unbaptized infants are separated from the direct vision of God remains an open question. Even if one is inclined to think that Limbo exists, still, the case of some human infants and the case of an entire race composed in part of adults are different. The unbaptized child never had exercise of free will, and therefore could not choose the good, whereas those ETIs who arrived at the age of reason could. The unbaptized children in the next life would not be afflicted by possessing only natural happiness because they would realize that they never had what was proportioned for them to obtain eternal life; they never were capable of choice. One is only reasonably afflicted if one is deprived of that which one in some manner had an aptitude of possessing.[16] The mature ETIs who were capable of choosing the good would be reasonably afflicted upon being denied supernatural happiness if they had gone on to choose the good, for in doing so they prepared themselves for a grace that was denied them.[17] It does not seem in keeping with God's goodness that he create a race of beings, who in spite of their good choices, are destined to be unhappy, their natural longing to know the essence of the ultimate cause of things left ultimately unsatisfied.

I am going to proceed on the supposition that ETIs would in fact be called to supernatural happiness, *not* that they would have to be called to it. I recognize that the issue is highly controversial, but to engage in a lengthy debate about it here would take us too far from our main purpose.[18] In addition to the *probable* argument just given that ETIs, like the angels and man, would be called to supernatural happiness, this view appears to have some support in Scripture. Ep. 1:8-10 states that it is God's will that everything is to be brought under Christ as a head, and this better accords with intelligent species being in fact created for the beatific vision rather than with them not being capable of attaining it, though God was under no obligation to have created them so.

Thus far the possibility that ETIs are not called to a supernatural life has been eliminated. To give an idea of how I will proceed in the rest of this chapter, here is an outline of the remaining theoretical possibilities that need to be considered if one is to determine what possible relation ETIs could have to Christ. I will also indicate here the alternatives that I will argue ought to be eliminated as impossible. The alternatives I do not eliminate, I regard as possible.

An ETI group is either unfallen or fallen or composed of both unfallen and fallen members (for the sake of simplicity the "mixed" group will be treated as a special case). An unfallen group could either be created blessed or such that it must merit beatitude. I eliminate the former possibility, leaving two pairs of possible situations for unfallen ETIs who must merit beatitude: First, either they receive the grace by which they achieve blessedness through Christ or they do not; second, either Christ becomes incarnate as one of them or he does not. As for the fallen, I have serious reservations about their existence. If these reservations are set aside, fallen ETIs are either going to be redeemed or left unredeemed. I reject the latter possibility, leaving two possible situations for the redeemed: Either they are redeemed by Christ's sacrifice on the cross or they are not. I eliminate the latter possibility, leaving two possible situations for ETIs redeemed by Christ's death on Calvary: Either Christ also became incarnate as one of them or he did not. Again, some of the things that I accept as possible, I will later argue are improbable.

On the assumption that ETIs are called to supernatural life, I will begin by examining the possibilities pertaining to the unfallen, the first of which is that they could either achieve beatitude through their free choices or they could be created in glory. There are a number of reasons why it does not seem fitting that ETIs be created blessed. To paraphrase Aquinas (*ST* I, q. 62, art. 4): Perfect happiness is natural to God alone. It is not the very nature of a creature to be happy, but happiness is an ultimate end. Ultimate ends are achieved through a being's operations. Human efforts alone, however, do not suffice to achieve beatitude. The beatific vision, then, has the notion of a reward which is only fittingly given to one who has merited it.[19] Inductively, one can see that God generally tests the love of the intelligent beings he creates, rewarding with eternal beatitude those who choose to follow his commands though they were capable of choosing other. An exception would seem to be the baptized infants who die before they reach the age of reason. They were not, however, created in glory, but they obtain it through another's act, rather than through their own acts; and as Aquinas puts it, this is an act of "*superexcedentis gratiae.*"[20] As for a particular individual being created in glory, Aquinas says that this can happen from some special privilege, as some believe is the case of the Virgin Mother of God.[21] It would seem unfitting, however, to create an entire species of beings capable of choosing between two options in which no individual ever exercised its capacity, and it would also seem unfitting to grant an entire species of intelligent creatures so great a privilege without any individual merit involved.

How then would unfallen ETIs who must merit their beatitude stand to Christ and his Church? Christ would be their head and Lord, as he is head and Lord of the angels, although he is not their redeemer. And, they, like the angels, would belong to the Church triumphant.

One might object that the *CCC* speaks as if the angels were not part of the Church:

Christians of the first centuries said, "The world was created for the sake of the Church." God created the world for the sake of communion with his divine life, a communion brought about the "convocation" of men in Christ, and this "convocation" is the Church. The Church is the goal of all things, and God permitted such painful upheavals as the angels' fall and man's sin only as occasion and means for displaying all the power of his arm and the whole measure of the love he wanted to give the world. "Just as God's will is creation and is called 'the world,' so his intention is the salvation of men, and it is called 'the Church.'"[22]

However, the *CCC* says elsewhere:

From infancy to death human life is surrounded by their watchful care and intercession. "Beside each believer stands an angel as protector and shepherd leading him to life." *Already here on earth the Christian life shares by faith in the blessed company of angels and men united in God.*[23] (emphasis mine)

The passage cited earlier (*CCC* #760) said that "God created the world for the sake of communion with his divine life," and that "the Church is the goal of all things." Here the angels are acknowledged to share in this communion. It seems then that Aquinas's reasoning is in accord with the Church's position when he says: "Both angels and humans are ordered to one end, which is the glory of divine fruition. Whence, the mystical body of the Church is made up not only of humans, but also of angels."[24] A distinction is sometimes made between the Church and the Kingdom of God,[25] and one might use it to argue that the angels are not members of the Church Triumphant, but are citizens of the Kingdom. Even if this were conceded, Christ remains head and Lord of the angels who are our fellows in the heavenly kingdom, and the same would be true of any ETIs that existed and shared the beatific vision with us.

A variation on the scenario where the ETIs did not sin, are not in need of a redeemer, would have the Word becoming incarnate as one of them for reasons other than redemption. This variation calls to mind two questions: First, is a second incarnation possible? And if a second incarnation is possible, would its occurrence have any impact on the relation of Christ to ETIs? For example, would Christ be displaced as head and Lord of the ETIs, if the Word became incarnate as ETI?

Although human redemption is the chief reason given in Scripture and Church tradition for the Incarnation of Christ as a human being, other reasons for his Incarnation are given as well, e.g., given that like likes like, Incarnation leads to a more intimate friendship between the divine person and the individuals sharing the nature that he united to himself.[26] And certainly if God so chooses, he is able to become incarnate as another human-type being. For the assumption of a created nature by a person infinite in power cannot exhaust the person's ability to assume other created natures. As Aquinas puts it:

> That which is able [to do something] in one case and not in another has its power limited to one. The power of a divine person is, however, infinite, and it ought not be said that a divine person had assumed one human nature in such a manner that another could not be assumed to its personhood, for that is impossible, because an uncreated thing cannot be comprehended by a created thing. It is manifest therefore that whether we consider the divine person according to power, which is the principle of the union, or according to its personhood which is the term of the union, it must be said that the divine person, besides a human nature which it has assumed, is able to assume another numerically different human nature.[27]

A second incarnation is within God's power. However, that God actually chooses to do so appears to be eliminated by what he tells us in Scripture, namely, that there is only one Lord, Jesus Christ:

> And even if there were things called gods, either in the sky or on earth—where there certainly seem to be "gods" and "lords" in plenty—still for us there is one God, the Father, from whom all things come and for whom we exist; and there is one Lord, Jesus Christ, through whom all things come and through whom we exist. (1 Co. 8:5-6)

> His state was divine, yet he did not cling to his equality with God, but emptied himself to assume the condition of a slave, and became as men are; and being as all men are, he was humbler yet, even to accepting death, death on a cross. But God raised him high and gave him the name which is above all other names, so

that all beings in the heavens, on the earth and in the underworld, should bend at the name of Jesus and that every tongue should acclaim Jesus Christ as Lord, to the glory of God the Father. (Ph. 2:6-11)

If the Second Person became incarnate on another planet as an ETI, there would appear to be a Lord other than Jesus Christ, true God and true man, since what would be true of the Second Person as having an ETI nature would not be true of the Second Person as having a human nature. One solution proposed in response to this difficulty is that "one Lord" applies to Christ in his divine nature alone.[28] Thus, the Second Person incarnate as an ETI would not be a Lord other than our Lord Jesus Christ. However, this interpretation does not accord well with the passage from Philippians, which implies that it is the Word incarnate as man who is given the name "Lord."[29] The Word in his divine nature is eternally Lord as begotten by the Father.

On the other hand, the Second Person is not two Lords despite that fact that he is Lord in both his human and in his divine natures. St. Thomas, commenting on 1 Co. 8:6: "There is one Lord Jesus Christ through whom all things are," says:

> It is manifest, however, that Jesus, the name of that man through whom all things are, belongs to the Word of God. If therefore the Word of God and that man are one Lord, there are neither two Lords nor two sons, as Nestorius was claiming. From this it follows further that there is one person of the Word of God and of [that] man.[30]

If the Second Person is not two Lords by his human and divine natures, why would he be two Lords by two created natures? It seems rather that just as Christ is a person in both natures, but not two persons, so too if he became incarnate in two human natures, he would be Lord in both, but again only one Lord because it is the person who is Lord, and there is only one person in the two or three natures. As counter-intuitive as it sounds, then, worshipping the one Lord ETI would not be different from worshipping the one Lord Jesus Christ, if indeed the supposed Lord of the ETIs would not be a Lord other than Our Lord Jesus Christ because of the unity of the person assuming those two natures.

A number of other passages from Scripture pose a similar sort of problem.[31] They refer to Christ as the head of all things:

> Such is the richness of the grace which he has showered on us in all wisdom and insight. He has let us know the mystery of his purpose, the hidden plan he so kindly made in Christ from the beginning to act upon when the times had run their course to the end: that he would bring *everything* together *under Christ, as head,* everything *in the heavens and everything on earth.* (Ep. 1:8-10) (Emphasis mine)

A question pertinent for our purposes is whether Christ is the head of the angels in his humanity or only in his divinity. Aquinas maintains that:

> The head causes an influx of sensation and motion to all members of the body....[S]omeone can understand "to flow into" ("influere") in two ways according to the spiritual sense and mode. One mode as principal agent: and thus it belongs to God alone to provide an influx of grace in the members of the Church. In another mode instrumentally: And thus even the humanity of Christ is a cause of the said influx; because as Damascene says...as iron burns on account of the fire conjoined to it, so were the actions of the humanity of Christ on account of the united divinity, of which the humanity itself was an instrument. Christ, nevertheless, according to the two last conditions of head [i.e., governance, influence] is able to be called head of the angels according to human nature,[32] and head of both according to divine nature; not, however, according to the first condition [namely, sameness in nature], unless one takes what is common according to the nature of the genus, according as man and angel agree in rational nature, and further what is common according to analogy, according as it is common to the Son along with all creatures to receive from the Father, as Basil says, by reason of which he is said to be the first born of all creatures, Col. 1:15.[33]

Aquinas maintains, then, that it is the union of the human nature to the divine nature in the person of Christ which makes that human nature an instrument for governing and exercising causality over all creatures.

Before that union Christ "would have been the head of the Church only according to his divine nature, but after sin [which Aquinas takes to be the main reason for the Incarnation] it is necessary that he be head of the Church also according to his human nature."[34]

Duns Scotus was of another opinion than Aquinas, holding that the angels received the grace by which they attained beatitude through Christ:

> Even if the glory of any one of the Angels had been willed, what was willed prior to that was the union of human nature to the Divine Word and the predestination of Christ to be the Son of God. For everyone who wills in an orderly way, wants first the end and those things which are closer to the end, and then, proceeding from there, those things which are means. Therefore, first the plenitude of all graces and gifts was willed to the soul of Christ, so that there would be nothing of grace creatable by a sole creation that was not willed to his soul and effectively brought together in it; therefore, from this plenitude descends and is received all of the supernatural gifts and graces that are found in those beneath Christ. I.e., with an eye to the one of highest grace and immediately willed, after willing the end, everything is given by means of which all who are capable of grace and charity are graced by God. Therefore, Christ is not only the head of humans, but also of Angels, because all have received in one way or another, and they receive from the fullness of grace that was either foreseen or was brought together in Christ.[35]

Aquinas rejects the notion that the angels achieved beatitude through grace that comes instrumentally through Christ on the grounds that an agent has to exist in order to act. Aquinas points this out on the occasion of explaining how people who lived before Christ were saved:

> It cannot be said that the sacraments of the old law conferred the grace of justification through themselves, that is, by their own power, because then the passion of Christ would not have been necessary, as is maintained by Gal. 2:21: "If justice is from the law, there was no point that Christ die." But neither can it be said that they had the power of conferring the grace of justification through the power of the passion of Christ. As is manifest from

what was said above, the power of the passion of Christ is joined to us through faith and the sacraments, nevertheless in a different manner; for the continuation which is through faith comes to be through an act of the soul; the continuation, however, which is through the sacraments comes to be through the use of external things. Nothing prevents that which is posterior in time to move an agent according as it is apprehended and desired by him. But that which does not as yet exist in the nature of things, does not move according to the use of external things. Whence an efficient cause is not able to exist posterior in being in the order of duration like the final cause can. Thus, therefore, it is manifest that the sacraments of the new law suitably derive justificatory power from the passion of Christ, which is the cause of human justification; the sacraments of the old law, however, do not.[36] Nevertheless through faith in the passion of Christ the ancient Fathers were justified, even as we are.[37] For the sacraments of the old law were certain protestations of this faith, insofar as they signified the passion of Christ and the effect of it. Thus, therefore, it is manifest that the sacraments of the old law did not have in themselves some power by which they worked to the conferring of justifying grace, but only signified the faith through which they were justified.[38]

It is plain, then, that the Word as man could only be a head of other beings upon actually becoming incarnate as man.

An ETI nature united to the divine nature in Christ would also be an instrument of governing and exercising causality in regard to all creatures—again from the time of the union onwards. If a second incarnation took place, would it then necessarily follow that there would be two heads (and two Churches)? If so, those Scriptural passages that affirm that Christ is the sole and unique head of all would eliminate the possibility that a second incarnation actually occurred. Now, after the Word's incarnation, Christ as man is the sole head of both men and angels. Granted that he is not head of the angels as sharing the same nature (at least not strictly speaking), he still is their head in his human nature as their governor and source of grace. Christ would stand in a similar manner to ETIs if a second incarnation occurred. He would not be their head as being of the same nature, but he would be their head in his human nature as their governor, and from the time of the Redemption onwards, he would be their source of grace as well. If this is so, it seems that ETIs could belong to the mystical body of which Christ is the head. However, one wonders then what would be the status of the Word in his hypothetical ETI incarnation, given that as such he would be head of ETIs as their governor, and possibly as an instrumental source of grace for them (supposing that they, like the angels, were not in need of redemption); in addition the Word-made-ETI, unlike Christ, would be like in nature to the ETIs, and on that account would rightly be called their head. At first sight it might seem that there were two persons—Christ and the Word-made-ETI—both of whom had a legitimate claim to headship. Of course, this cannot be the case, since the Word is one divine person regardless of how many times he becomes incarnate. Even when one grants this point, it still seems counterintuitive to say that Christ and the Word-made-ETI would not constitute different heads. The solution to the similar question of whether an ETI incarnation would imply that there were two Lords does not apply so neatly here, for the reason that headship, as least in one sense, is clearly attributed to the person due to his nature,[39] unlike lordship which seems to be an attribute first and foremost of the person.[40]

Yet another concern that arises in regard to a second incarnation is whether it would affect the central place that Christ has in the universe, a placed defined by his bringing about the new creation to which the original creation was ordered.[41] It seems that given the unity of the natures in the divine person, a second Incarnation as ETI would pose no problem here, for one could rightly say that ETI incarnate has a central role in the universe, although not in the Word's assumed ETI nature. This can be gathered from Aquinas's explanation of a similar problem, namely, whether "the Lord of glory was crucified:"

> [T]he first doubt concerns the fact that he says that the Lord of glory was crucified. For the divinity of Christ is not able to suffer anything, according as Christ is called the Lord of glory. But it ought to be said that Christ is one person and individual substance (hypostasis) existing in both natures, namely, the divine and the human. Whence he is able to be designated by the name of either of the two natures, and by whichever name he is signified, it can be predicated of him what belongs to either nature, because there is only one hypostasis underlying both. And in this manner we can say that a man created the stars, and that the Lord of glory was crucified, but nevertheless he did not

create the stars according as he is man, but according as he is God, nor was he crucified according as he is God, but insofar as he is man.[42]

One cannot attribute what belongs to one of Christ's natures to him in his other nature, but one can of course attribute it to his person. Thus, one cannot say that ETI incarnate as ETI brings creation to its perfection. However, one can say that ETI incarnate brings creation to its perfection if one means by that that the person who is ETI incarnate brings creation to its perfection.

I do not see then that the Scriptural passages concerning the Lordship, Headship, or centrality of Christ in the plan for the universe *necessarily* exclude a second incarnation. However, given that questions which pertain to the hypostatic union are of the greatest difficulty, I remain open to the possibility that someone more versed in theology could show that I am mistaken. Indeed, I had originally taken the opposite position, and continue to harbor doubts on the matter. Then there is the further question of whether there are any other passages in Scripture that speak against a second Incarnation. A careful reading of the New Testament leads me to think that this is not the case. However, a passage from the *CCC* gives cause for pause:

> The unique and altogether singular event of the Incarnation of the Son of God does not mean that Jesus Christ is part God and part man.... He became truly man while remaining truly God.[43]

Perhaps I have overlooked some passage in Scripture speaking decisively of there being only one Incarnation. Or perhaps the arguments examined above which I did not regard as eliminating a second Incarnation were judged by the Church in fact to do so. Or perhaps what I will later offer as merely probable arguments that God became incarnate only once, will be seen by the Church as providing adequate grounds for the *CCC's* statement here. For some dogmas which were eventually pronounced by the Church are not spelled out word for word in Scripture. For example, Scripture never says that Mary was conceived without the stain of original sin. It is true that the angel says of Mary that she is "full of grace" (Lk. 1:28). But without the guidance of the Church one could not be sure that this statement applies to Mary from the very first moment of her existence. Similarly, without the Church's guidance, it seems quite logical to understand the Scriptural statement that "Christ is the savior of the whole human race" (1 Tim. 4:10) to include Mary, and thus to be indicative that she must have at some moment existed under the slavery of sin (which of course was at the root of Aquinas's mistake concerning the Immaculate Conception[44]).

There are reasons to think that the *CCC* does not intend to say here that there has been only one single Incarnation of the Word. Both "singular"[45] and "unique"[46] have a certain range of meanings. Taken in the narrow sense, "singular" means relating to a single instance, and "unique" means one of a kind. Taken in the broad sense, "singular" means unusual or exceptional, and "unique" very rare or very unusual. The context makes it clear that the main purpose of the statement is to address the manner of union of the two persons, and not to address whether the Incarnation is a one-time event. This provides an explanation of why no clarification is offered as to the ambiguity of "singular" and "unique." Furthermore, to my knowledge there is no traditional teaching on the uniqueness of the Incarnation, and so it would be strange for the matter to be addressed in passing here.

Thus far in speaking about incarnation, I have been speaking about the Second Person of the Trinity. The other two persons of the Trinity are of course also *capable* of assuming a rational nature.[47] However, given that Scripture says that everything is to be brought under Christ as head (Ep. 1:10), it cannot be the case that the incarnation of another person of the Trinity has *in fact* occurred. For if another person became incarnate, that person would be head by nature of the race in question. Given the equal majesty of the three persons, that head could not be subordinate to Christ, yet this would have to be the case if Christ indeed is the head of all things in heaven and on earth.

I am going to proceed then as if a second incarnation of the Word is not necessarily excluded either by Scripture or by Church teaching. I am not doing so in a spirit of contention, but rather of legitimate doubt. If further clarification by the Church made it plain that Catholics are to deny that a second Incarnation ever took place, I would willingly yield to its judgment.

Let us now consider the case of fallen ETIs: How they would relate to Christ? Colossians 1:18-20 states that:

> As he is the Beginning, he was first to be born from the dead, so that he should be first in every way; because God wanted all

perfection to dwell in him and all things to be reconciled through him and for him, everything in heaven and everything on earth when he made peace by his death [literally "blood"] on the cross.

There are no grounds to take Christ's reconciliation of all things in heaven and all things in earth to exclude any extraterrestrial species that might be in the heavens. Granted that a person who had no reason to think ETIs might exist would most likely interpret "everything that is in heaven" to refer to the angels who are in a state of blessedness, rather than to the part of the material universe surrounding the earth,[48] still it is plain that "everything in heaven and everything on earth" is meant to be an exhaustive division of "all things."[49] Similarly, all perfection would not rightly be said to dwell in him if his cross and resurrection were not what had wrought the salvation of all those in need of salvation.

Col. 1:18-20 indicates, then, that fallen ETIs, if they are redeemed, are not redeemed by any one other than Christ on the cross.[50] This rules out the possibility that another person of the Trinity become incarnate to save ETIs. I cannot countenance that God would leave them unredeemed, since it is not in keeping with his goodness that he would create a kind of rational being destined for supernatural happiness none of whose members achieved the end for which they were created.[51]

There are two other passages in Scripture that support this reading of Colossians 1:18-20. John 12:32 recounts Christ saying: "When I am lifted up from the earth, I will draw all things to myself." Hebrews 10:12, 14-15 also indicates that Christ offered one sacrifice for the sins of all:

> He, on the other hand, has offered one single sacrifice for sins....
> By virtue of that one single offering, he has achieved the eternal perfection of all whom he is sanctifying.

This last passage is somewhat weaker than Colossians 1:18-20 and Jn. 12:32 in that it could be argued that the "all whom he is sanctifying" is meant to refer only to all on earth. On the other hand, it better accords with the other two passages if it is understood to refer to all sanctified sinners without qualification.

A scenario that does not appear to conflict with the Scripture passages that we have looked at so far would be one in which Christ's sacrifice on the cross on earth makes satisfaction for the fallen ETIs as well as for us.

Although Scripture says that it is fitting that Christ belong by blood to the race he came to save, it remains the case that Christ did not have to become man, nor having done so did he have to die in order to redeem us, but rather the human race could have been saved in many other ways. Similarly, there are many different ways that God could have saved fallen ETIs. However, the Scripture passage just cited indicates that, in fact, all who are saved are saved by the death of Christ. It is of course possible that ETI salvation be accomplished by means of the one sacrifice of Christ on the cross, since it is a sacrifice which is infinite in its saving power.[52] As Beilby Porteus puts it:

> [I]f the Redemption wrought by Christ extended to other worlds, perhaps many beside our own; if its virtues penetrate even into heaven itself; if it gathers together all things in Christ; who will then say, that the dignity of the agent was disproportioned to the magnitude of the work…?[53]

So far, it appears that Christianity is not incompatible with ETI existence as such, but only excludes its existence under certain circumstances. Both the scenario in which fallen ETIs are redeemed through Christ's sacrifice on Calvary, as well as that in which ETIs are not in need of redemption, neither conflict with the role of Christ as universal Lord and Redeemer, nor with "the grandeur attributed to the Church itself,"[54] as Abbé Joseph Filachou feared. For if the ETIs are redeemed by Christ's death, they belong to the same Church that humans do. If the ETIs did not fall, they would be in a situation similar to that of the good angels who along with human saints are counted as members of the one and same Church triumphant that has Christ as its head. This appears to be the case even if the Word became Incarnate as one of them, for the Word incarnate in ETI flesh would be one and the same head as Christ. Thus, ETI existence does not exclude the Catholic teaching that: "It is in the Church that Christ fulfills and reveals his own mystery as the purpose of God's plan: 'to unite all things in him.'"[55]

There remains yet another passage of Scripture concerning the relation of Christ to those whom he saved which needs to be looked at carefully. Aquinas's commentary on this passage is of interest, whence I am also including the Latin translation that he used:

> Decebat enim eum propter quem omnia, et per quem omnia, qui multos filios in gloriam adduxerat, auctorem salutis eorum, per passionem consummari. Qui enim sanctificat et qui sanctificantur, ex uno omnes. Propter quam causam non confunditur fratres eos vocare.... Quia ergo pueri communicaverunt carni et sanguini, et ipse similiter participavit eisdem, ut per mortem destrueret eum qui habebat mortis imperium, idest diabolum; et liberaret eos qui timore mortis per totam vitam obnoxii erant servituti. Nusquam enim angelos apprehendit, sed semen Abrahae apprehendit. Unde debuit per omnia fratribus assimilari, ut misericors fieret, et fidelis pontifex ad Deum, ut repropitiaret delicta populi. In eo enim in quo passus est, ipse et tentatus, potens est et eis qui tentantur auxiliari. (Heb. 2:10-18)

As it was his purpose to bring a great many of his sons into glory, it was appropriate that God, for whom everything exists and through whom everything exists, should make perfect, through suffering, the leader who would take them to their salvation. For the one who sanctifies, and the ones who are sanctified are of the same stock; that is why he openly calls them brothers.... Since all the children share the same blood and flesh, he too shared equally in it, so that by his death he could take away all the power of the devil, who had power over death, and set free all those who had been held in slavery all their lives by the fear of death. For it was not the angels that he took to himself; he took to himself descent from Abraham. It was essential that he should in this way become completely like his brothers so that he could be a compassionate and trustworthy high priest of God's religion, able to atone for human sins. That is, because he himself has been through temptation he is able to help others who are tempted. (Heb. 2:10-18)

One could read "For the one who sanctifies, and the ones who are sanctified are of the same *stock*" (Heb. 2:11) as an explanation for why "As it was his purpose to bring a great many of his sons into glory, it *was appropriate* that God" make perfect their leader. In other words, the appropriateness of Christ suffering to save mankind lay in his being of the same stock as they. This could be true, without it necessarily being the case that Scripture intends to affirm this here. Aquinas, looking at the Latin, does not take "ex uno" ("from one;" the Greek reads "ex henos") to refer to "one stock" as does the English translation, but to one Father.[56] Accordingly, Aquinas understands this passage to give as the reason why Christ is not discomfited to call the ones he sanctifies brothers "because they are from the same Father."[57] Having the same father also qualifies men and angels as brothers, even though they are not of the same nature: "Angels are called our brothers and consorts; but this would not be except according as they have the same father and have been adopted to the same inheritance with us."[58] Thus, the line that reads: "For the one who sanctifies, and the ones who are sanctified are of the same stock; that is why he openly calls them brothers" would not eliminate the possibility that there were ETIs in need of sanctification, for they, like the angels, could be adopted brothers of Christ.

I think that the next lines in that passage are more telling for our debate. Up until now I have been maintaining that one could say that Christ's sacrifice on the cross saved all who are saved, humans alone being saved by the Second Person's taking on the same nature as they, the other rational beings also being saved through him, without him taking on their nature for that purpose. This does not, however, seem consistent with what Hebrews next says (2:14), namely, that the Word took on the same blood and flesh as humanity *since* the children were all of the same blood and flesh, so that by his death he could set free all those who had been held in slavery. Note that it does *not* say that he would not have taken flesh as man if the children were not all of the same blood and flesh. However, what would be meant by saying that the Word became man *because* the human race was descended from one set of first parents, if those saved from the slavery of sin and death included non-human beings? The most natural explanation of the stated rationales behind the Incarnation and Passion—"*since* the children share the same blood and flesh, he too shared equally in it, *so* that by his death he could...set free those who had been held in slavery all their lives by fear of death" (emphasis mine)—is that given the unity of the human race, the sacrifice of a man who was God would make appropriate satisfaction for the sin of the entire race: "[S]in entered the world through one man, and through sin death…. [I]f it is certain that death reigned over everyone as the consequence of one man's fall, it is even more certain that one man, Jesus Christ, will cause everyone to reign in life who receives the free gift that he does not deserve, of being made righteous" (Rom. 5:12, 17). It does not make sense to say that the Word shared in human nature in order to free ETIs and humans from the slavery of sin and death, *because* the children share the same blood and flesh.[59]

If ETIs were saved through the cross of Christ, the passage from Hebrews would have to read or be read differently. It would have to say (or be understood to say) something to the effect that the Second Person took on the same blood and flesh as humanity as is appropriate for saving those on earth who are held in slavery, whereas he saved other beings elsewhere from the slavery of sin not because he shared their flesh and blood, but through some sort of application of the Passion to them. For example, the qualification could have been added that he took on human flesh in order to "set free *humans* who had been held in slavery...." rather than "all those who had been held in slavery" as the English translation reads. (The Greek and Latin simply say "those", "toutos" and "eos" respectively.) In this way the door would remain open to the possibility that setting free ETIs from this slavery could be a secondary purpose for the Word's incarnation as man and death on the cross, albeit it was not the reason he took on specifically human flesh.[60] Of course, one could argue that a qualification of this sort is understood but left unstated because Scripture is ordered to human salvation. I find this line of interpretation contrived, and think that Heb. 2:14 is best read as excluding the possibility that *fallen* ETIs exist.

The following lines, speaking of it being essential[61] that Christ become "completely like his brothers so that he could be a compassionate and trustworthy high priest...because he himself has been through temptation he is able to help others who are tempted" (Heb. 2:17), would also have no applicability to any ETIs that he would have come to save, providing a further indication, albeit a weaker one than Heb. 2:14, that there are no such fallen beings.

Rom. 5:15-19 supports my reading of Heb. 2:14 insofar as it speaks of sin coming into the world through one man having as counterpart salvation coming into the world through one man:

> Adam prefigured the One to come, but the gift itself considerably outweighed the fall....If it is certain that death reigned over everyone as the consequence of one man's fall, it is even more certain that one man Jesus Christ, will cause everyone to reign in life who receives the free gift that he does not deserve, of being made righteous. Again, as one man's fall brought condemnation on everyone, so the good act of one man brings everyone life and

makes them justified. As by one man's disobedience many were made sinners, so by one man's obedience many will be made righteous (Rom. 5:15-19).

On the hypothesis that fallen ETIs exist, the full story would be "as one man and one or more ETIs' fall brought condemnation on everyone, so one man's good act brings everyone life." One could say that this passage from Romans only mentions humans since it is addressed to humans, and that it could be understood to say that sin came into *our* world through one man, and salvation came to it through one man. However, this passage does give the impression that God intended there to be a correspondence between the fallen and the redeemer, one to one. Such correspondence is present in the case of Adam and Christ, the new Adam. It is not however present in the case of ETI fallen and Christ: Christ is not the new ETI, and given the disparity in nature, it is hard to regard ETI fallen as "prefigur[ing] the One to come." And even if ETI fallen were Christ's counterpart, there would still be two fallen heads of races to one redeemer.

I think that the Colossians 1:18-20 text is about as clear-cut as it can be when it comes to excluding the possibility that there exist beings who are saved in some manner other than through the cross of Christ, because it contains the explicit qualifications that Christ was to be first in every way and was to reconcile *all* things, both "in heaven and in earth." This reading also accords well with the cosmic import that the Church has traditionally attributed to Christ's Incarnation, Passion, and Resurrection, something that I will elaborate on in chap. 15.

In the case of Hebrews 2:14, I am more hesitant about judging its meaning, for although I am sure that it means to affirm that Christ desired to free man from sin and death by becoming one of us, I am not absolutely sure it means to exclude that other rational creatures are saved in some way derivative of the cross of Christ. Caution must always be exercised in interpreting Scripture, even with statements that seem quite straightforward. For sometimes statements of that sort have to be nuanced on the basis of other Scriptures or Church teachings, and end up meaning something somewhat different from what one would think at first sight. For example, Christ says: "You must call no one on earth your father, since you have only one Father, and he is in heaven" (Mt. 23:10). What could be plainer than that? Yet Catholics are not forbidden to call both priests and male parents, "Father." Further examination of Scripture reveals passages where St. Paul calls himself "father," e.g., "You might have thousands of guardians in Christ, but not more than one father and it was I who begot you in Christ Jesus by preaching the Good News." (1 Co. 4:15, 16).[62] Thus Christ's apparently straightforward explicit admonition cannot be taken at face value.

Of course, I leave the final judgment as to how to interpret these passages of Sacred Scripture to the Catholic Church. I am going to proceed, however, as if the interpretation given above of Col. 1:18-20 is correct, and as though that of Heb. 2:14 is only probable, although I strongly suspect that it is correct. The advantage of not going with my hunch that Christ came to save only members of Adam's race is that in the case it is wrong, I will not be at fault for failing to consider the scenario of fallen ETIs saved by Christ.

Given my position on Heb. 2:14, it is fair to ask whether I really think that belief in Christianity and in ETI existence are compatible. Paine states without qualification that the two beliefs cannot be held in the same mind. I think that Paine is wrong because I think that belief in unfallen ETIs is not necessarily excluded by Christian belief, which is what I try to show in chapters one and two. However, I would tend to agree with Paine if he had made the more restricted statement that some belief in ETI is excluded by Christian belief, namely, in fallen ETIs. Still, there are two reasons why I do not affirm without reservation that there is a partial conflict between the two beliefs. First, I have concluded that there is this partial conflict based on my reading of Heb. 2:14, a reading that could be mistaken (I am not even a theologian).

Even if I was correct, there is a second and more important reason for not asserting that the two beliefs are in part incompatible, namely, the absence of any Church teaching on the matter (as I endeavor to show in Part I). Heb. 2:14 may in fact exclude the existence of fallen ETIs. However, because there is neither an official interpretation of this passage, nor any official censure of belief in fallen ETIs, a person can be a good Catholic and adhere to all that the Catholic Church teaches, and still believe in fallen ETIs. There are doubtlessly cases where Scripture indicates some truth, but Catholics are not bound to profess that truth. For example, Lk. 1:43 may well indicate that John the Baptist, while in Elizabeth's womb, was cleansed from original sin at the moment of the Visitation: "For the moment your greeting reached my ears, the child in my womb leaped for joy." The person then who denied John's cleansing would be holding a position incompatible with Scripture, but not incompatible with the essential teachings of the Catholic faith which all Catholics are bound to profess. As Aquinas notes:

> Things pertain to the faith in two ways. In one way directly; as are those things which are principally handed on to us by God, e.g., that God is three and one, that the Son of God became incarnate, and things of this sort. And to opine what is false concerning such things entails heresy, chiefly when obstinacy is present. Those things which indirectly pertain to the faith are those from which something contrary to the faith follows; as if someone were to say that Samuel was not the son of Elcana; for it would follow from this that divine Scripture was false. Therefore, someone is able to hold a false opinion concerning things of this sort without danger of heresy, before it is considered or determined whether something contrary to the faith follows from it, and especially if he does not adhere to it with obstinacy. But after it becomes manifest that from a given position something follows that is contrary to the faith, and mainly if this is determined by the Church, to commit such an error would constitute heresy. And for this reason, there are many positions that are now reputed heretical, which in the past were not reputed so, for now it is more manifest what follows from them.[63]

If the Church ever made an official pronouncement that Christian belief and belief in ETIs are incompatible, then belief in ETIs would be matter for heresy.

In sum, I maintain that some, but not every, form of belief in ETI existence is compatible with Christian belief. The forms of belief in ETI existence which I think are in fact incompatible with Christian belief are: belief in fallen ETIs who are not redeemed by Christ, and belief in fallen ETIs without qualification. The latter belief, however, I see as compatible with Christian belief in the sense that it does not appear to unambiguously compromise any doctrine essential to the Christian faith.

Chapter 2

Something Wrong with Being Special?

I give you thanks that I am fearfully, wonderfully made.

—Psalm 139

Thus far we have seen that the argument that Christianity and ETI existence are mutually exclusive on the grounds that Christ could not have any meaningful relationship with ETIs does not stand up under scrutiny. Christ could relate to unfallen ETIs in a manner similar to how he relates to the angels, and to fallen ETIs as their savior (although Heb. 2:14 does cause serious doubts as to this possibility). Now it is time to consider the other main line of argument opposing Christianity with ETI existence, namely, that the specialness of mankind and of the planet earth as portrayed in Scripture is incompatible with the existence of other intelligent life forms. Certainly, if man's specialness, as delineated by Scripture and Church doctrine, amounts to uniqueness in the strong sense, then Christianity is incompatible with ETI existence. However, not every form of specialness is equivalent to uniqueness in the strong sense of the word. There is a need to define the different meanings of "special" if we are to discern whether Christianity's assertions regarding human specialness would be rendered absurd if ETI were discovered.

One might wonder why I cast the second point of debate concerning the possibility of ETI existence on the assumption that Christianity is true in terms of human specialness when neither Church documents nor Scripture ever say "humans are special" in those exact words. "Special," however, is used in regard to humans in at least one Church document, and it is also used in many works of theology. The encyclical *Evangelium vitae* says: "Human life is sacred because from its beginning it involves 'the creative action of God,' and it remains forever in a special relationship with the Creator, who is its sole end."[1] In the same vein, it was not uncommon for catechetical works in the last century to speak of the "special creation" of each human soul. Aquinas speaks of how God's providence extends in a special way to rational creatures.[2] Moreover, Church documents often mention features of human beings that can be termed "special," even if they do not use the word (this will be clear from what follows). Largely as a consequence of the usage of "special" in Catholic theology, those seeking to drive a wedge between Christian belief and belief in ETI existence often use this word in their arguments, and those rebutting their arguments often employ the same term, so I will do so as well.[3]

"Special" is not only a term that can be ambiguous because of its many meanings, it is also a term that is inherently vague. These two things make it particularly easy to misunderstand the force of arguments based on human specialness, be they against or in favor of ETI existence. It is all too easy to slip from taking specialness as corresponding to unique in the weak sense to taking it as corresponding to unique in the strong sense. And it is easy to slide from affirming specialness in one respect, to affirming it in some other respect. Thus, precautions must be taken to avoid both equivocation and imprecision.

Webster's Collegiate Dictionary (11th edition, 2003) devotes twenty-one lines to defining the word "special" and explaining its usages in comparison to other words like it in meaning. The meanings of the word include:

> 1: distinguished by some unusual quality; esp: being in some way superior; 2: held in particular esteem; 3 a: readily distinguishable from others of the same category: UNIQUE; 3 b: of, relating to, or constitutive of a species: SPECIFIC; 4: being other than the usual: ADDITIONAL, EXTRA; 5: designed for a particular purpose or occasion.

Meanings 3b, 4, and 5 do not relate to any ETI-Christianity arguments, while 1, 2, and 3a, do. There is not much difference between 1 and 3a. If something is readily distinguishable from others of a category, it must have some unusual quality, and generally if something has an unusual quality it will be readily distinguishable. Meaning 1 does add that the unusual quality is generally in the line of an excellence or superiority, and this is the way it will be understood here. "Unique" is given as a synonym of 3a, but it seems to correspond more closely to the weak sense of unique, i.e., very rare or very unusual, as opposed to one of a kind. Certainly if something was unique in the strong sense it would be special, but not vice versa. Given the close interconnection in meanings 1 and 3a, I will consider them as one in the discussion below. The second meaning of "special" relevant to the Christianity ETI debate is 2: "held in particular esteem." Note that the latter expression contains an ambiguity which will be addressed later on.

In addition to the word having two meanings relevant to our discussion, both of these meanings generally require further specification in order for them not to be vague. That someone be called "special" because of being distinguished by an unusual quality does not tell us much until the quality is specified, e.g., a child can be called special due to being musically gifted, or extraordinarily well-behaved, or mentally retarded, or exceptionally coordinated. So just to say that the human race is "special" is hardly a statement one can agree or disagree with unless it is specified as to what.

We must endeavor then to discern both which meaning of special is being used, and then how that meaning is specified, in the arguments that pit Christianity against ETI existence. Here is a list of the chief ways in which ETI existence is supposed to conflict with Christianity's claims regarding human specialness, accompanied with what sense of "special" is being used or implied, the specification also being stated: 1) Man is made in the image of God. As such he is the pinnacle of creation, and thus is that to which all other things in the universe are ordered (the earth having a corresponding importance, as man's abode, in comparison to other planets). Accordingly, man has dominion over all of the earth (unusual as superior); 2) the destiny of the universe depends upon man (unusual as superior); 3) God has a special relationship with the human race because of a) ordering all things to man; b) becoming incarnate as man; c) redeeming man; d) tying the destiny of the universe to man (held in particular esteem).

"God created man in the image of himself, in the image of God he created him, male and female he created them" (Gen. 1:27). The *CCC* #355 quotes this verse, and adds the following comment: "Man occupies a unique place in creation: (I) he is 'in the image of God'...." I think that it is natural to assume that "unique" here means one of a kind, rather than very unusual. The statement seems to indicate that other created beings are not in the image of God—man alone is. This is why at least one ETI proponent suggests that: "The assertion that 'God created man in his own image' is ticking like a time bomb in the foundations of Christianity."[4] But is this true?

Man is the image of God in virtue of his intellect and free will. This certainly makes humans superior to all the other created beings explicitly mentioned in Genesis, for these other beings are incapable of knowing and loving their creator. Humans are not, however, the only being that God created in his image—this is also true of the angels.[5] We are not then unique as being the only being created in God's image. Plainly the *CCC* statement that appears to say the contrary (#355 quoted just above) is not meant to address the question of whether man alone is created in the image of God. One could maintain that it is intended to answer the question of whether humans are unique as being the only beings in *material* creation created in God's image. But then one could also maintain that it is intended to answer the question of whether humans are unique as being the only being *on earth* created in God's image. In order to determine which, if either, of these two is more likely to be the case, it is helpful to look at another reference in the *CCC*.

CCC #256 at first sight seems to rule out the existence of other rational material beings in the universe: "'Of all visible creatures only man is able to know and love his creator.'" Read out of context, this certainly sounds like a denial of ETI existence. Put in context, the first thing to note is that the document it quotes, *Gaudium et Spes*, reads: "For sacred Scripture teaches that man was created 'to the image of God,' is capable of knowing and loving his Creator, and was appointed by Him as master of all earthly creatures…"[6] It does not say man is the *only* visible creature created to the image of God. Second, and more importantly, the next line of the *CCC* reads (and here it quotes *Gaudium and Spes* directly): "He is 'the only creature *on earth* that God has willed for its own sake'" (emphasis mine).

Church statements that say that humans are the only creatures on earth that God has willed for their own sake neither affirm nor deny that humans are the only creatures in the material universe willed for their own sake. Church statements which seem to indicate that humans are the only material rational beings God wills for their own sake may well be leaving out the qualification "on earth" for the sake of brevity, and thus one cannot conclude that they mean to affirm or deny that humans are the only creatures in the material universe willed for their own sake. Such statements are made not to answer the question whether man is the only material rational being in the universe, but to tell us how we humans are related to God so that we can understand our dignity, a dignity that lies in being created in the image of God, in being able to know and love God. It is not reasonable to take such statements as if they were magisterial pronouncements on ETI existence when the question is not even raised. If ETIs were discovered, this would not in any way affect the human specialness or uniqueness that consists in our being the only life form created on earth in the image of God. To date, the Church has left open the question of whether we are the only intelligent material life form in the universe.

The expression "special creation" is related to the notion that humans are made in the image of God.[7] The human powers of intellect and free will (in virtue of which humans are in the image of God) can only be rooted in an immaterial soul. Thus, each human soul has to be specially created by God; purely natural processes cannot produce something that is immaterial. If there existed another type of rational material being, the soul of each individual of that type would also have to be specially created, for the exact same reason that holds in the case of humans.

Another thing directly related to our being created in the image of God is the notion of "special providence:"

> ...it is manifest that divine providence extends to all things. Nevertheless it is necessary that some special notion of providence be observed in regard to intellectual and rational natures before all other creatures; for they excel other creatures both in the perfection of their nature and in the dignity of their end. In the perfection of their nature, certainly, because only the rational creature has control over its acts, freely moving itself to acting.... In the dignity of the end, however, because only the intellectual creature arrives at the ultimate end of the universe by its operation, namely, by knowing and loving God; other creatures cannot arrive at this ultimate end except by a certain sharing in its likeness.[8]

God's providence for rational creatures is special in contrast to the providence he exercises over non-rational beings. It would be extended to any race of rational beings.

Another thing that follows upon man's being created in the image of God is that he is the pinnacle of creation, and thus that to which all other things in the universe are ordered. Just as the statement that "humans are unique as being created in the image of God," is not to be taken as an answer to the question of whether we are the only beings in material creation that are such, so too the statement that all things exist for man must not be taken as saying one way or another "for man only." Man is certainly portrayed in Genesis as being the pinnacle of material creation *on earth*. We alone on earth are made in the image of God, and are set in dominion over "the animals living on earth" (Gen. 1:28), with the seed-bearing plants given us for food, and after the deluge, animals as well (Gen. 9:3, 4). Ps. 8 also affirms our supremacy over material creation:

> Yet you [God] have made him [man] little less than a god, you have crowned him with glory and splendor, made him lord over the work of your hands, set all things under his feet, sheep and oxen, all these, yes wild animals too, birds in the air, fish in the sea....

The reason that we have this supremacy follows upon our nature as rational beings. Rational beings are naturally ends in themselves, because they are able to reflect on their acts, and exercise self-control.[9] They can then not only pursue goods, but they can pursue them understanding that they are goods, and thus they can realize a higher level of goodness than beings lacking reason (or intelligence) can. Non-rational beings have a natural ordering to those things which are ends in themselves, contributing instrumentally to a good they themselves cannot realize. Thus, rational beings rightly use plants and animals for food, clothing, transportation, etc.[10]

Rational beings existing elsewhere, however, would also be the end of the non-rational beings, and have natural dominion over them. The natural dominion of rational beings does not mean, of course, that any rational being can make use of just any non-rational thing. There is a matter of ownership. Thus, if the ETIs came to earth they could not use or take our property without permission.[11] Even if they were more intelligent than we are, this would not give them justification to use us as their slaves, nor would we lose our rights to our property any more than a non-technological society does when it comes into contact with a technological society. Perhaps we would have an obligation to share the earth with them. But this sort of question is not radically different from the question regarding human immigration into one country from another. It is not a matter, then, of our being deprived of our dominion over the earth, but at most perhaps being obligated to share this dominion with other rational beings. Filachou's claim that ETI existence would conflict with "the importance presupposed [in Scripture] of the role of man on earth"[12] is thus unfounded.

The *CCC* seems to go further than simply asserting that the material things *on earth* exists for man, the most excellent being *on earth*:

> God created everything for man, but man in turn was created to serve and love God and to offer all creation back to him: What is it that is about to be created, that enjoys such honor? It is man—that great and wonderful living creature, *more precious in the eyes of God than all other creatures*! For him the heavens and the earth, the sea and *all the rest of creation exist*. God attached so much importance to his salvation that he did not spare his own Son for the sake of man. Nor does he ever cease to work, trying every possible means, until he has raised man up to himself and made him sit at his right hand.[13] (emphasis mine)

How is the assertion that not just the material things on earth, but "all the rest of creation" exists for man to be understood? Perhaps it is left understood that it is all *material* creatures which exist for man, e.g., *CCC* #353 states that: "He [God] destined all material creatures for the good of the human race. Man, and through him all creation, is destined for the glory of God." This would not as such exclude that material creation also exists for the benefit of other rational creatures who would have the same rights to it that man does. As before in *CCC* #256, the absence of the qualification all *material* creation in *CCC* #358 cited above is most likely simply for the sake of succinctness. Still the affirmation that man is "more precious in the eyes of God than all other creatures," leaves a lingering doubt as to whether other intelligent beings exist for man.

Here it is helpful to consider the relation of angels to man. The ultimate end of the angels is the beatific vision, and thus they are not ordered to man in the same way as the plants and other non-intelligent things in the universe are. The angels do, however, in a qualified way exist for man:

> Christ is the center of the angelic world. They are his angels: "When the Son of man comes in his glory, and all the angels with him...." (Mt. 25:31). They belong to him because they were created through and for him: "for in him all things were created in heaven and on earth, visible and invisible, whether thrones or dominions or principalities or authorities—all things were

created through him and for him" (Col. 1:16). They belong to him still more because he has made them messengers of his saving plan: "Are they [the angels] not all ministering spirits sent forth to serve, for the sake of those who are to obtain salvation" (Heb. 1:14).[14]

All the angels are ordered to Christ, who is both God and man, in a general way because they are his creatures, and in a special way because they are his ministers. As the latter they also are ordered to us. They are not, however, ordered to us in the manner in which material creation is ordered to us. Rather, as Aquinas puts it:

> [A]ngels are more noble than man according to the condition of nature; whence they are not for the sake of man in the said mode [i.e., as inferior things are], but only as from them some utility comes to man; as if it were said that the king was instituted in office for the sake of some rustic, to whom came the utility of peace due to the laws of the king.[15]

Is it the case that man is more precious to God than the angels? When speaking of individuals, it is reasonable to think that some angels are more blessed than some individual humans are or will be, and thus are more loved by God.[16] For according to tradition, the just are to take the places in the celestial hierarchy vacated by the fallen angels.[17] Be that as it may, God nonetheless has a certain predilection[18] for mankind: "For it was not the angels that he took to himself; he took to himself descent from Abraham" (Heb. 2:16, 17). Nor did he shed his blood for the angels.

Would the ETIs be ordered to man? Since they are not purely material beings, but possess an immaterial soul, they are ordered to eternal life as their ultimate end. So they would not exist for man in the same way plants and animals do. The ETIs, like the angels, would exist for man, insofar as they exist for Christ for whom all of creation exists. This would be true even on the supposition that the Word became Incarnate as one of them, for Christ and this supposed Incarnation would be the same person. The ETIs, however, do not seem to exist in any way for the sake of mankind. To date they have not benefited any human, unlike the angels who protect us and have brought messages to us. Nor did they play a role in the economy of salvation, as did the angels.

Up until now we have been examining man's superiority insofar as he is the final cause of material creation, i.e., that to which all material creation is in some way ordered. We have seen that this neither excludes other rational animals from enjoying a similar station, nor does it imply that immaterial intelligences are subservient to man,[19] other than to Christ (those who help man do so not as instruments or slaves, but rather as parents do children, or teachers, students). Yet another question arises regarding man's role as efficient cause in the universe. A passage from the *CCC* (#1042), quoting *Lumen Gentium*, makes it sound as if all of creation is destined to the glory of God through man:

> At the end of time, the Kingdom of God will come in its fullness. After the universal judgment, the righteous will reign forever with Christ, glorified in body and soul. The universe itself will be renewed: "The Church...will receive her perfection only in the glory of heaven, when will come the time of the renewal of all things. At that time, together with the human race, the universe itself, which is so closely related to man and which attains its destiny through him, will be perfectly re-established in Christ."[20]

The angels achieved their beatitude (and the demons merited eternal punishment) through choices made prior to the Fall of Adam and Eve. Thus it is without human intervention that the angels achieved with God's grace the end to which he ordered them, and in doing so glorified God. As mentioned earlier, before Christ was incarnate he infused grace into the angels only in his divine nature, and thus the angels did not achieve their individual ends through Christ as man.[21]

While the angels did not achieve their destiny through man in the sense that the God-Man or other humans were the efficient cause of their salvation, some theologians speculate that in order for the angels to achieve their final end, an act on their part involving reference to man was required of them:

> Many theologians have conjectured...that the mystery of the Divine Incarnation was revealed to the Angels, that they saw that a nature lower than their own was to be hypostatically united to the Person of God the Son, and that all the hierarchy of heaven must bow in adoration before the majesty of the Incarnate Word;

and this, it is supposed, was the occasion of the pride of Lucifer....[T]he advocates of this view seek support in certain passages of Scripture, notably in the words of the Psalmist as they are cited in the Epistle to the Hebrews: "And again, when he bringeth in the first-begotten into the world, he saith: And let all the angels of God adore him" (Heb., i, 6; Ps. xcvi, 7).[22]

Suarez is one of the theologians in question. He argues in favor of the view that God revealed to the angels the future Incarnation of the Word as man.[23] The angels who fell did so because they rejected the Incarnation, not in the sense that they did not believe it would take place, but in the sense that they refused to "adore Christ as Lord, and recognize him as their head, and venerate him."[24] If this scenario was what actually occurred, it could be said that the angels achieved their salvation by reverencing Christ as known to them by faith. Granted that the grace whereby they achieved their salvation came to them directly from God, and not through the Word *Incarnate*, their situation does not seem all that different from the just in the Old Testament. The people in the Old Testament were justified not by grace coming to them through Christ, but by their faith in the future coming of Christ,[25] while the angels achieved salvation not by grace coming to them through Christ, but by their reverencing of Christ who was revealed to them as the Word destined to become Incarnate at a future time. Christ is the savior of all men, people in the Old Testament included. So perhaps Christ could be regarded as in some way responsible for the angels' achieving glory if the Suarezian scenario is correct, granted that the humanity assumed by the Word after the angels' fall is not the efficient cause of the grace by which they achieved glory. Of course, not all theologians subscribe to Suarez's views, and no definitive teaching has been made by the Church on these points.

Does *CCC* #1042 require one to believe that the ETIs have to achieve their destiny through man? For ETIs existing before the Incarnation and Redemption, Christ as man could not be the efficient cause through which they achieved their beatitude. As to whether ETIs existing before Christ's coming would achieve their destiny through man in another mode, similar to the mode of faith of those in the Old Testament, or to the mode by which the angels, on the Suarezian scenario, reverenced Christ's coming, this is hidden to us. We are not even sure of what happened in the case of the angels, whom we know to exist. In addition, the *CCC*'s statement that the universe "attains its destiny" through man admits of other interpretations compatible with the angels not achieving their destiny in any manner through man.

Another way one could take the statement that the universe "attains its destiny" through man is as an affirmation that the final completion of the universe is attained when all things give glory to God. The angels were not holding up the universe from achieving this end, and the same would go for unfallen ETIs, if such there be. It was the human race that stepped outside of God's original plan for creation when our first parents sinned. Thus, that the universe achieve its destiny through man could be taken to refer first and foremost to the restoration of fallen man that Christ brought about.[26] Then in a complementary way, it could refer to the realization of the redemption in the individuals who cooperate with Christ's salvific grace.[27] Certainly Christ's sacrifice is infinite in its redeeming power. However, as St. Augustine notes, God creates us without our cooperation, but cannot save us without it. Now, inasmuch as any fallen ETIs there might be would achieve their destiny through the sacrifice of the God-Man, they would achieve their destiny through man. As for the other sense of the universe achieving its destiny through man, if fallen ETIs too attain their eternal salvation, they too play a role in the achievement of the universe's destiny, though a certain priority is assigned to man, the race God became incarnate as, in a way similar to the Gospel being announced first to the Jews, the chosen people, and then to the Gentiles.[28]

This leads us to the third apparent conflict between Christianity and ETI. Could God favor man while regarding other intelligent races as being of secondary importance? Robert Jastrow, who leans in favor of ETI existence, states the conflict thus:

> [S]ome of the older races [of ETI] might be...superior in their moral and ethical values and religious beliefs. Does this not create problems for the traditional Judeo-Christian view of the Deity as being very much concerned with the affairs of the particular race of intelligent beings that exists on our planet?
>
> A logically impeccable answer is that the Deity is omnipotent and can be concerned with the affairs of as many intelligent races on as many planets as the Deity wishes. But it seems to me that the image of a God whose attention is divided among trillions of intelligent races inevitably dilutes the relationship between God

and humankind which is the essence of the Old and New Testaments.[29]

William Whewell argues in basically the same way, although unlike Jastrow he comes down decidedly in favor of Christianity. Whewell maintains that the specialness of the human race (and planet earth) would be lost if there were other planets inhabited by intelligent life forms:

> The earth…can not, in the eyes of any one who accepts this Christian faith, be regarded as being on a level with any other domiciles. It is the Stage of the great Drama of God's Mercy and Man's Salvation…. This being the character which has thus been conferred upon it, how can we assent to the assertion of Astronomers, when they tell us that it is only one among millions of similar habitations…?"[30]

Both Jastrow and Whewell seem to think that God could not have special interest in our planet if there were other planets inhabited by intelligent beings. Yet God's caring for countless inhabitants of countless worlds would in nowise prevent him from choosing our planet and race to be unique insofar as the Word became Incarnate as a man and performed here the redemptive act through which all things are reconciled. God is omnipotent, and thus his attending to other rational beings on other worlds would not diminish or dilute the attention and care he bestows on our world.[31]

Jastrow not only seems to underestimate God's omnipotence when he suggests that there is opposition between God caring for other material rational species and his according humans special status, but he also seems to erroneously suppose that God always treats equals in the same manner, and unequals according to merit. For the latter view seems to be the reason why Jastrow regards it as problematic for God to be more concerned with humans than with a morally superior ETI race. The same supposition may also underlie Whewell's fear that if ETIs exist the earth would be on the same level as other planets. For supposing that God treats equals in the same manner, and assuming that one race of material rational animals is pretty much the same as another, it would follow that each ETI inhabited planet would be the site of a redemption story like that of earth's. This supposition, however, runs counter to the lesson of the parable of the workers that arrived late and yet received the same wage as those who had worked all day (see Mt. 20:1-16), namely, God is fair to all, but he is generous to whom he chooses to be generous. The question of why God chose the human race (and the earth) for purposes of the Redemption, rather than some other race, is the same sort of question as why God chose the Jews to be his people, and why certain individuals receive the privilege of baptism while others never even hear the name of Christ. God can certainly choose, and indeed has chosen, to grant favor to whom he wills while offering to all the possibility of salvation.

Given that our planet has been shown favor, Monseigneur de Montignez offers an argument by fittingness for why Christ would have come to earth rather than to some other planet inhabited by intelligent beings:

> Because our earth is of insignificant size and contains "probably the most disgraced" creatures in the cosmos, it served as the ideal locale for that "annihilation of the divinity" which is the incarnation. As Christ chose "Bethlehem...the least among the cities of Judah" for his birthplace, so also he selected the earth as the location for the founding of his Church and his redemptive actions.[32]

This account supposes that there exist other intelligent races more intelligent and more virtuous than the human race, and thus that the human race is not special as being superior in these ways (indeed when it comes to intelligence, we are lesser than the angels). The reason we are special is due to the favor that God showed us by saving us as one of us. Our race is elevated to a privileged position in virtue of the Word's taking on human nature for the purpose of the Redemption.

Ultimately, it is foolishness to accuse God of favoritism. God's good will and pleasure are unfathomable to us, and thus our inability to know with certitude why God condescended to become incarnate on planet earth rather than elsewhere to save sinners is not a reason for denying that God has chosen to confer special dignity upon the human race. The accusations leveled in the ETI debate against the "particularism" of Christianity are based on the underlying assumption that God could not have a chosen people or a chosen species. But again, although we rightly maintain that God is all-good and all-just, it is not for us to dictate how God is to distribute his gifts to his creatures.

God not only has a special relation with the human race, he also has another sort of special relation with baptized human individuals. For it is through baptism that humans become adopted children of God. That baptized humans have this special relation to God does not mean that individuals of another nature cannot have a similar relation. All beings of a rational nature are capable of becoming adopted children of God. Indeed, the angels are also called sons of God,[33] and since they are not so by nature, this can only be because they have been adopted by God. ETI individuals, then, could also have a special relationship with God as his adopted children.

To recapitulate, then, the ways in which God has a special relationship with man, God has favored man by: 1) ordering all things to man; 2) redeeming man; 3) assigning to man the completion of the universe's destiny; 4) becoming incarnate as man. Our analysis has shown that none of these forms of special favor is incompatible with ETI existence.

First of all, as we have seen, God would not order ETIs to man given that he created ETIs free and capable of achieving the beatific vision. Other things in material creation would have a natural ordering to all beings of a rational nature, granted one such being might have priority over another in a given part of the universe, as man would on planet earth, and ETIs on their respective planets. It remains the case, though, that God holds us in esteem in ordering non-rational material beings to our good, rather than vice versa.

Secondly, the redemption performed by Christ could be applicable to ETIs, as it is to man. However, we are special in that the Word redeemed us by becoming one of our race (the numerous benefits entailed by this will be spelled out in a later chapter). Also, the actual event by which Christ redeemed sinners took place on our planet alone.

It is important to keep in mind that although the human race excels the animals in being created in the image of God, this does not mean that the race as a whole possesses any special excellence when it comes to achieving what rational creatures by nature are able and meant to achieve. Aristotle thought that most humans were bad. If this view is perhaps overly pessimistic, still it would be hard to deny that mediocrity is the order of the day. Granted, we are all affected by original sin, so one cannot evaluate what the race would have been like if Adam and Eve had not sinned. Still it would be absurd to claim that the majority of individuals constituting the human race are in fact special because they possess exceptional goodness. Everyday life in every age has shown the contrary to be the case.

Scripture's evaluation of mankind also leaves no room for pride: "The number of fools is infinite"[34] (Qo. 1:15). We are special chiefly because Christ made us special, elevating our race by his Incarnation and Redemption. To give a parallel: There was nothing special about the tax collector, the fishermen, etc. whom Christ chose to be his twelve closest disciples. It was his choosing them that made them henceforth special. Thus, it is questionable whether it is accurate to say that the human race is special in the sense that God held it *in esteem*, for this would seem to imply that our race possessed goodness of a sort apt to elicit high regard for it on God's part, when rather our race is special in the sense that we have been the object of God's favor and mercy. Given that word usage changes with time, it is hard to say for sure whether or not the expression "to hold in esteem" nowadays always implies excellence on the part of the thing esteemed, or whether it can also mean "to prize" for whatever reason. In any case, the ambiguity here as to word usage should not obscure the fact that I'm not claiming that humans as a group exhibit exceptional wisdom and virtue, but rather I'm claiming that God treasures us, as can be seen from the fact that he sent his only Son to die for us despite our pathetic condition: "[W]hat proves that God loves us is that Christ died for us while we were still sinners" (Rom. 5:9).[35]

The third reason for human specialness concerns humanity's role in bringing about the universe's destiny. Now, the first cause of the completion of the universe's destiny is Christ,[36] the man who is God. His death made possible the forgiveness of our sins, and gave us the grace to live a supernatural life. Those who cooperate with Christ's saving graces, be they humans or ETIs, are secondary causes of the universe being brought to the completion of its destiny. That humans do so does not entail that other beings are excluded from also doing so, albeit humans would have a certain priority over other rational species, inasmuch as the human species was the one that God chose to unite to himself in the person of Christ in order to save all who are saved.

Lastly, what of the specialness that accrues to humanity due to the Incarnation—does it eliminate the possibility of other intelligent life forms? Any species that a divine person would unite to himself by assuming its nature would by that very reason be elevated in dignity, and Christianity teaches that this happened in the case of our species. If there were other intelligent material species and incarnations of divine persons occurred in many of them, then one would not say our race was special in the sense of being distinguished from others. In comparison with all intelligent natures, however, we would still be somewhat special given that God did not become incarnate as an angel. Looked at from yet another point of view, in light of the singular favor shown us which need not have been shown us, we can say that the Incarnation makes us special because God, in his goodness, showed us this particular favor. As for whether the human race has the further specialness that we are the sole intelligent species which the Word became incarnate as, nothing we have seen so far indicates conclusively that this is the case. The *CCC* passage to this effect is unfortunately ambiguous. I think at most probable arguments against a second Incarnation can be made (as I will attempt to do in the next chapter). Again, even if it is true that the Word never united itself to any other material intelligent being, and thus that the human race is special for this reason, this would not entail that God had no care for the hypothetical ETIs. For again, fallen ones could be redeemed through Christ's death on Calvary. And unfallen ones would still be related to him as their Lord and Head, as is the case of the angels. Their relationship would be somewhat closer or more distant, depending on whether a Suarezian-type scenario did or did not obtain in their case. The concern that God's lavishing attention on the human race would be incompatible with his caring for intelligent beings elsewhere is unfounded, for he is omnipotent. And that God show more favor to one person or group than another falls to his good pleasure.

In sum, the existence of ETI is not a threat to the specialness that Christianity acknowledges man to possess be it at a natural or a supernatural level. As rational beings, humans will always belong to the top grade of material beings (and thus will always have a general right to make use of non-rational material beings). Also, as rational beings, their souls will always be the product of special creation, and they will always be the object of God's special providence. On the supernatural level, it will always be the case that both the redemption of all the saved and the destiny of the universe is accomplished by a human being whose nature God united to himself in the person of the Word. The appearance of ETIs would take away none of the specialness belonging to us due to all the above. Nor is the existence of ETI precluded by any of these forms of human specialness.

The above considerations provide in large part a response to the oft-made claim that Christianity has been losing ground ever since Copernicus and Darwin showed that the earth and humans are not special, and stands to lose even more ground once ETIs are discovered, as that would put an end to any remaining illusions that the earth or ourselves are special. Now, even if ETIs made an appearance, we would still be unique in the universe, for the reasons given above. And if our planet proves to have ETI-inhabited planets as rivals, what of it so far as Christian belief is concerned? Christians regard the earth as special because it was the planet God made for us, and because it was the place where the Word became incarnate and wrought our Redemption. ("We believe in God, the Father, the Almighty, Maker of heaven and earth.... For us men and for our salvation he [the Son of God] came down from heaven.") Thus, the notion that the discovery of ETI would somehow cause the earth to slip a notch lower on the scale of specialness, than it supposedly slipped when heliocentrism became accepted,[37] in a way that would affect Christianity is based on a misunderstanding of the importance Christianity places on the earth. Again, Christians would have no problem acknowledging that planets inhabited by other beings created in the image of God would be special compared to uninhabited ones. Still, the earth remains unique as being the planet where the Redemption took place.

The arguments pitting Christianity against ETI existence on the grounds humans are special have not held up.[38] Nor did those we saw earlier that opposed the two beliefs on the grounds that the Gospel's claim concerning the central role of the God-Man in the universe would be nonsensical in a universe populated with intelligent beings alien to man. "Christ is the center of the angelic world"[39] even though he neither assumed an angelic nature nor was responsible for the angels' attainment of beatitude as an efficient cause thereof.

Chapter 3

The Bible's Silence on ETI

> All scripture is inspired by God and can profitably be used for teaching, for refuting error, for guiding people's lives and teaching them to be holy.
> —2 Timothy 3:16, 17

A final type of scriptural argument in favor of the position that Christianity and ETI existence are incompatible remains to be considered, namely, the argument from Scripture's silence about ETI. Philip Melanchthon, a collaborator of Martin Luther, gives an argument of this sort. He points out that Genesis recounts that on the sixth day of Creation God finished the work he had been doing, and on the seventh day he rested from all the work he had done. Melanchthon infers from this that anything that Genesis does not mention God to have created in the first six days was never created by him at any later time. And then he applies this reasoning to the case of ETIs.[1] Centuries earlier, certain medieval authors had argued in a similar manner against the existence of their version of ETI, namely, animate stars, on the grounds that the scriptural account of the last judgment does not mention the presence of such beings, although it does mention humans and angels.[2]

Alternately, the absence of mention of ETI in Scripture is used by those who think that the discovery of ETI existence would spell the end of Christianity as proof that the Bible is a parochial anthropocentric document or more generally an unreliable document. As the philosopher Roland Puccetti notes:

> [T]he prospect of extraterrestrial intelligence, concerning which the principal sacred writings of Christianity, Judaism, and Islam

are absolutely silent, generates a profound suspicion that these terrestrial faiths are no more than that.[3]

Both of the above arguments are based on a lack of understanding of what the purpose of Scripture is. As Vatican II explains:

> Through divine revelation, God chose to show forth and communicate Himself and the eternal decisions of His will regarding the salvation of men.[4]

> Therefore, since everything asserted by the inspired authors or sacred writers must be held to be asserted by the Holy Spirit, it follows that the books of Scripture must be acknowledged as teaching firmly, faithfully, and without error that truth which God wanted put into the sacred writings for the sake of our salvation.[5]

Scripture is meant as a work directed specifically to humans for their benefit. It is not a work in cosmology. Things that have no relevance to human salvation are not found in it.

One cannot then infer that something does not exist because Scripture and Tradition do not mention it. (Scripture and Tradition[6] are the only two acknowledged sources for Catholic magisterial teaching.) One can, however, infer that if a thing exists that is not mentioned by Scripture or Tradition, it is unimportant for Christians as Christians to know that it exists. Thus, for example, as John Wilkins points out, Genesis does not mention that God created the other planets, yet plainly they are part of God's creation.[7] There is nothing surprising about this omission since such knowledge is not helpful to us for purposes of saving our souls.[8] Likewise, if ETIs are not mentioned by Scripture or Tradition, this does not mean that they do not exist. However, it does mean that knowledge about them is of no profit to us when it comes to our ultimate destiny. In this way the putative ETIs stand in sharp contrast with the angels who "are a truth of the faith."[9] Angels played and still play a role in regard to our salvation, and are thus are repeatedly mentioned in Scripture.

Chapter 4

What Church Documents and Tradition Say about ETI

> One of the more wonderful and nobler things sought after in nature is whether the world is one or whether there are many worlds....
>
> —St. Albert, *Commentary on De Caelo et Mundo*

Having scrutinized Scripture for any indication of compatibility or incompatibility between Christianity and ETI existence, and having considered statements in Church documents which appeared to pronounce on the question of human uniqueness, but in fact did not do so, it is time to determine whether any Church document indicates what Catholics are to think about ETI existence. There is also a need to examine what tradition has to say on the matter, given that traditionally held views have the force of doctrine when they have been constantly maintained throughout the Church's history.[1] I will begin with tradition as it will provide a context for understanding the Church documents.

The Church Fathers and Doctors rarely say anything about ETI existence, but speak more often about the related question of pluralism. Pluralism is the claim that there are many worlds. While some pluralists maintain that these worlds are inhabited, this is not an essential tenet of pluralism. Pluralism takes two forms, depending on the meaning given to the word "world." Sometimes "world" ("mundus" or "kosmos") is used to refer to an earthlike planet, and at other times it is used as a synonym for "universe." The earliest advocates of pluralism, Democritus and Epicurus, understood "world" to mean "universe," and the vast majority of subsequent thinkers reflecting upon pluralism followed their lead. I am plainly most interested in those passages where there is some question of the existence of a "world" in the minimal sense of a planet at least potentially habitable by some life form. Still, some of the arguments against many universes can be adapted to argue against many earthlike planets as well, and thus they also merit mention here.

My position on the early Church Fathers (from the first through the eighth century) and the Doctors of the Church (from 170 to 1280, i.e., from Hippolytus of Rome to St. Albert[2]) is that all of them who explicitly raise the question of whether there is one world or many, or who at least take an explicit stand on the question, reject pluralism, with the exception of Origen. There are also Fathers and Doctors who speak of many worlds, without at all having pluralism in mind. For them, the word "worlds" signifies non-contentious theological concepts such as the present order destined to pass away as opposed to the eternal order of heaven (the present world as opposed to the world to come).

Given how little has been written on what the tradition has to say about pluralism, I take particular issue with the erroneous claims that appeared in a review in the Roman Catholic journal, the *Rambler*, most likely penned by the editor, Richard Simpson (1820-76). According to Michael Crowe's summary:

> The first review...begins with the information that Catholic authorities had made no *de fide* declaration for or against pluralism. Although St. Augustine and St. Philastrius of Brixen included this doctrine in lists of heresies, St. Clement of Rome, Clement of Alexandria, St. Irenaeus, Origen, and St. Jerome all affirmed it.[3]

Simpson, as I will show, is mistaken about the views of most of the patristic authors whom he mentions. As a consequence, he presents a misleading picture of what patristic authors thought.

I am going to begin my survey of tradition by looking to what St. Albert and St. Thomas have to say about whether there is one world or many worlds, for they are the ones who treated the topic the most extensively.

St. Albert takes up the question of many worlds as it is posed in Aristotle's *De Caelo*. Although the question actually concerns the existence of many universes, rather than of many earthlike planets, it is useful to examine the arguments Albert gives there, for many of them can be adapted to answer the question of the existence of many earthlike planets.

A physical argument that Albert gives is that there can be only one lowest place, and one highest place, and so there can be only one center in existence, and one heaven. This argument could be adapted to argue that there is only one earth, for according to the physics of the ancients, all heavy material moves towards the sole center that exists.[4]

A second argument Albert gives against a multiplicity of universes goes as follows: "Since nature is able to realize completely all works through the things which are in this world, it will appear to be superfluous that there are entirely different worlds."[5] This sort of argument is what I'm going to term a "redundancy" argument, and it too can be adapted to the questions of whether there are many earthlike planets, as we shall see later on.

Albert proffers a third argument when commenting upon the view of the Hesiodists who hold that there is a plurality or infinity of worlds:

> It would be strange (mirabile) if what they said were true, because according to it, although every civil good is perfected through communication among the citizens, the gods, whom they call creators of the worlds, did not make it such that there is communication among the citizens of the diverse worlds; for the good of the worlds is not perfect without communication of its citizens.[6]

This argument would also apply to diverse earths, for lack of communication among the inhabitants of different earthlike planets would be incongruous for the same reason that lack of communication among diverse universes is.

Albert regards all the above arguments as having "little more strength than dialectical proofs by way of sign."[7] His supposedly knock-down *propter quid* argument turns on the notion that although form in principle is communicable to more than one matter, if there is no matter apt to receive it, it cannot in fact be communicated. In other words, if all the material capable of holding an edge were used up in knives, though the form of knife existed in the artisan's mind, he could not make another knife, at least not without first destroying an existing one. Or to give Albert's quaint comparison: "If, therefore, one nose was formed from all flesh which is or can be and in it snubness was present, then there could not exist any other snubness except that one, and snubness of nose would never be found except in that nose."[8] He then argues that the form of our world actualizes all the matter, and so there is no matter left to receive the form of world a second time. I shall omit his reasoning to this conclusion, because it lacks any applicability to the question of many earth-like planets.

Aquinas, like Albert, takes up the question of whether there are many universes in the context of commenting on Aristotle's *De Caelo*. He also addresses "Utrum Sit Mundus Tantum" in the *Summa Theologiae* (I, q. 47, art. 3), and when commenting on Bk. XII of Aristotle's *Metaphysics*.[9] Aquinas affirms the uniqueness of the world, giving all of the three sorts of arguments that Albert gives, and a couple of others as well. I do not intend to go over them here, with the exception of one physical argument, as virtually all of them will be referred to later on, given that they prove applicable to the ETI question. My main goal at this point is to establish that nothing in tradition supports the notion that a plurality of inhabitable planets exists. The argument that Aquinas gives most clearly directed to that point is derived from Aristotelian natural philosophy. It is similar to an argument that Albert gives, only Aquinas makes specific mention of the planet earth ("terra"), and not just of the universe ("mundus"):

> The universe is made up of all its matter. For it is not possible for there to be another earth than this one, because all earth, wherever it is, is born naturally to this center. And the same reasoning holds for the other bodies which are parts of the world.[10]

Turning now to the patristic authors, those who consider the question of a plurality of worlds plainly come down on the side of a negative answer, with the exception of Origen (185-254), and several reject by name the pluralist views of atomists such as Democritus and Epicurus. Since several of the Fathers contrast their views with Origen's view, it is worthwhile to consider it first. Origen endorses both many universes, and many earthlike planets, with the twist that the universes do not exist simultaneously, but sequentially, and this would seem to be his position on earthlike planets as well:

> But this is the objection which they generally raise: they say, 'If the world had its beginning in time, what was God doing before the world began? For it is at once impious and absurd to say that the nature of God is inactive and immovable.... [W]e can give an answer in accordance with the standard of religion, when we say that not then for the first time did God begin to work when He

made this visible world; but as, after its destruction, there will be another world, so also we believe that others existed before the present came into being. And both of these positions will be confirmed by the authority of holy Scripture. For that there will be another world after this, is taught by Isaiah, who says, 'There will be new heavens, and a new earth, which I shall make to abide in my sight, saith the Lord;' and that before this world others also existed is shown by Ecclesiastes, in the words: 'What is that which hath been/Even that which shall be/And what is that which has been created/Even this which is to be created: and there is nothing altogether new under the sun. Who shall speak and declare, Lo, this is new? It hath already been in the ages which have been before us.' By these testimonies it is established both that there were ages before our own, and that there will be others after it. It is not, however, to be supposed that several worlds existed at once, but that, after the end of this present world, others will take their beginning...."[11]

Origen considered that each time around the new world would not be identical with the previous ones, and that as far as inhabitants are concerned, each new world would not have the same population as the others, for births and deaths in the worlds would be unlikely to occur at the same rate.[12]

Augustine (354-430) in the *City of God*, without naming Origen, both denies Origen's position that there existed a series of worlds,[13] and attacks the view that is at the root of Origen's position, namely, that it would be absurd to think that God was idle before the creation of our world.[14] Augustine was in fact familiar with Origen's *De Principiis*, as he mentions it by name in the *City of God*, in another context.[15] Augustine's rejection of Origen's sequential universes entails rejection of Origen's sequential earths.

St. Jerome (343-420) explicitly condemns Origen's position on at least two occasions. In one passage, Jerome says:

> Among the many evil doctrines of Origen, I consider the following especially heretical: that the Son of God is a creature; that the Holy Spirit is a minister; that there are innumerable worlds (mundos) which succeed one another throughout eternal centuries....[16]

Jerome also condemns Origen's innumerable worlds, and at length, in Letter 124 to Avitus. There he notes that Origen "maintains a plurality of worlds; not, however, as Epicurus taught, many like ones existing at once, but a new one beginning each time that an old comes to an end."[17] Jerome elaborates on this view of Origen, quoting him extensively. He then goes on to ask the rhetorical question: "In speaking thus does he [Origen] not most clearly follow the error of the heathen and foist upon the simple faith of Christians, the raving of philosophy?"[18] Admittedly, Jerome does not level any argument specifically against the plurality of worlds as such. His objections to Origen were directed against his unorthodox theological views, such as the view that demons could come back in a new world as human beings,[19] and that sin is the cause of each new world.[20] It remains the case, however, that Jerome does plainly not agree with Origen's sequential pluralism.

Let us turn now to the patristic authors whose criticisms of pluralism are not directed specifically against Origen's views. Hippolytus of Rome (170-235) describes in some detail Democritus' views that there are infinite universes, explicitly noting that Democritus regarded some of these universes to be "destitute of animals and plants, and every species of moisture,"[21] the implication being Democritus thought that other universes harbored life (and thus contained earthlike planets). While Hippolytus does not actually critique this view, it is plain that he rejects it, for he recounts it in a work entitled: *The Refutation of all Heresies*. Hippolytus both rejects Democritus' infinite universes, and the earths that come with these universes.

Philastrius, Bishop of Brescia (4th century; died before 397) also lists pluralism in his book on heresies:

> There is another heresy that says that there are infinite and innumerable worlds, according to the empty opinion of certain philosophers—since Scripture has said that there is one world and teaches us about one world—taking this view from the apocrypha of the prophets, that is from the secrets, as the pagans themselves called them; there was also the Democritus who asserted there to be many worlds; he agitated the souls of many people and stirred up doubtful opinions with his diverse errors, since he proclaimed this [i.e., the plurality of worlds] as proceeding from his own wisdom.[22]

A careless reading of certain patristic authors might lead one to think that they endorse pluralism, when they are simply affirming that God is able to make many worlds. For example, St. John Chrysostom (345-407) says:

> For with God nothing is difficult: but as the painter who has made one likeness will make ten thousand with ease, so also with God it is easy to make worlds without number and end. Rather, as it is easy for you to conceive a city and worlds without bound, so unto God it is easy to make them; or rather again it is easier by far.[23]

Chrysostom here is only affirming God's power to make many worlds; he is not making a case for the actual existence of many worlds. Athanasius (297-373),[24] St. Basil (329-379)[25] and St. Bonaventure (1217-1274)[26] also affirm that God is capable of creating many worlds, but do not adopt the position that God actually did so.

When all is said and done, patristic authors speak more often about there being only one universe than about there being only one earth. Still, all those who do consider the many-earths question, even if only implicitly, all give a negative answer. The Fathers and Doctors that reject Origen's sequential universes, implicitly reject his sequential earths along with them. Similarly with those who reject the infinite universes of Democritus and Epicurus; they also implicitly reject any other earths that might be supposed to come with each universe. The question of whether there could be another earthlike planet in our universe almost never comes up, perhaps in part because the philosophers (and Origen) who proposed many earthlike planets always proposed multiple universes as well. Once the patristic authors had addressed the greater question posed by the philosophers, they had little motivation to pose the more limited question about the earth, especially given that there was no ambiguity in Scripture on that score: "In the beginning God created the heavens and the earth." Of course, a major reason why the question of whether there might be other earths did not come up is the influence that the geocentric theory exerted, positing as it did that all heavy elements in the universe accumulated on the earth as attracted to the earth's center. It was only much later when heliocentrism became widely accepted, and the earth was recognized to be one planet orbiting a star amongst many other planets orbiting stars, that the question of whether there were many earth-like planets came to the fore.[27] Before that time, Aquinas is the only Christian theologian who explicitly argued that there is only one earth in this universe. In the final analysis, then, every church Father and Doctor who paid some sort of attention to some version of many earths, always rejected the notion, with the single exception of Origen.

There is a small group of patristic authors who speak about there being more than one world. In their case, however, it is plain that they do not mean inhabitable worlds of the sort referred to by the advocates of pluralism. A case in point is one early Christian writer whose works were initially attributed to St. Clement of Rome (1st century):

> But the world that now is, is temporary; that which shall be, is eternal. First is ignorance, then knowledge. So also has He arranged the leaders of prophecy. For, since the present world is female, as a mother bringing forth the souls of her children, but the world to come is male, as a father receiving his children from their mother, therefore in this world there come a succession of prophets, as being sons of the world to come....[28]

It is plain that the two worlds spoken of here offer no encouragement to the proponents of ETI.

St. Clement of Rome also mentions many worlds:

> The ocean, impassable to man and the worlds beyond it, are regulated by the same enactments of the Lord. The seasons of spring, summer, autumn, and winter, peacefully give place to one another....The ever-flowing fountains, formed both for enjoyment and health, furnish without fail their breasts for the life of men....All these the great Creator and Lord of all has appointed to exist in peace and harmony....[29]

The least forced interpretation of this statement is to take the worlds referred to here to mean something along the lines of the Old World and New World.

Perhaps it was guilt by association that led Simpson to incorrectly list Clement of Rome as an endorser of pluralism. Origen quotes the above-cited passage from St. Clement of Rome in the context of discussing the different meanings which the term "world" has. Initially, Origen takes Clement of Rome to be referring there to peoples on other parts of the earth who are separated too far from us to be reached.[30] A little further on, however, he attributes to Clement the wish that "the globe of the sun or moon, and of the other bodies called planets...be each termed worlds,"[31] although he does not go so far as to pin belief in the existence of many inhabitable worlds upon Clement. Simpson, however, does charge Clement with pluralist views, but this is hardly supported from the passage cited above which has a less-forced, non-pluralist interpretation. (This is the only passage to my knowledge where Clement speaks of "worlds.")

A final consideration concerning the Fathers' and Doctors' views on pluralism concerns the word "aiônes." This word is used by both a number of biblical writers and patristic authors, and is sometimes translated as "worlds." The question then arises: Do these authors intend any endorsement of pluralism by their use of "aiônes"?

In the singular, "aiôn" properly names concepts associated with time: lifetime, age, generation, (long) space of time, etc; in the plural it signifies ages and eternity.[32] According to Grimm's *Greek-English Lexicon of the New Testament*, "by metonymy of the container for the contained, hoi aiônes denotes the worlds, the universe, i.e. the aggregate of things contained in time."[33] However, when one looks at the Scriptural references accompanying Grimm's claim, there is no reason to take "aiônes" as denoting anything other than all of creation or the universe: "[God] spoke to us through his Son...through whom he made everything there is" [di' hou kai tous aiônas epoiêsen] (Heb. 1:2). "It is by faith that we understand that the world was created by one word from God...." [Pistei vooumen katêrtisthai tous aiônas rêmati theou] (Heb. 11:3).

Indeed John of Damascus (?650-?750) takes up the meanings of aiôn and aiônes, and his treatment includes reference to Heb. 1:2:

> He made the ages who exists before the ages, of whom the divine David says: "From eternity to eternity thou art" [Ps. 89:2]; and the divine Apostle: "By whom also he made the ages" [Heb. 1:2].
>
> Now, one should note that the term *age*...signifies a great many things....Still again, this whole present life is called an age, and so is the age without end to come after the resurrection. And again, that is called an age which is neither time nor any division of time measured by the course and motion of the sun...but which is co-extensive with eternal things after the fashion of

some sort of temporal period and interval. This kind of age is to eternal things exactly what time is to temporal things....

Before the framing of the world, when there was no sun to separate day from night, there was no measurable age, but only an age co-extensive with eternal things after the fashion of some sort of temporal period and interval. In this sense, there is one age in respect to which God is said to be of the ages, and indeed, before the ages, for He made the very ages—since He alone is God without beginning and Himself creator both of the ages and of the things that are....God, therefore, is the one maker of the ages—He who also created all things and who exists before the ages.[34]

It is pretty clear from what John of Damascus says here that while it is legitimate to use "this age and the age to come" as interchangeable with "this world and the next,"[35] there is no justification for taking "aiôn" and "aiônes" as used in Scripture to signify other earthlike planets.

The patristic authors who use the word "aiônes" show no sign of pluralist leanings. For example, the Creed adopted by the one hundred and fifty Fathers assembled at the Council of Constantinople (381), and later reaffirmed by those present at the Council of Chalcedon (451), reads: "We believe...in one Lord Jesus Christ...begotten of his Father before all worlds"[36] [ek tou patros gennêthenta pro pantôn tôn aiônôn].[37] It is unwarranted to read this use of "aiônes" as an endorsement of pluralism given that the issue was not raised in either of these councils, and moreover, it was apparently not raised in any council prior to that at Chalcedon, for surely Augustine and Jerome would not have let this pass without comment.

I will conclude my consideration of tradition by addressing Simpson's claim that "St. Clement of Rome, Clement of Alexandria, St. Irenaeus, Origen, and St. Jerome all affirmed it [pluralism]." To the extent that Jerome considered it (as presented by Origen), he rejected it. St. Clement of Rome speaks of worlds in the sense of Old World and New World. Clement of Alexandria (c. 150-c. 215) quotes St. Clement of Rome's line about "an ocean illimitable by men and the worlds after it."[38] However, he does not make any pronouncement on pluralism at that point, which is not at all surprising since the theme he is treating is: "God can not be embraced in words or by the mind." Nor does he use the word "worlds" anywhere else in his writings. One wonders if Simpson's labeling of Clement of Alexandria as a pluralist is not yet another case of guilt by association. St. Irenaeus (?130-202) never uses the word "worlds." Nor does he show any sign of pluralist leanings. For example, he entitles a chapter: "There is but one creator of the world, God the Father: This is the Constant Belief of the Church."[39] And in this chapter he affirms:

> That God is the Creator of the world is accepted even by those very persons who in many ways speak against Him...all men, in fact, consenting to this truth: the ancients on their part preserving with special care...this persuasion, while they celebrate the praises of one God, the Maker of heaven and earth.... For even creation reveals Him who formed it, and the very work made suggests Him who made it, and the world manifests Him who ordered it.[40]

Simpson was incorrect about four out of five of the Fathers that he names as supporters of pluralism. Moreover, the impression one might get from his listing five Fathers in favor of pluralism and only two against is also incorrect. They were uniformly against it, with the exception of Origen.

Tradition, far from lending support to belief in the existence of ETI, does not even concede it a planet to establish itself on. At the same time, it must be keep in mind that the Fathers and Doctors do not generally directly address the possibility of the existence of many earthlike planets, but rather the existence of many universes. Aquinas is really the only one who considers whether our universe could contain many earths, and he comes to a negative conclusion based on erroneous views about the physical world.

Turning now to Church documents: It is not possible to examine every Church document for direct or indirect references to ETI. How then can one be reasonably sure that one has not overlooked any such document? In addition to the approach used in the previous chapter of looking to Church documents that speak about human uniqueness, another way of making sure that the pertinent references have been discovered is by checking what others researching the topic have come up with. Also, it is useful to try to find ecclesial cases where people were being tried as heretics for espousing belief in ETI existence. For there, if anywhere, one would expect that official documents on the subject would be brought forth

I discovered two Church documents pertinent to the Christianity-ETI debate by consulting other authors who have researched the topic. The first is a letter of Pope Zachary to Archbishop Boniface dated 752:

> For it was also intimated by your fraternal holiness, that one Virgilius has shown malevolence against you for the reason that he was confounded by you for straying from Catholic teaching.... Concerning his perverse and contrary teaching, which he spoke against God and his soul: If it will have become clear that he professes that there exists another world (alius mundus), and other men (alii homines) under the earth (sub terra), or the sun and moon (seu sol et luna), he, when counsel has been taken, is to be ejected from the Church, and deprived of sacerdotal honor.[41]

This passage is immediately preceded by a greeting (the kiss of peace of Christ), and immediately followed by further instructions as to how to deal with Virgilius. Pope Zachary's letter, dedicated in large part to questions concerning Baptism, elaborates no further on Virgilius's error, and thus gives us no clues for understanding what was at issue. Yet another difficulty in interpretation arises from the Pope's grammar: "Sun" and "moon" are in the nominative case, leaving one wondering what the Pope meant to say about them. Maybe he meant to condemn the notion of another sun and moon, and left out the word "another" ("alius," "alia") or maybe he meant to condemn the notion of human inhabitants on the sun and moon, and omitted the word "on" (L. "in")—in which case "sun and moon" should have been put in the ablative case. Yet another ambiguity is as to whether the other world referred to is a universe or a world under the earth.[42]

Supposing that the Pope did not intend "alius mundus" to refer to an inhabited land under the earth, it almost certainly refers to another universe rather than to another earth. For the patristic tradition that Zachary had to draw on never directly condemned the notion that many earths existed, whereas it frequently condemned the notion that many universes existed.

The "men under the earth" the Pope mentions more likely refers to the "Antipodes" Augustine speaks of, than to some sort of subterranean people. Augustine was of the view that:

But as to the fable there are Antipodes, that is to say, men on the opposite side of the earth, where the sun rises when it sets to us, men who walk with their feet opposite ours, that is on no ground credible. And indeed, it is not affirmed that this has been learned by historical knowledge, but by scientific conjecture, on the ground that the earth is suspended within the concavity of the sky, and that it has as much room on the one side of it as on the other: hence they say that the part which is beneath must also be inhabited. But they do not remark that, although it be supposed or scientifically demonstrated that the world is of a round and spherical form, yet it does not follow that the other side of the earth is bare of water; nor even, though it be bare, does it immediately follow that it is peopled....[I]t is too absurd to say that some men might have taken ship and traversed the whole wide ocean, and crossed from this side of the world to the other, and that thus even the inhabitants of that distant region are descended from that one first man.[43]

Was Pope Zachary censuring Virgilius in light of Augustine's incorrect position on the Antipodes? Or was the Pope concerned that Virgilius was maintaining there was another race of human beings that had not descended from Adam and redeemed by Christ? In either case, there is no reason to understand the Pope's condemnation to be directed against belief in ETI.[44]

The other Church document relevant to our debate is a letter written by Pius II, November 14, 1459, which begins "Cum sicut accepimus." [45] In this document Pope Pius II condemned the following propositions proffered by canon Zaninus of Solcia:

God also created another world besides this one, and that in its time many other men and women existed, and that consequently Adam was not the first man.[46]

The question to ask is whether Pius II unconditionally rejected the notion that God created another world inhabited by material rational beings or whether he only rejected the more qualified notion that God created a world that was populated by members of the human race, prior to creating our world. I think that the latter is more likely, for positing a prior world inhabited by members of the human race necessarily entails denying that Adam and Eve were the first parents of the entire human race, whereas positing a prior world inhabited by non-human material intelligent beings does not. One would expect Pius II to be concerned with any view that would have as a consequent that Adam and Eve were not the first parents from whom all us humans descended, for as was explained in the introduction, it is a constant teaching of the Church that the human race is unified insofar as all its members are descendants of one set of first parents.

There is no indication that Pius II intended here to condemn belief in the existence of other biological species of humans. The condemned proposition is simply one of a sundry list of errors espoused by Zaninus. (It is somewhat curious that a condemnation circulated in 1459 would be directed against the notion that there was another earth within this universe, given that the Copernican revolution which provided the impetus for speculation about ETI inhabited worlds was yet to be launched. Copernicus's *On the Revolution of the Heavenly Spheres* was first published in 1543.) Even if there were some reason to think that the Pope intended to condemn without qualification the view that there were other worlds inhabited by rational beings, one would not have to take an isolated teaching like that as the last word unless either it was clear that the Pope had the specific intention of defining a new dogma, or it was clear that the Pope was simply reiterating something that had been passed down in Sacred Tradition over the centuries—neither of which is the case.

The case of Giordano Bruno (1548?-1600) presents itself as a prime candidate for an ecclesial case in which official doctrinal documents concerning other inhabited worlds would have been pulled out, if any such documents existed. Bruno was burnt at the stake as a heretic, apparently for holding, among other things, that the universe was infinite and that it contained innumerable worlds.[47] Bruno envisaged the worlds that he postulated as being inhabited:

> If not exactly as our own, and if not more nobly, at least no less inhabited and no less nobly. For it is impossible that a rational being fairly vigilant, can imagine that these innumerable worlds, manifest as like to our own or yet more magnificent, should be destitute of similar and even superior inhabitants; for all are either themselves suns or the sun doth diffuse to them no less than to us those most divine and fertilizing rays, which convince us of the joy that reigneth at their source and origin and bring

fortune to those stationed around who thus participate in the diffused quality. The innumerable prime members of the universe are then infinite [in number], and all have similar aspect, countenance, prerogative, quality and power.[48]

From what we can tell, Bruno was not condemned for *populating* his innumerable worlds.[49] Yet, if the Church did in fact reject the notion of many inhabited planets, it is surprising that nothing was said on this point, especially when one takes into account that Church officials brought a total of eight counts against Bruno. The Church by that time had been dealing with Copernicanism for a good fifty years, and could not have been oblivious to speculations about ETI that it engendered. Yet apparently the Church did not see it fit to require the faithful to believe that there was but one sole planet in the universe populated by rational beings.

So far as I can see then, while Church documents do take a position on the existence of other lineages of human beings other than the one descended from Adam, they do not take a position on ETI existence. Tradition virtually never directly addressed the question of whether other planets in the universe might be inhabited by intelligent material beings. It is Scripture which raises questions about ETI existence by things that it says concerning Christ's mission and relation to other beings in the universe.

We have seen that the Christian teachings that the Word became incarnate as a human being and died on Calvary to redeem sinners (the privileged status of the human race is a derivative of these acts) are compatible with the existence of other intelligent beings in the universe. Scripture, however, does exclude ETI existence under certain conditions. Col. 1:15-20 excludes the existence of fallen ETIs who were not redeemed by Christ's death on Calvary. And Heb. 2:14 appears to exclude the existence of all fallen ETIs, for it says that Christ desired to share in the same blood shared by *all* the children, so that by his death he could free *all* those who were held in slavery by the fear of death. If there were fallen ETIs in need of redemption, then Christ did not set the captives of death free by means of offering flesh and blood that he shared in common with all of them. Again, since I am not entirely sure that my interpretation of Heb. 2:14 is correct, I am going to proceed as if fallen ETIs are not excluded by Scripture, though I strongly suspect they are. No scriptural argument has been found that would exclude the possibility of unfallen ETIs. It appears, then, that barring a new magisterial pronouncement to the contrary, the discovery of ETIs would not spell the end of Christianity, nor does Christianity exclude the possibility that ETIs exist, at least not unfallen ones. However, one can still wonder whether ETIs do in fact exist, and whether the Christian faith provides *probable* arguments for or against their existence. The latter question will be examined in the next section.

Part II

The Improbability of ETI Existence in Light of Christianity

CHAPTER 5

Plenitude or Redundancy?

> [S]ince there are two doubts concerning the stars which anyone could reasonably have, we should try to say what appears to us to be the case concerning them; in such a manner, however, that we repute the eagerness of a person considering questions of this sort more in keeping with…modesty than with audacity, i.e., presumption, which is the case so long as the one who considers doubts of this sort also loves arguments of little force in view of discovering the truth….
>
> —Aquinas, *Commentary on Aristotle's De Caelo et Mundo*

Humans naturally wonder about the things that are in the heavens. As Aristotle notes, the heavens are an unfortunate case of something we very much want to comprehend, but are unable to readily get answers about due to our inability to perceive things so very far away. However, Aristotle encourages us not to despair but to forge ahead, mindful of our limitations, and aware that the arguments we come up with will not have the demonstrative force that we should like. In this section, I will endeavor to give the strongest possible arguments against the existence of ETI, acknowledging that they will not have as much force as I might like, given the inherent difficulties of the subject. They will be drawn from the Catholic faith and from philosophy, the scientific facets of the question being left to others. I will also examine a probable argument drawn from theology and philosophy in favor of ETI existence, the argument from "plenitude."

A "redundancy" argument against the existence of another human-type species, whether it be fallen or not, can be patterned on a metaphysical argument which Aquinas gives when arguing against a multiplicity of worlds. It is helpful to contrast this argument with the aforementioned probable argument in favor of ETI existence that is based on what is sometimes called "the principle of plenitude." Crudely stated, the redundancy argument says if one has one good thing, one does not need another just like it, whereas the plenitude argument says the more the merrier when it comes to having different sorts of good things. Put this way, it seems that there is no reason not to agree with both, and so it is somewhat surprising that these propositions are used to argue to different conclusions in regard to ETI existence.

The principle of plenitude is understood in a variety of ways by different authors. My intention here is not to explain every variation, as this alone would take up a good part of a book.[1] Rather, I intend first to present Thomas Aquinas's account of this principle, which I hold to be basically sound, then to explain why another variant sometimes used in the ETI debate is to be rejected, and finally, to show the limitations of the Thomistic version.

Aquinas enunciates the position thus:

> …God produces things for the sake of communicating his goodness to creatures, and through them to represent his goodness. And because it cannot be adequately represented through one creature, he produces many and diverse creatures, so that what is lacking in one for the purpose of representing divine goodness, is filled up by others; for the goodness which exists simply and uniformly in God, in creatures is multiple and divided. Whence the whole universe more perfectly shares in and represents divine goodness than any other creature whatsoever.[2]

Thus, one version of the principle of plenitude is that a greater number of diverse creatures better represents God's goodness than a lesser number does. Aquinas takes as a corollary of this view that it "certainly agrees with the affluence of divine goodness that those things which are nobler are more abundantly produced in being."[3] For God's goodness is better reflected by a greater number of more noble things than by a greater number of less noble ones.

Now some have added a further qualification to the principle of plenitude, and this has led them to reason in the following manner about ETI existence:

The principle [of plenitude] lays down that a Creator such as is envisioned in the Christian tradition must bring to be all that is possible, out of the fullness of Divine power and goodness. It is the presumed nature of God that leads to the expectation that a plurality of inhabited worlds is not only possible, but in some sense necessary.[4]

What these authors fail to recognize is that there is no best of possible universes. God is infinite, and therefore no creation can exhaust his power. No matter how great in goodness is the universe he creates, it is also possible for him to create another even greater.[5] It would imply a contradiction for God to bring to be all that is possible in the fullness of his power and goodness, for that would imply that his infinite power and goodness could be exhausted. (The question is similar to that of whether God could create another omnipotent being.[6] A created being can never be the equal of the Uncreated one, and so it is not because God is lacking in power that he cannot do this, but because it is inherently contradictory and nonsensical.) Thus not all the things that could possibly exist do exist.[7] There is necessarily something arbitrary then as to which things actually exist to represent God's goodness, because God could just as well have created other things:

> God through his providence orders all things to divine goodness as to an end; not, however, in this manner that something accrues to his goodness through the things that come to be, but insofar as a likeness of his goodness is impressed upon things insofar as it is possible. Since it is necessary that every created substance falls short of the perfection of divine goodness, in order for a likeness of divine goodness to be more perfectly communicated to things, it was necessary for there to be diversity in things, so that what is not able to be perfectly represented by some one thing may be represented in a more perfect manner by diverse things in diverse ways.... Thus, therefore, that God love his own goodness is necessary; but that it be represented through creatures does not necessarily follow, since divine goodness is perfect without this taking place. Whence that creatures are produced in being, even if they do have their origin from the notion of divine goodness, nevertheless depends on the simple will of God. Having supposed, however, that God wants to

communicate his goodness to creatures according as it is possible through the mode of similitude, this explains why there are diverse creatures; it does not, however, follow from necessity that there be this or that measure of perfection, or this or that number of things.[8]

Thus, a correct reading of the principle of plenitude in no way necessitates any specific creature, but just some multitude of diverse creatures, and more of the better ones, supposing, of course, that God wills to create a universe. Thus, a plurality of inhabited worlds is in no wise necessitated by the principle of plenitude.

This principle, and more particularly the variant which states that there should be "more of better things," perhaps can be legitimately used to argue in a probable manner that, all things being equal, there should be other worlds inhabited by intelligent life forms. However, a question that needs to be addressed is whether the greater abundance of more noble things refers to the number of kinds of things or to the number of individuals within a kind or to both. In other words, is it fitting that God should create more of the higher levels in the hierarchy of beings, or that he should create more individual beings in the higher levels than in the lower, or both?

Aquinas was certainly aware of the problematic character of the question, due to the apparently conflicting views of his predecessors. The issue comes up in a discussion of the number of the angels:

> [T]he Platonists were saying that to the extent that something is closer to the first principle to that extent it is smaller in multitude; just as to the extent that a number is nearer the unit to that extent it is less in multitude. And this opinion stands up well as to the number of orders: three assist, while six minister.—But Dionysius held…that the multitude of angels transcends lower bodies in greatness by something immense, so that the higher incorporeal natures transcends all corporeal natures because what is better is more intended by God and more multiplied. And according to this, since those assisting are superior to those ministering, there are more assistants than ministers. [9]

According to these principles,[10] there should be fewer sorts of humans than animals, and more individual humans than animals, but the latter is not the case. Nor if one regards humans as the lowest of intellectual substances do the principles apply: There should be more sorts of the lower form, i.e., humans, and fewer individual humans than angels, but the former is not the case. Ultimately, Aquinas seems to acknowledge that the requirements of plenitude do not cash out as necessary laws:

> It does not therefore appear to be universally true that the more imperfect difference of a genus is multiplied in more species. For body is divided into animate and inanimate: nevertheless there appear to be more species of animate bodies than inanimate, especially if the heavenly bodies are animate, and all the stars differ from one another in species. But even in plants and animals there is the greatest diversity of species.[11]

Even if Aquinas's example is in some ways questionable, still, it is not hard to find other examples that show that sometimes there are more of inferior things. For instance, there are more beetles both in numbers and in species than there are apes. Thus, the version of plenitude which states that there should be more of better things is not a hard and fast rule, regardless of whether one looks to species or whether one looks to individuals.[12] And again there has to be some arbitrary cut-off point as to the exact number of better things that are to exist. More of better things, then, provides at most a feeble argument in favor of ETI existence.

On the other hand, one could argue that it would be redundant to create more than one human species, and it is not characteristic of intelligent agents to do things that are redundant. Before I investigate this line of reasoning, I wish to set forth an extreme view concerning the number of rational material species possible, as this will give greater credibility to the redundancy argument. The view in question holds that it is not even possible for other human species to exist because the conditions of the body suited for a rational soul are so narrowly constrained.

Thomas Aquinas argues in three different places[13] that there could be only one species of rational animal. One of his arguments turns on the need for a rational animal to have certain bodily features without which it could not be rational.[14] The animal in question would have to have a big brain so it could have ample imagination and memory, since thinking depends on imagining. It would also have to have a brain of such a sort as would dispose it for the use of language, since language is so intimately connected with thought. It would have to have a good sense of vision, since vision of all the senses brings one the most knowledge about things. For only the sense of sight readily discerns the forms of things, which most reveals what things are, and sight also allows one to perceive many things all at once. The animal in question would also have to have a good sense of touch, because while vision reveals much, it is also the sense that is most readily deceived, whereas touch puts one more directly in contact with reality. It would also have to have grasping appendages such as hands so as to be able to manipulate objects, for otherwise it would be difficult to inspect objects, and it would also need some means of locomotion, for otherwise its ability to acquire knowledge would be severely restricted.[15] Lack of mobility would also limit the scope of its choices, which would seem inappropriate in a material being with the unique capacity of free choice. To the extent that hypothetical beings endowed with a rational soul would have to have all the named abilities along with their appropriate organs, to that extent they would be physically like us in significant ways. Indeed, Aquinas thinks that this would be to such a point that they could not be called another species, taking "species" in the philosophical sense of the word (i.e., a different kind of thing with a different substantial form).

There are two questions one might raise concerning Aquinas's argument. First, are the constraints on the human body are as narrow as Aquinas thinks they are? And secondly, does his argument have bearing on the existence of another biological species of humans? As for the first question, Aquinas's position finds more support than one might first have thought. It is too easy to get into the habit of imagining intelligent life taking on all sorts of forms that are strange to us, while forgetting that imaginary things do not have to meet the physical constraints that real things do. Galileo asked whether it were possible for giant horses or men to exist. He came up with a physical proof that this is not possible unless the bones were made of harder and more resistant material or were thickened disproportionately.[16] Organisms, in order to survive, have to meet the environmental challenges set them. A given environmental challenge cannot be met by just any old structure, and thus similar and even the same structures or organs tend to develop in separate lineages in response to the same environmental challenges, a phenomenon referred to as convergent evolution. A commonly offered example is the bilateral symmetry and over-all stream-lined shape found in animals that move with any speed through water (fish, penguins, dolphins, etc.).[17]

What features are needed to live the life of a rational animal? Aquinas is not the only one to have a list. The evolutionary biologist and anthropologist C.O. Lovejoy names the following:

> Man is not only a unique animal, but the end product of a completely unique evolutionary pathway...We find, then, that the evolution of cognition is the product of a variety of influences and preadaptive capacities, the absence of any one of which would have completely negated the process, and most of which are unique attributes of primates and/or hominids. Specific dietary shifts, bipedal locomotion, manual dexterity, control of differentiated muscles of facial expression, vocalization, intense social and parenting behavior (of specific kinds) keen stereoscopic vision, and even specialized forms of sexual behaviour, all qualify as irreplaceable elements.[18]

Michael Denton is another biologist who has a list of features essential to being a rational animal. Denton points out that in order for human-like beings to be capable of science, they would have to possess the ability to make and manipulate fire, without which they would be unable to make scientific instruments. The ability to manipulate fire depends on having a body of a certain size with hands, vision, and a specific muscular capacity. An animal lacking any of these features would not be *Homo scientificus*.[19]

Denton takes things yet one step further and argues that the underlying chemistry making possible human organs and their activities is narrowly constrained, and that ETIs would not have some form of biochemistry radically different from our own.[20] This view is becoming more and more widespread, as David Darling notes:

> The idea that, with minor variation, life always ends up employing the same kinds of chemicals might seem to suggest a failure of imagination. Imagination, however, isn't the issue. It's relatively easy to invent fictional aliens whose blood resembles cleaning fluid or whose cells are filled with alcohol. The problems start when you have to fill in the biochemical details of how it would all work. Then in becomes clear that there may be only so many ways of assembling elements into the kinds of materials that might be biologically tenable.[21]

For instance, a number of scientists believe that the citric acid cycle is a must in order for complex multi-cellular organisms to exist, because without it they would not be able to harvest a sufficient amount of energy from glucose to stay alive.[22]

While people may be mistaken about whether a specific feature belongs on the list of bodily features necessary to being human, and while the underlying biochemistry may not be so constrained as some think, still the idea that certain features are required and certain physical constraints must be met is doubtlessly closer to the truth than the idea that an intelligent being can take just any form.[23] Modern authors are, however, more likely to think that more divergence from the present human form is possible than Aquinas did, due to their evolutionary perspective which takes into account historical factors in the development of bodily organs. They would, moreover, certainly maintain that it is extremely unlikely that we and another hypothetical human-like species would be capable of producing fertile offspring by interbreeding.

This leads to a closely related question one might have with Aquinas's argument that there can be only one human species, a problem which arises from the ambiguity of the word "species." It is unlikely that it ever crossed Aquinas's mind that there could be two human groups that were similar in important ways (eyes, large brain, etc.), but nonetheless reproductively isolated. Although Aquinas maintains that the differences between us and another human-like group would be insufficient for us and them to constitute two separate philosophical species, it is not clear whether or not he thought that the two groups would have to be so alike as to eliminate differences that would make for two biological species of *Homo*. Thus, it would be a mistake to take his argument to rule out ETI existence. It does, however, suggest a "redundancy argument."

Redundancy arguments are based on the general premise that intelligent agents do not do the same thing over and over without reason. Aquinas uses this sort of argument in regard to the question of whether there are many worlds:

> [N]o agent intends a material plurality as an end; for a material multitude does not have a definite term, but of itself tends to infinity; infinity, however, is repugnant to the notion of an end. When many worlds are said to be better than one, however, this is said according to a material multitude. This sort of better, however, is not in the intention of God as agent, because by the

same reasoning it could be said that if he made two, it would be better that there would be three; and so on *ad infinitum*.[24]

The notion that needless repetition does not befit an intelligent agent is generally accepted, and indeed it provides part of the grounds for Thomas Paine's objection to Christianity in light of ETI:

> ...are we to suppose that every world in the boundless creation had an Eve, an apple, a serpent, and a redeemer? In this case, the person who is irreverently called the Son of God, and sometimes God himself, would have nothing else to do than to travel from world to world, in an endless succession of deaths, with scarcely a momentary interval of life.[25]

It does not seem fitting for God to engage in this type of repetitive action (of course, as we have seen earlier, there is no need for God to do so).

Now we are in a better position to evaluate the redundancy argument against ETI existence that runs thus: given that another human-like species could not be all that different from our species, there is really no point in creating it.[26] One might object to this argument on the grounds that there are thousands of biological species of beetles, and so who is to say that even a relatively slight variation on our body plan on some other planet might not yield another human-type species that would add as much to the chain of being as the 76,305th species of beetle did? However, one might respond that the reason that there are so many species of beetles does not lie in the diversity they add to the world, which is relatively insignificant, but rather in the important role they play in the food chain: a lot of animals eat various species of beetle, while not many eat people. Still, if a human-like species differed from *Homo sapiens* as much as one species of great ape differs from another, there seems no reason for it to be deemed it redundant. Thus, the redundancy argument, at least as it has been stated so far, has not proved convincing. It would be premature, however, to dismiss it entirely, as there are some additional considerations which will be made later that will substantially buttress it.

A somewhat stronger probable argument against an ETI race is based on the notion that uniqueness is a perfection, assuming that it is added to something good. This notion is a matter of common experience. It is a compliment to be told that "they broke the mold after they made you." A circus artist is introduced as "the one and only...." Human individuals normally aspire to some kind of uniqueness, be it nothing more that a quirk of dress. We like to think that we are one of a kind. Sports articles used when an important record was broken command high prices at auctions. Works of art which are difficult or impossible to reproduce exactly, such as Michelangelo's Pietà or the Sistine Chapel, are especially prized for that reason.

Note that uniqueness is not unqualifiedly a perfection, but is only such on the condition that it is added to something good. For example, to be the only one in a group to lack an eye or to fail an exam is plainly not a perfection. People do sometimes act as if uniqueness was a perfection even when added to something bad, because of a strong desire to be set apart from others. For example, a student who is doing poorly in a course may brag about being the only one in class to never have cracked open the assigned textbook. Yet clearly the singular character of the student's laziness is not a perfection.

That uniqueness in certain cases constitutes a type of perfection is not only witnessed to by everyday experience, but also by authors of note. Plato in the *Timaeus* maintains:

> Wherefore, in order that this Creature might resemble the all-perfect Living Creature in respect of its uniqueness, for this reason its Maker made neither two Universes nor an infinite number, but there is and will continue to be this one generated Heaven, unique of its kind.[27]

And C. S. Lewis in *Perelandra* expresses the sentiment that repetition detracts from the perfection that belongs to a singular experience:

> For one draught of this on earth wars would be fought and nations betrayed....As he let the empty gourd fall from his hand and was about to pluck a second one, it came into his head that he was now neither hungry nor thirsty. And yet to repeat a pleasure so intense and almost so spiritual seemed an obvious thing to do....But for whatever cause, it appeared to him better not to taste again. Perhaps the experience had been so complete that repetition would be a vulgarity—like asking to hear the same symphony twice in a day.[28]

The notion that uniqueness is a perfection when added to something good suggests that it would be appropriate for the created nature that God assumes to be unique, and I intend to develop this line of argument more carefully later on. At this point, I will simply note that the argument given earlier against ETI existence (namely, that another material rational creature would be redundant), and the argument just suggested against it (appealing to the notion of uniqueness), are different, but complementary arguments. There is no point to doing something over and over when one can achieve one's goal without doing so. Moreover, if one can achieve one's goal without repetition, repetition is not only pointless, but may also detract from the goal to be achieved by depriving it of the excellence of being unique. (A person who had a life-size replica of Michelangelo's David in the living room would never add a second one with the intention of beautifying the room; whether good taste would allow adding a replica of Bernini's David is debatable.) There is no pre-set cut-off point for how many better things God should create, and God can achieve the goal of creating more of better things through the immense celestial hierarchy without creating a number of human-type races. Creating more than one human-type race is not required by the principle of plenitude, and it would subtract the perfection of uniqueness from the race.

In the next three chapters I will consider the following logical possibilities: The Word either became incarnate once or more than once. If the Word became incarnate only once, there is either only us or there is an ETI race or races in addition to us, and this race or these races are unfallen or fallen or mixed. If the Word became incarnate a second time, then there has to be a race other than us, and it is either fallen, unfallen or mixed. I will examine each of these alternatives, and will show that in every case the superior alternative is that we are the only material rational species.

Chapter 6

Probable Arguments that Humans are Unique on the Supposition of One Incarnation: The Case of the Fallen ETIs

> The grace of God could not have been more graciously commended to us than thus, that the only Son of God, remaining unchangeable in Himself, should assume humanity, and should give us the hope of His love, by means of the mediation of a human nature, through which we, from the condition of men, might come to Him who was so far off—the immortal from the mortal; the unchangeable from the changeable; the just from the unjust; the blessed from the wretched.
>
> —St. Augustine, *The City of God*

One argument that the human race is unique, as being the only species of rational animals that God has created, runs thus: It is an extraordinary thing that God would assume a material nature. Thus it is fitting that this be a one time event. And further it is appropriate that the nature that God assumed should be unique.[1]

Independent of the probable arguments for human uniqueness that can be formulated on the grounds that there was only one Incarnation, it is plainly important for my thesis "ETIs do not exist" to make a case that there was only one Incarnation, since a second incarnation presupposes the existence of a second rational species. If there is a second incarnation, there must be ETI. If there is not a second incarnation, there may or may not be ETI. So first I will argue against a second incarnation. After I conclude that there is good reason to think that there was only one

Incarnation, I will use this as a premise to argue in favor of human uniqueness (in the strong sense).

The Incarnation has been traditionally regarded by Christians as one of the central mysteries of the faith. It is an event beyond human expectations. Indeed, the Incarnation is so surprising an event that many regarded belief in its occurrence as ridiculous. As Aquinas puts it:

> Belief in the Incarnation is reputed by non-believers to be stupidity, according to the words of the Apostle: "It pleased God to save those who have faith through the foolishness of the message preached" (1 Co. 1: 21), for it seems stupid for someone to preach such a thing, not only because it is impossible, but also because it is unbefitting [of divine goodness].[2]

Aquinas goes on to enumerate more than a dozen reasons why someone would reject God's incarnation as man as something repugnant to divine wisdom and goodness. I will cite just a few in view of getting across what an unusual event the Incarnation is.

> For it befits divine goodness that all things keep their order. This, however, is the order of things: that God be exalted over all, while man is included among the least creatures. Therefore it does not befit divine majesty to be united to human nature.[3]
>
> Moreover, if it was fitting that God become man, it would be necessary that some advantage come from it. But since God is omnipotent, any given advantage could have been produced by his will alone. Since therefore it is fitting that anything come to be in the most direct manner possible, it was not necessary that God, for the sake of some sort advantage, unite himself to human nature.[4]

St. Anselm recounts similar objections against the Incarnation:

> [T]his question, both infidels are accustomed to bring up against us, ridiculing Christian simplicity as absurd; and many believers ponders it in their hearts; for what cause or necessity, in sooth, God became man, and by his own death, as we believe and affirm, restored life to the world; when he might have done this,

by means of some other being, angelic or human, or merely by his will. Not only the learned, but also many unlearned persons interest themselves in this inquiry and seek for its solution.[5]

...

Infidels ridiculing our simplicity charge upon us that we do injustice and dishonor to God when we affirm that he descended into the womb of a virgin, that he was born of woman, that he grew on the nourishment of milk and the food of men; and, passing over many other things which seem incompatible with Deity, that he endured fatigue, hunger, thirst, stripes and crucifixion among thieves.[6]

That the Eternal, Almighty, Impassible Word would enter time as a helpless infant[7] subject to hunger, thirst, and fatigue is already hard to fathom, even before one considers the more profound sufferings tied to his passion and death.[8] Why? Why did God "empty himself taking the form of a slave" (Ph. 2:7)? "Why is he filled with such goodness that the word of God made himself dried grass for us?"[9] "For what necessity and cause God, who is omnipotent, should have assumed the littleness and weakness of human nature for the sake of its renewal?"[10] The Incarnation is so extraordinary an event that Aquinas asserts that "there are reasons of this mystery which are incomprehensible to every created intellect."[11] Now, the Fathers and Doctors of the Church of course have responses to the arguments that claim that the Incarnation is absurd and unbefitting God's goodness. My point here is simply that the Incarnation is so unusual an event that many find in this reason to reject that it happened.[12]

If the Incarnation is rightly regarded as an extraordinary event, one can argue that it is fitting that it be a one-time event, something never to be repeated. Again, while I do not think that anything in Scripture eliminates the possibility of a second incarnation, nonetheless those passages Scripture which depicts Christ's coming on earth as the central event in the universe's history lend credence to the position that it would not be appropriate for such an event to occur for a second time:

> He has let us know the mystery of his purpose, the hidden plan he so kindly made in Christ from the beginning to act upon when the times had run their course to the end: that he would

bring everything together under Christ, as head, everything in the heavens and everything on earth. (Ep. 1:8-10)

I, who am less than the least of all the saints, have been entrusted with this special grace, not only of proclaiming to the pagans the infinite treasure of Christ, but also of explaining how the mystery is to be dispensed. Through all the ages, this has been kept hidden in God, the creator of everything. Why? So that the Sovereignties and Powers should learn only now, through the Church, how comprehensive God's wisdom really is, exactly according to the plan which he had from all Eternity in Christ Jesus our Lord. (Ep. 3:9-12)

The *CCC* echoes the above texts in affirming the centrality of Christ's role in the entire course of creation:

"Christ died and lived again, that he might be Lord both of the dead and of the living." [Rom. 14:9] Christ's Ascension into heaven signifies his participation, in his humanity, in God's power and authority. Jesus Christ is Lord: he possesses all power in heaven and on earth. He is "far above all rule and authority and power and dominion," for the Father 'has put all things under his feet.' [Ep. 1:20-22] Christ is Lord of the cosmos and of history. In him human history and indeed all creation are "set forth" and transcendently fulfilled.[13]

Col. 1:15-20 is worth citing again because of the plain witness that it bears to the centrality of Christ's death (which presupposes his Incarnation) in God's overall plan for the universe:

As he is the Beginning, he was first to be born from the dead, so that he should be first in every way; because God wanted all perfection to be found in him and all things to be reconciled through him and for him, everything in heaven and everything on earth when he made peace by his death on the cross.

Another incarnation would diminish the centrality of the Word's Incarnation as a human being, in the same way that anything no matter how valuable becomes only one among many when a second like it is found. That the circumstances surrounding another incarnation would be different does not change the fact that it would be essentially the same kind of event, an incarnation. Moreover, either the second incarnation would be of equal cosmic importance as the first, or one incarnation would have precedence over the other. If the two were of equal importance, then there would be no central event in the universe's history. If there was a hierarchy of importance, this would require some rationale, and at first sight it is hard to see how one incarnation could be of greater or lesser importance than another.

There is a further reflection that gives cause for pause, without absolutely ruling out a second incarnation. It concerns the manner in which the second incarnation would take place. If the Word assumed an ETI nature in the same manner in which he assumed human nature, he would have two mothers. If this is so, it is hard to see how Mary is "Mother of the Church" and "Queen over all things"[14] given that an ETI mother of God would seem to have equal claim to these titles. It is true that the second body to be assumed could be constituted from dust (as was Adam's), or from part of ETI's body (as Eve was formed from Adam's rib). Yet, as Aquinas points out in discussing the question of whether Christ should not have formed a brand new body for himself, rather than assuming human nature from Adam's stock, it would not have been appropriate for Christ to form a brand new body inasmuch as he was to serve as an example of how we ought to live.[15] Similarly, if ETI incarnate's body was formed from scratch, ETIs could give excuses for not exercising the virtues that ETI incarnate did, claiming that he was made of sterner stuff than they.[16] As for being taken from the body of an ETI in a manner similar to that by which Eve was formed from Adam, this manner of production has traditionally been taken as a symbol of Eve falling under Adam's authority,[17] and to fall under another's authority in this manner[18] would not be fitting on the part of the Lord of Lords:

> A man should certainly not cover his head, since he is the image of God and reflects God's glory; but woman is the reflection of man's glory. For man did not come from woman; no, woman came from man; and man was not created for the sake of woman, but woman was created for the sake of man. That is the argument for women's covering their heads with a symbol of authority over them, out of respect for the angels (1 Co. 11:7-11).

While these arguments may not be the strongest, they do give further support to the position that a second incarnation would not be appropriate.

In sum, three arguments have been offered against a second incarnation: 1) It is so extraordinary an event, that it is appropriate that it be a one time event; 2) Scripture and Church teaching supports the notion that the Incarnation (and subsequent death and resurrection of Christ) constitutes the central plan for the universe; 3) none of the possible sources from whence the ETI body could be assumed seem suitable. One would not then be entirely without reason if one took the *CCC* #464 statement that the Incarnation was a "unique and altogether singular event" to mean that the Word took on flesh only once, albeit it does not appear to have intended to say that.

By showing in a probable manner that a second incarnation did not occur, the necessity that a second intelligent species exist in order for a second incarnation to occur has thus also been eliminated in a correspondingly probable manner. However, that there be no second incarnation does not eliminate the possibility that ETIs exist. Now I will consider whether their existence is probable if there were only one incarnation.

The uniqueness of the Incarnation makes it reasonable to think that not only is the human race unique as being the only intelligent material being a divine person became incarnate as, but that it is unique as being the only intelligent material being. Creation was created with a view to the new Creation in Christ, and it is fitting that in this most extraordinary plan a nature that is unique be employed. This same sort of reasoning is behind the tradition of the bride wearing a dress and veil which will never be worn on any other occasion: singular occasions call for unique accoutrements.[19] The Incarnation is, of course, an incomparably more extraordinary event than a wedding.

Another way of seeing the fittingness that human nature be the sole rational material nature can be gathered from Aquinas's response to an objection to the Incarnation which reads:

> [S]ince God is the universal cause of all things, it is necessary that he aim chiefly at what is useful for the entire universe of things. But the assuming of human nature pertains only to what is useful for man. Therefore it was not fitting that if God should have assumed a foreign nature, that he would have assumed only a human nature.[20]

Aquinas responds:

> Since man is constituted from a spiritual and a corporeal nature, as a certain boundary of both natures, what happens in regard to human salvation seems to have pertinence to every creature; for lower creatures are seen to yield to man's use and in a certain manner are subject to him; higher spiritual creatures, however, namely, angelic ones, have in common with man the attainment of the ultimate end.... And thus it seems fitting that the universal cause of all things assume in the unity of person that creature which shares more in common with all creatures.[21]

Aquinas takes as a given that humans are the only intelligent material species.[22] However, an argument to that view is suggested from what is said here. The creation of human nature was for the sake of the Incarnation, which at the moment we are assuming is a one-time event. If God was going to unite in some sense all of creation in the Word, man is just the sort of being suited for this purpose. For man is a link between material and spiritual realms, being a composite of body and immaterial soul. Since human nature serves well the purpose of allowing the Word Incarnate to share most in common with creation, creating another species like it would be superfluous. Note that this redundancy argument is much more convincing than the rather insubstantial redundancy argument given earlier which reasoned that the creation of different variations on human nature would amount to pointless repetition.[23]

The case in favor of one sole species of rational material being finds further support when one considers in detail the benefits humans derived from the Incarnation, benefits that would not accrue to beings belonging to a race other than the one to which Christ belonged. In the case of some of these benefits, only a fallen race would miss out on them, but in the case of others, both fallen and unfallen alike would miss out. Aquinas lists eight of the benefits of the Incarnation in the *Summa Contra Gentiles*, Bk. IV, chap. 54, some of which coincide with three that can be discerned from reading Heb. 2:10-18:

> As it was his purpose to bring a great many of his sons into glory, it was appropriate that God, for whom everything exists and through whom everything exists should make perfect, through suffering, the leader who would take them to their salvation. For

the one who sanctifies, and the ones who are sanctified are of the same stock; that is why he openly calls them brothers.... Since all the children share the same blood and flesh, he too shared equally in it, so that by his death he could take away all the power of the devil, who had power over death, and set free all those who had been held in slavery all their lives by the fear of death. For it was not the angels that he took to himself; he took to himself descent from Abraham. It was essential that he should in this way become completely like his brothers so that he could be a compassionate and trustworthy high priest of God's religion, able to atone for human sins. That is, because he himself has been through temptation he is able to help others who are tempted.

It is not of small importance that the savior of the human race was of the race of Adam.[24] Rather Catholic tradition supported by Scripture affirms that God's becoming human was the most appropriate solution to what is sometimes referred to as the "divine dilemma." God in his mercy did not want the human race to be lost on account of original sin. Although God in his graciousness could simply have remitted the sin, mankind would not have fulfilled what justice demands by way of satisfaction. At the same time, no human being could ever make adequate satisfaction for an offense against the infinite God. It is only the God-Man, Jesus Christ, who is capable of making infinite satisfaction for this human debt.[25]

The passage from Hebrews indicates that the Incarnation not only brought us a savior capable of making due satisfaction for sin, but in addition one who could set an example for us that we could not dismiss, for he was "like us in all things except sin." To reach out to all and to set an example[26] for all, Christ took on human flesh in all its infirmity: tested at times by hunger, thirst, lack of a home, weariness, and the ultimate agony of the Passion, Christ is a model of obedience to the Father's will who is able to inspire those who "dwell in darkness and the shadow of death" (Lk. 1:79).[27] Hebrews mentions in addition that the Incarnation made it possible for the human race to regain the dignity it lost when it was conquered by Satan, for now one of its very own members can go on to conquer Satan.[28]

As was noted in chapter three, this passage from Hebrews seems to indicate that man alone is the intended beneficiary of Christ's redemptive act. If one does not view this text as providing an absolutely sure scriptural basis for ruling out fallen ETIs, it seems one must at least acknowledge that it provides a probable argument against fallen ETI existence. This passage does not, however, rule out unfallen ETIs.

Returning to the benefits that humans but not ETIs would reap: I will continue by presenting what Aquinas has to say in his very thorough treatment of the subject in the *Summa Contra Gentiles*. Again, some of benefits mentioned would only be benefits for a fallen species, whereas others would be benefits for fallen and unfallen species alike. Two of the three mentioned above, and one of the six mentioned below are applicable only to sinful species.

"The perfect happiness of man consists in the immediate vision of God. Someone might think, however, that man can never arrive at a state where the human intellect is directly united to the divine essence itself, as intellect to its intelligible object, on account of the immense distance between natures; and thus man would grow lukewarm in the pursuit of happiness, held back by the very despair of it. Through this that God wanted to unite human nature to himself in a person, he most evidently demonstrates to men that man can be united to God through the intellect by seeing him directly."[29]

Perfect happiness lies solely in the enjoyment of God. Yet man can be lead away from true happiness by ignoring his dignity and inhering in things beneath him. Now as far as man's ultimate end goes, there is no being above man other than God. "Therefore, God, by directly assuming a human nature himself, most fittingly showed that man's dignity is to attain happiness through the direct vision of God. Whence we see that subsequent to the incarnation of God a large part of humanity set aside the cult of angels, demons, or creatures of this sort, and spurning also carnal pleasure and all material things, dedicated themselves to worshipping God alone; to whom alone they look for the completion of their happiness...."[30]

"Because the perfect happiness of man consists in the sort of knowledge of God that goes beyond every created intellect...it was necessary that there be a certain foretaste of this sort of knowledge in man, by which he would be directed into that full knowledge of the blessed; and this is what faith certainly is.... It was necessary, therefore, in order for man to obtain perfect certitude about the truth of the faith that he be instructed by God himself, made man, so that man would receive divine instruction according to the human mode; and this is what is said [in the Gospel]: 'No man has ever seen God; it is only the Unbegotten Son who is near to his Father's heart who has made him known (Jn. 1:18);' and the Lord himself says: 'I was born, and I came into the world, to bear witness to the truth' (Jn. 18:37)."[31]

"[S]ince the perfect happiness of man consists in the enjoyment of God, it was necessary that the affect of man be disposed to desire the enjoyment of God.... It was necessary then that man tending towards perfect happiness be led to divine love. Nothing, however, so induces us to love someone as the experience of the love of that person towards us. The love of God for mankind in no wise could be more efficaciously demonstrated to man than through this that God wanted to unite himself to man in his person; for it is proper to love to unite the lover with the beloved to the extent this is possible."[32]

"Since friendship consists in a certain equality, those that are unequal as to many things do not seem to be able to be united in friendship. Therefore to the end that there would be a more familiar friendship between man and God, it was expedient for man that God would be man, because naturally man is a friend to man, and thus, when we know God visibly, we are taken up in an invisible love."[33] I think that this point especially strikes home when one considers how many devotions are addressed to Christ's Sacred Humanity: Devotions to the Sacred Heart, to the Holy Face, to the five wounds (as mentioned, for example, in the Prayer before a Crucifix), and in the Eastern Church, the use of icons of Christ. I do not think that one has to espouse cosmic racism or be oblivious to the suffering of animals, to acknowledge that it would be hard, if not impossible, to fully appreciate the sufferings of a savior of an alien race and to feel the same degree of love towards him that we spontaneously feel towards a savior of our own race. I do not deny that I am of the opinion that if ETIs exist, they would not look all that different from us. And I am fond of Yoda, a fictional rational animal with a not-quite human appearance. Still our inability to fully fathom an alien being's capacities for experiencing things and its reactions to them would make him a less than satisfying savior. The ideal savior both understands us as a result of his own experience, and can be understood by us in terms of our experience, rather than through extrapolation or guessing.

Sin as an offense against God removes man's confidence of being able to approach the One who grants man his eternal reward. Thus, man was in need of some way of obtaining remission for his sins, and also of knowing that his sins were in fact remitted. Therefore, "it was expedient that God become man, so that the remission of sins would come thus through God, and certitude of this remission would be obtained through the God-man.

Whence the Lord himself says: 'Know that the Son of man has power on the earth to forgive sins' (Mt. 9:6), etc.; and the Apostle says that 'the blood of Christ...cleanses our conscience from dead works, so that we may serve the living God' (Heb. 9:14)."[34]

Now if fallen ETIs were redeemed by Christ's sacrifice on Calvary, certainly that redemption would be the greatest gift granted to that race. However, the ETIs would not themselves have made adequate satisfaction,[35] nor would they have overcome their conqueror (supposing that it was the devil), nor would they have gained the most suitable model for their behavior, since Christ was not an ETI, but a human. Fallen ETIs saved through Christ would also not have the same assurance that they could achieve supernatural happiness, nor the same dignity to keep them from straying into idolatry that humans have as a result of God's uniting himself to us in the person of Christ. Furthermore, they would not have the same certitude that their faith was true and that their sins were forgiven that we have as the result of the Word's incarnation on earth. Finally, the ETIs would not be set aflame to love God in the same manner that humans are, as God did not unite himself to their nature in his person, nor would they have the same level of familiarity in their friendship with God.

In the case of fallen ETIs, it appears incongruous that God would show so much attention to the appropriateness of every last detail of human salvation, while not exhibiting like concern to a group resembling the human race from the point of view of both nature and need. One might object here that I argued earlier that it not contrary to God's goodness that ETIs be saved by the God-man, since God bestows his favor on whom he wills. However, I am not denying that God could have created ETIs and shown them relatively little favor compared to human beings. Rather I am saying that this is not probable on the grounds that even the minutest parts of salvation history seem painstakingly arranged as if man alone was being kept in mind. Why would God introduce in a plan that had been blocked out down to the smallest detail beings foreign in nature to Christ, given that they could only imperfectly profit from his coming? God is not only Lord of Creation, he is also Master of History.[36] It is thus impossible for the story of the universe be a series of unrelated episodes.[37]

As for the unfallen ETIs, they would lack a role model who was member of their own race, our greater assurance that supernatural happiness can be achieved, our increased awareness of our dignity that helps keep us from straying into idolatry, our great certitude as to the truth of our faith, the same motive for love of God, and the intimacy that we have in our friendship with God, all of which we have as a result of God's show of love in uniting himself to us. Again, God has no obligation to dispense gifts to any creature. Still, the close attention God has paid to man in comparison to the unfallen ETIs makes them appear as something of an afterthought. On the other hand, even if the unfallen ETIs would not share in the same favors just noted, they still could have a very intimate friendship with God, and a great motive for loving him, if he was present to them the way that he was present to Adam and Eve before the Fall. Perhaps, the situation could be somewhat like that of a mother with several children, one of whom is terribly sick. The mother would spend much more time with the sick child, and do many things specially for him, not because she loved him more than her other children, but simply because his condition required that she show him more attention.

A further question concerning fallen ETIs is how they would learn of the salvation wrought for them by Christ. It seems unfitting that they would never have the gospel announced to them. For then all of the members of a race who were saved would be saved in ignorance of their savior. (In the case of the human race this is true of only some of its members.) The alternative to this is that either the Good News is brought to them by God himself (in the same manner he spoke to Adam and Eve in the garden, or in a similar manner, or by the God-man), or through angels, or through ETI prophets, or through us. That God speak to them directly as he did to Adam and Eve does not seem likely at first sight, for on earth this was a privilege shown to unfallen humans and withdrawn after the fall. However, God did speak directly, if perhaps in a somewhat different manner, to many people after the Fall, e.g., Abraham, Moses, and Gideon.

Angels and ETI prophets cannot be ruled out as messengers of the Good News. Angels have delivered incredible messages, e.g., that the aged Elizabeth would bear a child, and that Mary was to be the mother of God (and that without the loss of her virginity). Prophets have also made astounding statements, e.g., Isaiah's predictions concerning Christ, the suffering servant. I was initially concerned that the Good News would lack any intrinsic plausibility for the ETIs, consisting as it would of something that happened in another world, a world that the ETIs may not know was inhabited or even that it existed. Finally, I do not think that what the ETIs would be asked to believe is more difficult to believe than God's promise to Abraham that he would be the father of many nations, or than Gabriel's announcement to Mary, or than the prophetic visions of the Apocalypse. If the veracity of ETI prophets was confirmed by signs—as for example, Elijah was shown to be a true prophet when his prayers resulted in a holocaust being miraculously set ablaze before the eyes of many onlookers (see 1 K. 18:20-40)—there would doubtlessly be ETIs who would believe their message.

Given that even angels or ETI prophets could bring the good news to ETIs, *a fortiori* Christ himself could bring the gospel to them, for he could certainly confirm that he was who he claimed to be by performing miracles.

As for earthling missionaries, the problem with this alternative is that it will be a long time before we develop means of space travel sufficient to get us across our galaxy. The ETIs could come to us first, assuming that their civilization is more developed and their technology more advanced. Or at least we could communicate with each other via radio waves. But there is a big fly in the ointment with these proposed solutions for circulating the Good News: While they might work for a limited part of the universe, it appears that they cannot work for the whole universe. As Roland Pucetti explains:

> Professor Milne's suggestion a decade and a half ago that we might succeed in spreading the Gospel to other beings in the galaxy through radiocommunication, and that they would then spread it to local galaxies, and they to 'the whole intergalactic universe', can hardly be taken seriously. It would require almost one hundred thousand years for a radiowave to reach the farthest star in our own galaxy, and about two million years to reach the nearest other galaxy. As we saw in Chapter 3, the farthest known galaxies, constituting probably only one-tenth the total intergalactic universe, are receding from us so rapidly that everything beyond them would be entirely inaccessible to us: even if we did not have to spread this message via ten thousand million intervening galaxies. Thus there is absolutely no hope of the Christian religion becoming known to all extra-human persons in the universe, if, in fact, the Earth is its sole point of origin.[38]

There does not seem to be any way for us to disseminate the Good News to all in need of hearing it. Assumptions that ETIs would not inhabit the galaxies out of our range, or that only unfallen ones would be in those galaxies seem offhand purely gratuitous, especially if ETI races are supposed to be so numerous as ETI proponents claim, but also if the "Rare Earth" school proved closer to being right, and intelligent life arose in but a place or two other than earth. Recently, however, a case has been made that the galaxies where it is possible for intelligent life to arise are galaxies that are near to ours.[39] But are these galaxies predicted to be so near ours that we might hope to possibly communicate with ETIs that might inhabit them? Scientists tell me no. Perhaps, however, someone will come up with reasons for why this distance should be revised, in the direction of yet an even smaller distance—or in the opposite direction. I acknowledge, then, that at present we cannot absolutely rule out the possibility that the only part of the universe capable of harboring intelligent life is sufficiently close to us to allow for communication between any intelligent inhabitants there and us. Given, however, that there is some reason to think inhabitable galaxies need not be that close to us, and no reason to think that they must be, this hypothesis is rather tenuous.

A somewhat better reason for not definitively ruling out the possibility of communication with the other intelligent life forms in the universe lies in our lack of certitude about the limitations on the capabilities of future forms of communication. The possibility of faster-than-light communication is currently rejected by the majority of scientists. But there are some physicists (and not just science fiction writers) who do not entirely rule it out, suggesting, for instance, that there might be short-cuts through space-time ("wormholes"[40]). Other physicists, however, question whether we could ever actually make use of them for purposes of communication. Nonetheless, given the incompleteness of our present understanding of the physical universe, it would be premature to entirely rule out the possibility that we could eventually communicate with all or at least most of the other intelligent life forms in the universe. At the same time, in light of our present knowledge, there is little reason for optimism.

Telepathy is sometimes offered as a solution to the communication problem. I have serious doubts that such a thing exists, but in any case, if it proceeds through causal means available in nature, it would be subject to the same restrictions mentioned above. It cannot be a direct transfer of ideas, since it belongs to the nature of embodied intelligences to grasp immaterial things starting from material things, rather than directly. One could suppose that telepathy involved transfer of information from one material rational being's mind to another's via angels.[41] Angels cannot transfer ideas into a human intellect, but can act directly on the human imagination, thus disposing a person to form certain ideas. But then there is finally not much difference between the Good News being communicated via telepathy as opposed to being communicated via angels—in the former case one simply labors under the illusion that the message has come directly from another embodied intelligence.

Despite future communication of the gospel across the universe via human inventions being a doubtful prospect, the problem of ETIs never hearing the Good News in not insoluble, given that God (be it the Trinity of Persons or the Word Incarnate) or angels or ETI prophets could bring it to them.

The likelihood that we are unable to communicate the Good News to all the fallen ETI races in the universe is somewhat similar to a more general objection against ETI existence, one that applies to the fallen and unfallen alike. This objection was already posed by Albert and Aquinas in their discussions of whether a plurality of worlds was possible. It has its root in something Aristotle points out in the *Metaphysics*, namely, that there are two ends and goods of the universe, one extrinsic to it, and one intrinsic to it. Aquinas elaborates on the illustration Aristotle gives to explain these two ends:

> [F]or the good of the army is in the order itself of the army and in the leader who presides over the army: but the greater good is in the leader than in the order: because the end is greater in goodness than those things which are to the end: the order of the army is for the sake of accomplishing the good of the leader, as the will of the leader lies in the realization of victory....[42]

For Aristotle the extrinsic good of the universe, in function of which all the parts of the universe are ordered, is the prime mover. Aquinas explains in more detail what the intrinsic order of the universe consists in:

> The order of the universe includes in itself both the conservation of the diverse things instituted by God, and the motion of them; because according to these a twofold order is found in things, namely, according as one thing is better than another, and according as one thing is moved by another.[43]

Aquinas elaborates on the latter of these notions when commenting on Aristotle's *Metaphysics*:

[T]hose who held that after number, there was magnitude, and after magnitude, sensible things, saying that the principles of each nature were other and other…make the substance "of the universe to be lacking connection," i.e., without order, so that one part, whether it is there or not, confers nothing on a different or second thing. And similarly they posit that many principles exist lacking interconnection. And this cannot be, because beings do not want to be badly disposed. For the disposition of natural beings is such that it is the best it can be. And we see this in individual things: each and every one of them is of the best disposition in its nature. Whence much more is it necessary to think that this obtains in the whole universe. But plurality of realms is not good: Just as it would not be good for diverse families which did not communicate with each other to be in one house.[44]

St. Albert, as the reader might recall, gave a similar argument, pointing out that "good of the worlds is not perfect without communication of its citizens."[45]

To relate this to the problem at hand: if there were no interaction between the human realm and the ETI realm, though the universe would possess the order of hierarchy (on the assumption that ETIs are not redundant), it would be lacking in the order of interactivity. This is unacceptable to Aquinas who sees that the individual parts in a lesser work, e.g., an animal body, do not function independently of each other, but are mutually interactive and dependent, and as such give unity to the whole[46]—from which he goes on to argue a fortiori that the parts of the universe, which is a greater work, should manifest even more mutual interactivity and co-dependency.

The notion that the universe's perfection lies in the interactivity of its parts is realized in the case of the angels. If the angels had never interacted with material creation they would for all practical purposes have been a quasi-separate universe, and this would have derogated from the order of the universe.[47] As a matter of fact, the angels played important roles in salvation history, among other things, tempting our first mother, and asking Mary if she would become the mother of God.[48] And they have important roles even in this day: some angels watch over human individuals, and devils are allowed to tempt humans up to a point.[49] Moreover, human salvation history has been traditionally thought to complement the angels' story in a certain way—so what humans do in a certain way affects them. Aquinas, among others, makes mention of this in his commentary on Ep. 1:8-10:

> The effect of this hidden plan [sacramentum—sacred secret] was to restore all things. For insofar as all things are made for the sake of man, all things are said to be restored..... *All things* he says *which are in heaven*, i.e., the Angels—not that Christ died for the Angels, but by redeeming man, the fall of the Angels was repaired.[50]

The angels not only interact with material creation, but also amongst themselves. Longstanding tradition (going back to Pseudo-Dionysius) has it that they speak with each other,[51] illuminate each other,[52] and cooperate among themselves in regard to their interactions with us.[53] Thus, although each angel is actually a species unto itself, it is far from being a world unto itself. One would expect the same to be true of an ETI species. Again, we cannot rule out that there is only one other intelligent material species in the universe, and it just happens to be only half a galaxy away; or that there are a multitude of such species, but they are still close enough that we could eventually communicate with them. We cannot rule out with absolute certitude that there exists some means of communication faster than is what is generally thought possible within the current paradigms in physics. At present, however, the prospects for interactivity via natural means look pretty bleak.

It was suggested to me that perhaps the angels supply the interconnections between ETIs and us by serving as guardians to both. In this way, the ETI world and our world would not be two entirely separate worlds but would be united via the angelic realm. While I do not deny that this would constitute some degree of interconnection (more than if the angels were removed from the picture), I do not think that it supplies the sort of connection which one allow one to regard the intelligent beings in the universe to constitute an interactive whole. Rational beings may be related in a significant manner without being cognizant of the relation, as for instance is the case of blood relatives who do not know each other at all; but they are not for so much interactive. The link between two people who are unknown to each other via one or a set of intermediary people (in the line of the so-called "six degrees of separation" proposed by Stanley Milgram) also does not qualify the two in question as interactive. Even if one person spoke to both of two people about the other (in ways favorable or unfavorable), this would not make them interactive. Interactivity is, however, possible through an intermediary who transmitted messages between the two. Now, although angels in the Old Testament delivered a variety of messages to a number of different humans, they never even brought news to us of the existence of ETIs, much less any message from them. Again, I reject the claim that this sort of communication is presently taking place. I also reject the *ad hoc* solution that God has charged the angels to start delivering messages between ETIs and us at some later date.

One might object that my insistence that communication must occur for intelligent species to be considered interactive is unfounded, given that the members of the body of Christ are organically united, but many of them do not know each other. The prayers offered for the Church at Mass by one of the faithful affect the other members of the Church, and vice versa. There is no reason to think that the same interaction would not obtain between the ETI faithful and us on the (questionable[54]) hypothesis that ETIs on their planet also celebrated the Eucharist. This hypothetical situation does not, however, offer a solution to the interactivity problem pertaining to ETI existence. If order is lacking at the natural level, it does not cease to be lacking when a supernatural order is established. Divine wisdom requires that there be a natural order among the parts of the universe, and especially among its principle parts. Thus, even if a Eucharistic interconnection were established, so long as the different groups remained ignorant of each other's existence, natural interactivity between them would be impossible. Despite the very real Eucharistic bond, we and they *in the natural order* would be "diverse families...in one house, which did not communicate with each other." Again, to superimpose a supernatural order on top of natural disorder, does not eradicate that disorder.

So far we have seen that fallen ETIs have five strikes against them: First, their existence would detract from the uniqueness of the nature the Word united to himself. Secondly, a second rational material species appears to be redundant when one considers that human nature already afforded the Word an assumable nature that in some way united all of creation. Thirdly, when one reflects on the multitude of ways in which the Incarnation and Passion were suited specifically to human salvation, it seems implausible that they were also ordered to the salvation of other rational material beings. Fourthly, Hebrews 2:10-18 seems to indicate that Christ desired to become man so that he could redeem all those living under the bondage of sin and death by being a member of their race. Fifthly, ETI existence would derogate from the perfection of the universe which lies in its being an interactive whole, that is, if we assume that the present pessimistic prognosis for future communication between earth and other habitable parts of the universe is accurate.

Chapter 7

Probable Arguments that Humans are Unique on the Supposition of One Incarnation: The Case of the Unfallen ETIs

> One goes into the forest to pick food and already the thought of one fruit rather than another has grown up in one's mind. Then, it may be, one finds a different fruit and not the fruit one thought of. One joy was expected and another is given. But this I had never noticed before—that the very moment of the finding there is in the mind a kind of thrusting back, or setting aside. The picture of the fruit you have not found is still, for a moment, before you. And if you wished—if it were possible to wish—you could keep it there. You could send your soul after the good you had expected, instead of turning it to the good you had got. You could refuse the real good; you could make the real fruit taste insipid by thinking of the other.
>
> —The Green Lady (the Eve) of Perelandra

As for unfallen ETIs, some of the same problems we have spoken about in regard to the fallen apply to them too: First, their existence undermines the uniqueness of the race the Word united to himself, although, on the other hand, a subdivision of intelligent material races into fallen and unfallen does make for greater diversity. Second, the limitations on how interactive they can be with other intelligent species is also problematic. Third, ETIs do not at first sight fit very well in the central story of the universe, the story of the Word made flesh who died for our sins, although again this could be explained by the fact that they do not share our need for God's special intervention.

It is worth considering how these probable arguments against unfallen ETIs stack up against the eloquent case that C. S. Lewis makes for a fictive unfallen race in his science fiction novel *Perelandra*. Lewis puts the following speech in the mouth of Ransom, *Perelandra*'s human protagonist:

> What had happened on Earth, when Maleldil was born a man at Bethlehem, had altered the universe for ever. The new world of Perelandra was not a mere repetition of the old world Tellus. Maleldil never repeated himself....When Eve fell, God was not Man. He had not yet made men members of His body: since then He had, and through them henceforward He would save and suffer. One of the purposes for which He had done all this was to save Perelandra not through himself but through Himself in Ransom. If Ransom refused, the plan, so far, miscarried....[Ransom] perceived that you might just as well call Perelandra, not Tellus, the centre. You might look upon the Perelandrian story as merely an indirect consequence of the Incarnation on earth: or you might look on the Earth story as mere preparation for the new worlds of which Perelandra was the first. The one was neither more nor less true than the other. Nothing was more or less important than anything else, nothing was a copy or model of anything else.[1]

I must acknowledge the persuasiveness of Lewis's defense of the unfallen race he describes. Lewis recognizes that the central role of Christ as redeemer must be upheld. The Perelandrians benefit from the redemption to the extent that Ransom's ability to prevent a second Fall is due to the fact that he is Christian. Thus, while they are not part of the Redemption story as playing a role in our salvation history, they are part of it by way of continuing it. Moreover, Lewis explicitly acknowledges that the Perelandrians' story would be to no purpose if it were simply a repetition of what happened on earth.

I cannot, however, agree with Lewis's view. Certainly, the alternative of regarding the Earth story as "a mere preparation for the new worlds of which Perelandra was the first" is not a viable alternative for a Catholic. The story of the redemption is the heart of God's plan for the universe. In the words of the *CCC*:

> In the Symbol of the faith the Church confesses the mystery of the Holy Trinity and of the plan of God's 'good pleasure' for all creation: the Father accomplishes the 'mystery of his will' by giving his beloved Son and the Holy Spirit for the salvation of the world and for the glory of his name. Such is the mystery of Christ, revealed and fulfilled in history according to the wisely ordered plan that St. Paul calls the 'plan of the mystery' and the patristic tradition will call the 'economy of the Word incarnate' or the 'economy of salvation.[2]'
>
> The eighth day. But for us a new day has dawned: the day of Christ's Resurrection. The seventh day completes the first creation. The eighth day begins the new creation. Thus, the work of creation culminates in the greater work of redemption. The first creation finds its meaning and its summit in the new creation in Christ, the splendor of which surpasses that of the first creation.[3]

Even if one adopts Lewis's other alternative, namely that one "might look upon the Perelandrian story as merely an indirect consequence of the Incarnation on earth," I still have difficulties with his overall view. First, Lewis seems overly optimistic about none of the other Perelandrians falling, after their first lady passed her test. The very existence of an unfallen race is highly questionable. It is not that ETIs would suffer temptations from the side of their animal nature, for it is reasonable to assume that if ETIs were created in the state of grace (which I argued in chapter 4 they would be), then their lower powers would be entirely subject to their higher powers.[3] The ETIs would be like Adam and Eve who were only capable of committing one sort of sin, that of not submitting to God.[5]

What renders it unlikely that an entire ETI race remains unfallen is that some of the angels who are superior in intellect and will in comparison to material rational creatures fell.[6] Aquinas, when discussing why it is that the majority of the angels did not fall, whereas it seems that it is the minority of human beings that are good, points out that it is not just that humans, unlike the angels, have been affected by original sin. It also finds an explanation in the "very condition of human nature."[7] Aquinas points out that while angels are naturally endowed with accidental perfections that direct their actions along the proper course, this is not true of humans, but rather: "the second perfections by which [human] acts are directed are not innate, but are acquired or infused." Our need to acquire habits to direct our actions correctly is rooted in the potential nature of our intellect which results in human nature "stand[ing] indifferently to all things intelligible and doable." Whence,

> since evil happens in many forms, but the good in only one manner, therefore [human nature] often lets itself go towards what is bad. For human nature thus considered is not yet as an agent that is perfected; for then an agent is perfect as to all its operations when it has been perfected by second perfections, which are the virtues; and therefore when it is determined through second perfections either infused or acquired, then it is determined to one, to which it tends in the greater number of cases....And therefore Cicero compares virtue to nature, saying that it is a voluntary habit, in the mode of nature, with reason consenting.[8]

It is true that Adam and Eve are thought to have possessed all of the virtues, since they were created in grace and endowed with original justice.[9] And I am supposing the same thing would be true of ETIs. Even the infused virtues, however, do not put humans on a par with the angels. They are special gifts, whereas the angels have the equivalent by nature. The gift of infused virtues does not change the fact that our nature does have a far greater amount of potency admixed with it than angelic nature. Virtue is like second nature, but it is not nature. Thus, human beings are more liable to go astray than angels.

One could also formulate an inductive argument that ETIs would fall, generalizing from the case of the human race and the case of the angels that every sort of intelligent being will have members who fall. I say "sort" rather than "species," for I agree with Aquinas's view that every angel is a species unto itself,[10] and thus that angels are only generically alike. Both members of the species "man" and the genus "angel" have fallen.

One might wonder whether had Adam and Eve past the test of the forbidden fruit, they would have been immediately confirmed in justice, i.e., would have become so fixed in the good that they could no longer fall. Aquinas argues that this could not be the case, because the only way to be confirmed in justice is to experience the beatific vision; however, when humans attain the beatific vision their bodies are spiritualized and their animal functions cease. Thus, on the suppositions that Adam and Eve resisted their initial temptation, and that they were thereupon confirmed in justice, there would be no human race. In the words of Aquinas:

> [A]ccording to certain people, if Adam when tempted had not sinned, he would have immediately been confirmed in justice, and all his posterity would be born confirmed in justice.... But I believe that this is false; for the condition of the body in the primal state corresponded to the condition of the soul; whence so long as the body was like those of animals, the soul was subject to change, having not yet been made spiritual. To generate offspring, however, pertains to the animal life; whence it follows that the sons of Adam would not be born confirmed in justice.[11]

Does the existence of an entirely unfallen race of ETIs, other than one that would be created in glory, imply a contradiction? Do some individuals belonging to a genus of fallible material creatures necessarily have to fail?[12] If this is the case, then it would be intrinsically impossible to create an unfallen race of the sort described. I am not sure what to say on this matter; my suspicion is that such a race is creatable. Even if one knew that such a race could be created, there would still remain the question of whether God in his wisdom would choose to do so. What we do know is that individuals of every sort of intelligent being that we know God to have created have fallen, and further that this fits with what one might expect given that all beings other than God lack the complete perfection that is found in him alone. (Note that this argument can be used to make an even stronger case against the existence of many unfallen races. For given that it is hard to envisage even one unfallen race, it is all the harder to think that there are many of them.[13])

Another objection to Lewis's position is that the Perelandrians' tie with Christ is a rather tenuous one. It is only indirectly through Ransom that there is any tie. By comparison, fallen ETIs are saved by Christ. The Perelandrian story does have the appearance, as Lewis himself suggests, of being "merely an indirect consequence of the Incarnation on earth," and not as an integral part of the plan for the universe.

The Perelandrian scenario raises the more general question as to what sort of relationship unfallen ETIs might have to Christ. Certainly they will know him as head and Lord in the eternal kingdom, but what about before that time? Working on our present assumption that the Word did not become incarnate in their flesh, it is certainly easier to envisage a relationship between such unfallen ETIs and God, than between them and Christ. It is not hard to imagine them walking with God in the like Adam and Eve did, but where and why would Christ enter their story? Still, if an unfallen race was more recent than ours, then Christ could walk with them, and in the case of older races he could make an appearance later in their history. It is true that in both cases he would be an alien to these beings. It is also true that they would not have the sort of relationship to Christ that the angels have (whose nature Christ does not share), given that they, unlike the angels, do not serve as messengers and guardians under Christ's command. Despite the comparatively weak association between unfallen ETIs and Christ, they would still have a relation to Christ insofar as he is their Lord and Head (albeit not their head as to likeness of nature), and he certainly could make himself known to them.

While there can be a connection between an unfallen world and Christ, there still remains a problem as to the lack of connection between an unfallen world and our world. While Christ's story, the angelic story and the human story form a unified interlocking whole, the unfallen, aside from the point of contact that Christ (or in *Perelandra*, Ransom) represents, constitute their own separate world. This is unacceptable given that: "The good of the universe, which consists in order and harmony, has more dignity than the good of any particular nature...."[14] Again, while future interaction between members of our world and those of a given unfallen world may be possible, it does not appear likely that this possibility extends to a multitude of unfallen worlds, due to the apparent limitations in the means of communication.

A mixed scenario, i.e., an ETI race composed of fallen and unfallen individuals, is certainly more likely than a race composed solely of unfallen individuals, given that someone is bound to fall somewhere along the line. However, if one asks how the mixed scenario compares to the alternative of human uniqueness, one sees that it is not a viable alternative, for it suffers from the combined incongruities of both of the unmixed scenarios. Furthermore, this scenario entails an additional unacceptable consequence, that of introducing division within the ETI race. Christ would be the savior of some ETIs, but not of others. Certainly in the case of the human race, God prized unity. This is clear from Rom. 5:12-19, quoted above: "[S]in entered the world through one man, and through sin death, and thus death has spread through the whole human race because everyone has sinned," etc. Augustine elaborates on this theme:

And God was not ignorant that man would sin, and that, being himself made subject now to death, he would propagate men doomed to die, and that these mortals would run to such enormities in sin.... But God foresaw also that by His grace a people would be called to adoption, and that they, being justified by the remission of their sins, would be united by the Holy Ghost to the holy angels in eternal peace, the last enemy, death, being destroyed; and He knew that this people would derive profit from the consideration that God had caused all men to be derived from one, for the sake of showing how highly He prizes unity in a multitude.[15]

Chapter 8

Probable Arguments that Humans are Unique on the Supposition of More than One Incarnation

The Lamb is the Lord of lords and the King of kings.

—Revelation 17:14

Thus far I have been arguing against ETI existence using as grounds that there has been only one Incarnation, which I have argued is most likely the case. It remains to be considered what would ensue if there was another Incarnation. A second Incarnation would entail the Second Person being united to either a fallen or unfallen ETI nature. I will begin with incarnation in a fallen ETI nature. (Many of the same problems ensue from a second incarnation as with a sole incarnation.)

In the case of humans, the Word assumed human nature to save us from sin, but the ETIs are already saved through Christ's cross, so there goes the need to assume an ETI nature to save them. All three of the benefits of having a member of one's own race as savior would be lost. Moreover, if the Word assumed a fallen ETI nature to be their teacher and/or friend, the ETIs would be faced with the situation of being saved by Christ who was a human being, and of having a divine teacher and/or friend who was also one of them, the two being the same person. This situation certainly seems baroque, and it would definitely make faith somewhat more difficult for ETIs than for humans. It is true that an ETI incarnation of the Word could perform miracles to manifest his divinity and to confirm that what he said was true. Still, one of the motives of credibility that we humans have for the Christian faith would be lacking to the ETIs, namely, historical records (other than Scripture) that mention Christ and the early

Christians. Also, it is hard enough to understand that Christ is one person in two natures (many Christians are essentially ignorant of this), so adding yet another nature is liable to be confusing to the ETIs, and thus not conducive to faith. ETIs are often depicted as having intelligences greatly superior to ours. Nevertheless, they are subject to experiencing the same difficulties humans experience in attempting to understand immaterial realities (such as the hypostatic union), since they acquire intellectual knowledge starting from sense experience. Although they are unlikely to need us as missionaries, since the Word doubly Incarnate presumably would impart the Good News to them, still the interactivity problem applies to them. For all these reasons, a second incarnation in a fallen nature does not seem likely.

As for a second incarnation involving union with an unfallen ETI race, this situation does not fare much better given what we know about Christ and the plan for the universe. At first sight, it does not seem to be incompatible with the notion that the plan for the entire universe revolves around Christ, since on this supposition the same person who is Christ is incarnate as ETI. And there is no reason why unfallen ETIs would be ignorant of these things. The bizarre situation that would arise if the Word became Incarnate as a member of a fallen ETIs race is not applicable here, since unfallen ETIs are not in need of the salvation Christ wrought through his death on the cross. However, when one starts filling in the details, it becomes harder to envisage the story of the universe as being essentially Christ's story on this hypothesis. For example, the Word could become incarnate as ETI in the beginning of the ETI story to prevent the ETIs from falling, and then later in the history of the universe become incarnate a second time as man to restore man to friendship with God. If this situation obtained, then the prevention of the ETI fall would be attributable to Christ, *but not in his human nature*. Even if the prevention of an ETI fall was subsequent to our fall, it would still not seem correct to attribute this act to the Word incarnate as man rather than as ETI, granted Christ and the ETI incarnation would be the same person. There are other scenarios, e.g., that the Word would become incarnate a second time to be teacher and friend to ETIs. However, then it would not be Christ in his human nature who was the ETIs' teacher and friend. Also, the ETI incarnation would be head of the ETIs in one manner that would not be true of Christ, namely, as to nature. While none of these scenarios entails the denial that the story of the universe is Christ's story, the claim does appear somewhat strained.[1] To my mind, tension of this sort inevitably arises when the uniqueness of the Incarnation is denied.

The supposition of a second incarnation in the flesh of an unfallen race is also rendered questionable on account of the interactivity problem. While Christ would be a link between humans and ETIs in virtue of the second incarnation, this of itself would not make the two groups as groups interactive. The interactivity required by a well-ordered universe poses problem for all ETI scenarios.

I will now evaluate the comparative likelihood of the various ETI scenarios. This may seem at first sight out of keeping with my main purpose, which is to argue against ETI existence by showing the unsuitable consequences which follow from positing it. However, since some consequences are more unsuitable than others, an evaluation of the relative (im)probability of scenarios provides a way of clarifying the extent to which the various forms of belief in ETIs impact on the Christian faith.

The Word becoming Incarnate as an ETI to a race of unfallen ETIs from some points of view is the least unacceptable of the ETI scenarios. Fallen ETIs square poorly with the notion that sin came through one man, Adam, and salvation came through one man, Christ, the New Adam. For this reason, positing the existence of fallen ETIs involves a more serious incongruity than positing the existence of unfallen ETIs does, as questionable as that latter is. Fallen ETIs also appear to be much more redundant than unfallen ETIs; it is hard to envisage their story as other than a superfluous subplot in the Redemption story. Comparing the two possible types of unfallen ETIs, the existence of a group in whose flesh the Word would become incarnate seems at first sight less problematic, for these ETIs would be led to a more familiar love of God, as well as be reassured that their intellect could be directly united to the divine essence itself, and so forth, through the God-ETI. Still, there are two things attached to this scenario which render it questionable. The first is that a second Incarnation would detract from the uniqueness of the first. Related to this incongruity is a second: Although it would be still be correct to say that Christ is the central figure in the universe—even though he would not be the center of the ETI world insofar as he is incarnate as man—it would plainly be true in a weaker sense than would be the case if there was one sole incarnation. Once again, all ETI scenarios appear to suffer from the inability to meet the requirement that "all things ought to be ordered in one order."[2] Ultimately, then, the ETI scenario which appears to be the least objectionable is that of an unfallen race to whom Christ appears or reveals himself in some other way, without the Word becoming incarnate a second time.

To sum up the probable arguments against the existence of ETIs given in this part: To start with, three arguments were given against a second incarnation, the first being that it is appropriate that an extraordinary event be a one-time only event, and the second being that Scripture and Church teaching regard the new creation in Christ as *the* purpose for which the universe was created to start with. A third argument is that all of the possible modalities for a second incarnation seem to be unsuitable. Discrediting the likelihood of a second incarnation is beneficial to my overall argument, since if there was good reason to think a second incarnation likely, by that very fact, there would be reason to think that a second rational material species existed.

After arguing that a second incarnation is improbable, I went on to give six probable arguments that ETIs do not exist on the assumption that God became incarnate only once. The first is that given that the Incarnation is a unique event, it is appropriate that the species assumed be unique, for good things that are unique are prized as having greater worth than those that are not (this argument turns on the nature of uniqueness). The second is that if the Incarnation was to profit all of creation, it was suitable that there be a species linking both spiritual and material realms; the human species serves just this purpose, and so a second human-like species would be superfluous to this end (this argument turns on the principle that intelligent agents do not engage in redundant activities). The third, which only argues against fallen ETI existence, is that Hebrews 2:10-18 indicates that Christ desired to belong to the same race as those he was to redeem so that they could be redeemed in the most appropriate manner (this argument is Scripturally based). The fourth is that the benefits of the Incarnation and Passion are directed to human well-being in such a specific way that it is hard to see the Incarnation and Passion as ordered to the benefit of some other material rational being (this argument is based on the notion that the story of the universe has a coherent plot, in function of which one can recognize episodes that would detract from the story's unity). The fifth argument is that in order for the universe to be a well-ordered whole, there would have to be interaction among the parts of primary importance, namely, the intelligent beings—something which is apparently impossible (this reduction to the absurd is based on the concept of order in the universe, and also relies on scientific evidence concerning the possibility of communication among all the supposedly inhabited planets). The sixth argument, which applies only to unfallen ETIs, is that given some individuals of a kind of being superior in nature to ETIs fell, it is unlikely that all members of ETI species would remain unfallen (this argument is based on a comparison of human and angelic natures).

I think that it is quite unlikely that God became incarnate more than once. However, on the assumption that this is the case, there are still a number of unacceptable consequences that would follow from ETI existence. The unfallen suffer from some of the same problems named above, i.e., their very existence is questionable and their connection with other intelligent races is a highly doubtful prospect. As for the fallen, positing a second incarnation does nothing to remedy any of the problems outlined in the previous paragraph (with the exception of the sixth, which did not apply to fallen ETIs). Moreover, the fallen ETIs would have a faith that was hard to understand, for the God-ETI would not be their savior in his ETI incarnation, but in his human incarnation.

Part III

Weaknesses in Arguments in Favor of ETI Existence

CHAPTER 9

Weaknesses of Arguments in Favor of ETI Existence Derived from Science

> Established fact in astrobiology remains a scarce commodity.
> —David Darling, *Life Everywhere*

In order to strengthen my case that the existence of ETI life is not probable on the assumption that Christianity is true,[1] I intend now to show that the arguments commonly offered to establish that the existence of ETI life is probable are not cogent. A good number of the mistakes in reasoning that I am going to address here have already been pointed out by other authors, most notably, Ernan McMullin and Michael J. Crowe (who in part takes inspiration from McMullin). I will try to stay on as general a level as possible, despite the almost irresistible attraction of examining the details of the contemporary research that has bearing on the ETI question. I am not a scientist, and therefore am not in position to arbitrate the purely scientific aspects of the debate. The other reason I prefer to stay away from the details is to keep this book from becoming prematurely dated. Scientists continually come up new means of observations and ingenious experiments with the result that a hypothesis that is of questionable value one day, sometimes seems more realistic the next, and may end up becoming well-supported with time. For instance, not so long ago it was thought that there is no life on Mars.[2] But then the controversial Martian meteorite ALH 84001[3] with its purportedly biogenic traces gave some reason to keep looking. Later on, photographs of deep, v-shaped channels on a southern portion of Mars suggested that there may have been water on Mars.[4] Still more recently the NASA Odyssey spacecraft using a gamma-ray spectrometer detected signs of water ice on Mars'

South Pole. Subsequently, even more conclusive evidence of ice was discovered by the Mars Express orbiter, using an infrared camera. The probes presently on Mars have gathered geological evidence of liquid water, and perhaps in the not too distant future, other probes will verify its presence directly,[5] and maybe even discover traces of life. I will occasionally stray a bit from the realm of generalities and logic because the scientific details are ever so fascinating.

In order for extraterrestrial life to exist, there must be a planet that is inhabitable, life must take hold on it, and it must evolve to the point of intelligence. There are numerous problems with the manner in which people have determined the likelihood of each of these things.

The most common mistake made by some of those who hold that ETI life exists, is to estimate the likelihood that intelligent life exists elsewhere in the universe on the basis of insufficient evidence. This is especially true in regard to the origin and development of life, and to a lesser degree true in regard to the production of earthlike planets. One form this error has often taken in the debate involves confusing necessary conditions with sufficient conditions. Astronomers on the whole compared to biologists have historically been more prone to people the skies. Biologists have traditionally been more reserved about doing so because they are aware of how ignorant we are about the origin and evolution of life on earth. The astronomers' tendency has been to think that once there is reason to think that the habitations needed for life are out there, life comes along with them, at least in a certain percentage of cases.

For years the Miller-Urey experiments were brought forth as evidence that it was easy for life to begin. Stanley Miller (who worked in Harold Urey's laboratory) passed a spark through reducing gases that he thought were likely to compose the earth's early atmosphere. The result was numerous simple carbon compounds which when dissolved were concentrated into amino acids, simple acids, purines and pyrimidines, which are constituents of living things. The conclusion drawn from this, that life arises easily, is problematic from a logical point of view. There is a big difference between the formation of a few of the chemicals found in life as we know it, and an actual living thing. Having the ingredients does not insure getting the final product (this is even more true when one only has some of the ingredients). This is a typical case of confusing necessary with sufficient conditions.

In addition, there is a scientific problem with the relevance of the Miller-Urey experiments to the question of how life originated on earth.

These experiments only work in a reducing atmosphere, but most scientists no longer think that the atmosphere of the early earth was reducing,[6] although this cannot as yet be absolutely ruled out.[7] Theories of the origin of life other than Miller-Urey's surface scenario have been proposed and are being tested, a front-runner being that life arose in deep sea vents. Researchers try to reproduce in the laboratory the temperature and pressure conditions found in deep sea vents, and depending on the chemicals that are added, have had some success in producing a few of the constituents of living things.[8] However, even David Darling, the optimistic author of *Life Everywhere*, acknowledges that:

> If synthesizing life in the laboratory is an Everest expedition, scientists are roughly at the stage of boarding the plane to Kathmandu. They've shown how *some* of small molecular subunits of life can be made under conditions that might have existed on the young earth.[9]

Darling calls to our attention another problem with synthesizing life in the laboratory and the origin of life. It may turn out that life synthesized in the laboratory will be little like what actually arose in nature, either because our initial conditions are unlike those that obtained in nature or because the ingredients or processes used are different. However, in light of the fact that physical and chemical laws have to be respected, there is some reason to hope that at least some degree of similarity between our experiments and nature's will one day be achieved.

If we do not know how life began here (assuming it did begin here), we are not in a good position to estimate how likely it is to have begun elsewhere. Some try to argue in an inductive manner that it is probably easy for life to arise under suitable conditions basing themselves on what happened on planet earth. They generally point to two facts: first, that life originated rather rapidly here. On an earth that is approximately 4.5-4.6 billion years old, life appears to have taken hold 3.5-3.8 billion years ago. Life actually shows up more quickly than these numbers would lead one to believe, for the earth was subject to heavy comic bombardments capable of sterilizing its surface until 3.8 billion years ago.[10] Life then only took at most .3 billion years to appear (300 million years), and perhaps as little as 10-20 million years.[11] There are some, however, who regard this relatively short delay as evidence that life did not begin on earth. They hypothesize that life emerged elsewhere (Mars being a top contender), and was carried to earth by meteorites.[12]

The second reason invoked in favor of thinking that life begins with relative ease are genetic analyses that suggest that members of the Kingdom Archaea are closest to the putative common ancestor of all life.[13] (The rooting of the Tree of Life, and the relationships of the major lineages remain controversial.) The Archaea are unicellular organisms that live in extreme environments such as hot springs and thermal vents, in temperatures ranging from 70-113C. Since submarine hydrothermal vents are rich in chemicals needed for life, and come with a source of chemical energy, and are a relatively stable environment compared to a surface bombarded by ultraviolet radiation and cosmic debris, some have proposed that life originated there.[14] If this is the case, it may be that life can take hold more readily than was thought when people were working on the assumption that a warm pond or soup was required. Perhaps these extreme thermophiles even arose before the cessation of the cosmic bombardments of the earth that caused catastrophic heating.[15] It may be the case, however, that the common ancestor of all life arose in more moderate conditions, and that life only later adapted itself to the extreme conditions found in sea vents.

Our uncertainty as to whether life did in fact originate on earth casts a shadow of doubt over any kind of generalization about the ease with which life arises starting from the case of our planet. And even if we were sure that life originated here, to reason inductively to the conclusion that life generally originates quickly, starting from one case, is plainly a hasty generalization. Also, our uncertainly as to the conditions under which life arose here (assuming it did) leave us unable to determine how likely it is to arise elsewhere. We can eliminate certain temperatures as too extreme for active metabolism. While organisms from what are thought to be the most ancient lineages are presently able to live in very hot places, this was not necessarily true of their ancestral forms. It would be useful to know whether life can only arise under such extreme temperatures or whether warm pond scenarios might not also yield life. Moreover, there are many other factors required for life besides the appropriate temperature, factors which remain unknown other than at a very general level, e.g., we can be pretty sure that the primordial life form will be carbon based.[16] To the extent that we are ignorant of what constitutes suitable conditions for the origin of life we lack a basis for gauging whether life is easy or hard to come by, and the extrapolations of the prevalence of life in the cosmos, typically made by ETI proponents, remain without a solid foundation.

As Ernan McMullin points out, various additional factors invoked in the extrapolation of how much life is out there in no way compensate for our fundamental ignorance concerning how readily life originates.[17] People will call upon the long periods of time to justify the population of other planets. However, if the origin of life is extremely improbable, the amounts of time in question may still fall short of what would be necessary. As Frank W. Cousins[18] puts it, if monkeys typing randomly would take 10x years to produce Hamlet, 10y may be huge period of time, but still not enough time, if it is less than 10x years. Again, what we need to know, and do not know, is whether the origin of life is extremely improbable or not. Similarly, the large numbers of planets[19] (assuming for the moment that these estimates are accurate) will also not result in hordes of ETIs if life originates only under very special conditions.[20] Invoking the uniformity of nature, as ETI proponents often do,[21] affords no help to their cause, because again we do not know how likely it is for the conditions sufficient for life to arise to obtain—life may be uniformly nowhere other than here.

I am not at all pessimistic that scientists will continue to make progress in figuring out the conditions under which life originated on earth, allowing for plausible estimates of how common it might be elsewhere. While a lot remains to be discovered, some progress has been made, e.g., we are now closer to knowing what the atmosphere of the early earth was like than we were in the past. And the discovery of life in thermal vents made us aware that inhabitable conditions are not as narrow as we first thought, and this has opened up investigation as to whether life might have arisen under extreme conditions. The debate between the Rare Earth school and the Life Everywhere school is bearing fruit, narrowing down what are and what are not constraints for life's appearance here.

It is plainly not enough for life to originate for there to be ETI, it also must evolve to the very high level of complexity requisite for intelligence. Here too our present state of knowledge does not allow us to make a reliable estimate of how likely this complexification is to occur on other planets. There are two main bones of contention. The first concerns the ease with which animals originate. The second regards the role that contingency plays in the evolution of specific kinds of life forms.

As to the first issue: Based on evidence from the fossil record, it was thought until fairly recently that while prokaryotic life took hold quickly, in less than .3 billion years, it took an additional two billion years to arrive at the more complex eukaryotic life forms, the first of which were unicellular.[22] (Prokaryotes do not have their genetic material organized within a membrane-enclosed nucleus as eukaryotes do. They also lack membrane-enclosed organelles and a cytoskeleton, characteristic features of eukaryotes.) Recent discoveries in the fossil record have shortened the gap between the first life forms and the origin of eukaryotes to approximately one billion years (this is acknowledged by proponents on both sides of the debate alike). Starting from what was thought to be the time delay for the origin of eukaryotes, be it shorter or longer, people have argued that complex life will be correspondingly easier or harder to come by in the rest of the universe. Either way, an extrapolation is being made from a single case. Moreover, if one is going to engage in such questionable reasoning from one case, the relevant case is not just the time it took for eukaryotes to evolve (the first of which again were unicellular), but the time it took for the eukaryotic lineage to develop to the stage where it could possibly give rise to intelligent life forms, namely, to the animal stage. It took about 2.3 billion years after life originated to get the first animals, about half of the life of the earth.[23] (It is of course possible that new discoveries in the fossil record may cause this number to be revised downward.)

The other major issue in the evolution of intelligent life forms revolves around the role of contingency in evolution. It would be hard to deny that contingent events have had a huge impact on the evolutionary history of our planet. The organisms that went extinct when a giant meteorite hit the earth 65 million years ago were not ill-adapted; they were unlucky.[24] Some, however, go so far as to hold that the contingent element in evolution is so great that it is unlikely that human(-like) intelligence would evolve again on planet earth, if one could go back and time and watch things evolve anew. Most will recognize this as being the position of Stephen Jay Gould who sees:

> the pageant of evolution as a staggeringly improbable series of events, sensible enough in retrospect and subject to rigorous explanation, but utterly unpredictable and quite unrepeatable. Wind back the tape of life to the early days of the Burgess shale; let it play again from an identical starting point, and the chance becomes vanishingly small that anything like human intelligence would grace the reply.[25]

Gould developed this view as a result of studying the Burgess Shale which contains a wealth of fossils dating from the time of the Cambrian explosion. Gould observed that there were many more body plans among the arthropods of the Cambrian period than are found in arthropods extant today. This led him to ask why in many cases the ancient species that represented a certain body plan went extinct without any related species succeeding them, while in comparatively few cases they ended up as part of a continuing lineage. Gould maintains that there is nothing to suggest that the species representing the body plans that were lost when they went extinct were less adapted to their environment than species belonging to lineages that continued. It appeared to him that it was simply a matter of luck that certain lines got wiped out, and not others (whence his metaphor "decimation by lottery").[26] A consequence of this is (in the words of David Darling) that if life's tape were replayed "the odds are that the insignificant little chordate worm that represented the earliest rendering of our own body plan would have fallen by the wayside."[27]

Not all scientists agree with Gould's radical contingentism. Scientists such as D'Arcy Thompson and Simon Conway Morris point to the presence of convergence in evolution. It may be the case that the destiny of any specific lineage is subject to chance events which may redirect it or put an end to it. However, this does not mean that a species bearing certain features is not eventually going to arise to meet a specific environmental challenge. Wings are eventually going to evolve to allow organisms to move about in the sky. Fins and streamlined shapes are eventually going to evolve to allow organisms to move themselves efficiently through water. Conway Morris thus disagrees with Gould:

> Gould argues passionately that were we "to replay the tape of life" from the time of the Cambrian explosion, we would end up with a different world. Among its features would be an almost certain absence of humans or anything remotely like us. [But] this whole argument...is based on a basic confusion concerning the destiny of a given lineage...versus the likelihood that a particular biological property or feature will sooner or later manifest itself as part of the evolutionary process.[28]

Without going into more detail concerning this debate,[29] it seems safe to say that both convergence and chance would play a role in the organisms we would see if the tape were replayed. However, acknowledging the influence of convergence does not of itself constitute grounds for concluding that human-like intelligence would repeatedly evolve; there also has to be some reason to think that this would be a feature that would be converged upon.

Darling tries to make a case that human-like intelligence would be converged upon claiming that intelligence is "a more or less ubiquitous characteristic of life." There are a number of problems with his argument. First, he conflates human-like intelligence with ability to adapt to the environment in ways that enhance survival, an ability which all organisms share to a greater or lesser extent, while labeling the position that there is a significant difference between human and non-human intelligence as "anthropocentric."[30] The latter view is hardly shared by all biologists. As Ernst Mayr dryly remarks: "With all my bias in favor of birds, I would not say that a raven or parrot has the amount and kind of intelligence to found a civilization."[31] It is Darling's failure to distinguish different meanings of the word "intelligence" that allows him to regard it a more or less widespread in the realm of living things. While all organisms manifest behavior in which they use appropriate means to achieve their goals—which is what it means to act intelligently—not all of them understand what they are doing. For example, the young gull that pecks at a red spot on its parent's bill to get the parent to regurgitate food will also peck on a red spot on a piece of cardboard. Indeed, organisms can act in an adaptive manner even in the absence of awareness, as in the case of plants that grow towards light.[32] Thus, the fact that intelligent behavior in the sense of "adaptive" behavior is often encountered in organisms has no bearing on whether evolution converges on human-like intelligence.

If we overlook this gross equivocation, the other problem with Darling's reasoning is that intelligence, as he understands it, is not something that develops in response to a specific evolutionary problem posed in a specific niche. Sharks, seals, and many fish are streamlined so as not to waste energy moving through their liquid environment. But what exactly is the environmental challenge to which human-like intelligence is the solution? Common sense would seem to indicate that the ability to take in information from one's environment and subsequently adjust one's behavior to benefit oneself is certainly a feature one would expect to evolve. Again, all organisms to some extent are capable of adapting some of their behavior in response to the environment. Some do so by way of taxis, whereas others do so instinctively, and yet others are capable of learning. Adjusting behavior to cope with the environment is a generic feature as ubiquitous as respiration or growth, things which are adaptive across the board. Why should the form of intelligence peculiar to humans evolve, rather than these other kinds? Darling's argument that human-like intelligence will be converged upon is thus not any more convincing than one that would conclude that human metabolism will be converged upon because metabolism is something evolution converges upon.

There is also another very important nuance regarding the question of whether human-like intelligence is or is not converged upon that is generally overlooked in scientific discussions of the matter. Strictly speaking human-like intelligence cannot evolve. This goes back to our starting assumptions concerning human nature, based on what the faith holds, though arguably quite defensible on grounds of reason as well (here is not the place to pursue the matter). Human-like intelligence is the ability to form and consider abstract ideas. Only an immaterial power is capable of such a feat. As a consequence, evolution, being a material process, cannot possibly produce a human-like intellect. Evolution can, however, produce features which are needed for the exercise of human-like intelligence.[33] For instance, it can produce brains endowed with high-capacity imagination and memory. It can also produce certain features facilitating language learning and allowing for speech production (as well as all the other features, named in chapter five, that are seen to be essential or virtually essential to humans). Granted that human-like intelligence cannot of itself evolve, it is however reasonable to think that God would not allow life to complexify on another planet to the same level that it did on earth in the primate lineage, and then arbitrarily decide not to intervene so that matter can progress to the highest level it could attain—that of being informed with the rational soul. Henceforth we are going to assume these qualifications when we refer to the biologists' position concerning the evolution of human-like intelligence, and in the interest of time will not keep reiterating them, despite their importance.

Returning now to our consideration of the biologists' views on the evolution of human-like intelligence: Ernst Mayr argues against the position that convergence is likely to bring about human-like intelligence repeatedly. Mayr begins his argument against the repeated evolution of human-like intelligence by tracing the evolutionary history of *Homo sapiens*, after which he comments:

> In conflict with the thinking of those who see a straight line from the origin of life to intelligent man, I have shown that at each

level of this pathway there were scores, if not hundreds, of branching points and independently evolving phyletic lines, with only a single one in each case forming the ancestral lineage that ultimately gave rise to Man.

If evolutionists have learned anything from a detailed analysis of evolution, it is the lesson that the origin of new taxa is largely a chance event. Ninety-nine of 100 newly arising species probably become extinct without giving rise to descendant taxa.[34]

Mayr thus espouses a contingentist position similar to Gould's. He next takes up the objection that given that convergent evolution produces highly improbable organs such as eyes in two different lineages, the cephalopods and the vertebrates, it is also possible that it produce the improbable feature, human-like intelligence, in two different lineages. Mayr responds by pointing out that:

The case of the convergent evolution of eyes is, indeed, of decisive importance for the estimation of the probability of convergent evolution of intelligence. The crucial point is that the convergent evolution of eyes in different phyletic lines of animals is not at all improbable. In fact, eyes evolve whenever they were of selective advantage in the animal kingdom. As Salvini-Plawen and I have shown, eyes evolved independently no less than at least 40 times in different groups of animals (Salvini-Plawen and Mayr 1977). This shows that a highly complicated organ can evolve repeatedly and convergently when advantageous, provided such evolution is at all probable.[35]

So what reason is there to think that the evolution of high intelligence is or is not probable? Mayr turns to the history of life on earth to make his case that it is incredibly improbable that human-like intelligence (as opposed to the sort of intelligence present in other mammals and in birds) evolve:

There were probably more than a billion species of animals on earth, belonging to many millions of separate phyletic lines, all living on this planet earth which is hospitable to intelligence, and yet only a single one of them succeeded in producing intelligence.[36]

Now the factual claim that Mayr makes will not be entirely agreed on by all scientists, some of whom think that man may have had multiple origins. However, they are talking about two separate origins, and these from a not very distant common ancestor, not ten or the forty Mayr refers to in the case of the eye, some of which cases belong to lineages that diverged in the very distant past. So the convergentist argument for ETI is not what one might have first thought.

While the view that evolution on the replay would never give much if anything similar to what it gave the first time around is not compatible with intelligent life arising elsewhere in the universe, the convergentist view has no necessary connection with espousing "life everywhere." Either one does think that life can readily arise and complexify to the level of being intelligent or one does not. One need not deny convergentism in order to affirm that intelligent life arose just once in the universe, if one regards intelligence as a feature highly improbable to arise.

Although the case Darling makes in favor of evolution converging on human-like intelligence was not convincing, and the empirical evidence gives no support for human-like intelligence being a feature that is converged on, we must avoid two possible mistakes in concluding that human-like intelligence is not something converged on. First, just because Darling did not propose a plausible selective pressure that is bound to elicit human-like intelligence as an evolutionary response, does not mean that such a pressure does not exist.[37] Secondly, that human-like intelligence has not arisen repeatedly is not necessarily due to the lack of any tendency for such intelligence to evolve, but may rather be due to difficulties involved in its realization. As we saw in chapter five, there is reason to think that there are fewer body plans compatible with human-like intelligence than there are body plans compatible with wings. In addition, perhaps the comparative availability of incipient structures and the facility with which they undergo modification is lesser in the case of human-like intelligence. Moreover, it may be the case that there are substantial liabilities attached to intelligence, as C. O. Lovejoy suggests:

> [A]n increased information-processing capacity in the nervous system is actually a reproductive liability both pre-natally (since a complex nervous system requires a long gestation period) and

post-natally (since it takes longer to raise and teach the young). Intelligence has no a priori advantage, but it is a clear and unmistakable reproductive hazard. Thus for this reason alone we would expect such capacity to be selected for 'only in rare instances'.[38]

Conway Morris, in his recent book *Life's Solution*, makes a case that human intelligence is converged on by pointing to how evolution repeatedly produces characteristics that are closely associated with human intelligence, such as the abilities to communicate, to use tools, to farm, to make music, and to form complex social units. According to Morris, evolutionary convergence on traits that we associate with our species indicates that "if we humans had not evolved then something more-or-less identical would have emerged sooner or later."[39] Mayr, however, would ask why no other human-like being has evolved. Conway Morris admits that the most promising humanoid contender, the dolphin, is unlikely to ever evolve to our level.[40]

We will leave off here with the questions: Is intelligent life converged upon?[41] Is intelligent life so difficult to arrive at that the case of man is a never-to-be repeated lucky strike? Or should the origin of human intelligence be described in some other manner? Answers to these questions would be worth having before we went extrapolating about what is likely to happen elsewhere.

Turning now to estimates made of inhabitable planets, some of the same sorts of problems arise estimating them as do with estimating the probability of life originating and complexifying. One big problem, as Crowe points out, is that a planet may be similar to earth, without it being similar in those ways crucial for life to begin and complexify[42]—we do not know yet what all the crucial factors are. We do have some sketchy knowledge. We know enough to eliminate some planets as uninhabitable, e.g., gas giants, ice ball planets, and planets in general on which liquid water is not present. We also know the temperature extremes that life on earth tolerates, granted this does not necessarily correspond to the temperatures under which life originated. I am optimistic that break-throughs will eventually occur with origin of life experiments. It is not a waste of time to try to figure out how many earthlike planets are out there, using both empirical and theoretical means, for in the meanwhile we can expect that advances will be made on the problem of the origin and evolution of life, such that scientists can then devise further astronomical tests to sort out or at least to come closer to sorting out the potentially life-bearing earthlike planets from non-life-bearing ones.[43] I do not doubt at all that estimates of earthlike planets and then of habitable ones will improve. It must be keep in mind, however, that finding earthlike planets at this point is not equivalent to finding planets where life is able to arise and evolve.

Also rearing its head in estimates of habitable planets is the contingency problem—perhaps the formation of such planets does not occur with predicable regularity, but depends upon rare fluke events. A number of scientists have defended the view that the earth would not be hospitable to life if it were not for its unusually large moon.[44] The claim is then that while there may be other earthlike planets out there, the chances that they have a moon like ours are extremely slim.[45] Others take the opposite position arguing that the moon is neither necessary for life to develop on a planet, and/or that such moons in any case are not rare.[46] There is a similar debate about the importance of Jupiter in our solar system.[47] Realistic estimates of habitable planets cannot be made until these debates are settled.[48] Again, I am not pessimistic that scientists will eventually sort things out, and that a solidly-based consensus view will emerge. My only point is that until contingency issues such as these are resolved, it is too early to be extrapolating on the number of habitable planets out there.

It is worth noting that values for the likelihood of earth-like planets, and for the likelihood that these planets are inhabited are two of the factors in a formula for calculating the likelihood of communication with ETIs called the Drake Equation (after Francis Drake who proposed it in 1961):

> N = R x fp x ne x fl x fi x fc x L…The number (N) of detectable civilizations in space equals the rate (R) of star formation, times the fraction (fp) of stars that form planets, times the number (ne) of planets hospitable to life, time the fraction (fl) of those planets where life actually emerges, times the fraction (fi) of planets where life evolves into intelligent beings, time the fraction (fc) of planets with intelligent creatures capable of interstellar communication, times the length of time (L) that such a civilization remains detectable.[49]

As we can see from our lack of knowledge as to the prevalence of earth-like planets, and as to evolution of intelligent life on such planets: "the Drake Equation is just a mathematical way of saying who knows?"[50] If one puts in "optimistic" values, the formula yields a large number of planets in our galaxy that have intelligent inhabitants with whom we could communicate. If one puts in "pessimistic" values, it is likely that the only place with intelligent inhabitants is here.[51]

Chapter 10

The Fermi Paradox

If they existed, they would be here.

—Enrico Fermi

There is a well-known science-based argument against ETI which goes by the name of the Fermi Paradox, after Enrico Fermi who proposed it in 1950. It goes like this: if there exist moderately long-lived ancient civilizations possessing advanced technological capabilities, simple math shows that one of them would have colonized our galaxy by now, and so they should already be here. But given they aren't here, it logically follows that they do not exist. Admittedly, a discussion of this argument does not really belong in this section, which is devoted to weaknesses in arguments *for* ETI. However, it has to be looked at somewhere, due to the popularity that it has in the literature. I will consider it only briefly, since it is not my intention to present scientific arguments in favor of our being alone, as interesting as they might be.[1]

There is a lot of speculation involved both in the Fermi Paradox itself, and in attempts to refute it. Those who reject the Fermi Paradox, and maintain that ETIs do exist, propose a variety of reasons for why they have not yet communicated with us. Some of the more commonly enunciated reasons include: 1) ETIs went extinct; 2) there exist means for ETIs to get here in principle, but cost and/or risk makes their implementation unfeasible; 3) ETIs are trying to communicate with us, but we are not advanced enough to recognize it; 4) they don't want to come here; 5) they are here.

As far as their not being here because they went extinct, this is mere speculation. Some claim that technological societies have a negligible life span, based on the notions that such societies would either self-destruct in a nuclear war (or something equivalent) or would so pollute their planets and/or exhaust their natural resources that they would die out. But self-destruction through war is a choice not a necessity, and there is no reason every technological civilization would go this way. As for pollution and exhaustion of resources, our technological society at present is more and more aware of the need to fund scientific research to address these problems, e.g., by developing renewable sources of energy, by recycling, etc., and this is what we would expect any intelligent technological civilization to do—perhaps this would not extend their life-span indefinitely, but it would seem to make it more than negligibly long. It is also speculated that civilizations that were running out of resources might develop means of obtaining resources from other nearby planets. Sometimes it is argued that ETI civilizations would be forced to colonize in order to avoid extinction, because their sun would eventually exhaust itself, as "hundreds of millions of solar-type stars have run out of hydrogen fuel and ended their days as red giants and white dwarfs."[2] On the other hand, a sun like ours is supposed to have a total stable life-span of 10 billion years. But then again:

> Some scientists are convinced that the end of life on Earth will be caused by an increase in the sun's energy output....As we have seen, the amount of energy being produced by the sun—and indeed, by most stars—increases over time.... Some scientists have predicted that temperatures on Earth will become too high for animal life within several hundred million years from now.[3]

I do not think we know enough to gauge how long an ETI race might last.

What about the explanation which gives as reason for ETI absence that it is not feasible for them to implement the technology available with the goal of travel to another planet? First, I have to say I wondered whether scientists were not being overly sanguine in supposing that the requisite technology will exist in ETI civilizations. One of the more prominent scenarios for the colonization of space in the literature is the one proposed by Barrow and Tipler. It involves "self-replicating universal constructor[s] with intelligence comparable to human intelligence" being launched to other stellar systems in every direction. Once the universal-constructor probes (called von Neumann machines) arrived in their new stellar system, they could construct more copies of themselves along with rockets to launch them, and the same process would repeat itself every time a probe got to a new planet.[4] Alternately, the probes could construct fertilized ETI eggs and artificial wombs in which they could grow.[5] The reason for using probes instead of people is that time estimates for a flight to a nearby star range from hundreds of years[6] to between 10,000-100,000 years.[7] With human colonizers, something would have to be done to avoid inbreeding.

It seems to me that space colonization is much more problematic than it is generally presented as being. For one, the construction of these von Neumann probes is easier said than done. For another, it seems that a lot of things could go wrong in a process that is supposed to take 50-300 million years, and galactic colonization is estimated to take this long.[8] Contrary to what one might expect, these doubts are not voiced by many ETI proponents, who all seem pretty sold on the possibility of space travel. For example, Carl Sagan does not hesitate to calculate a time for the colonization of the galaxy, and in fact comes up with a value that agrees fairly closely with the one that Tipler calculates and uses in support of the Fermi Paradox.[9] Paul Davies, however, does question the feasibility of Tipler's project:

> ...Tipler's assumptions about the feasibility of constructing von Neumann machines—in effect, living computers with superhuman intelligence added—strike me as being exceedingly simplistic. We have absolutely no idea what obstacles of principle may exist to frustrate such attempts, let alone the practicalities. The same applies to space travel: the recent failure of the Mars Observer mission underscores how vulnerable technology is in space. The assumption that a man-(or alien-) made machine could operate flawlessly over millions of years in a hostile environment stretches credulity.[10]

Although there may be more realistic alternatives to Barrow and Tipler's scenario, it seems that any attempts to colonize space will inevitably entail mistakes leading to disaster and frustration, putting at least a damper on future attempts, and possibly putting an end to them in some cases. Then again perhaps ETI technology is bound to eventually become so advanced that insuring ETI astronauts' safety would no longer be an issue. The point can be further argued back and forth, but I will leave off here with my speculations.

As realistic as colonization projects may or may not be, expense is certainly a reason for why our exploration of space falls short of our technological capabilities, and the same may be a cause holding back more advanced civilizations as well. There are no hard facts from which to extrapolate whether an advanced civilization could afford the requisite technology or not. We neither know how expensive the as yet non-existent technology is, nor do we know how wealthy the as yet undiscovered ETIs are. In the absence of evidence to the contrary, "They can't afford it" provides a plausible excuse for ETI absence. Then the question becomes: if they can't afford space travel, why aren't they talking to us using the cheaper alternative of electro-magnetic communication of some sort?

If we suppose that ETIs are trying to communicate with us, this leads us to the third response to the Fermi Paradox, namely, we are not advanced enough to recognize their messages or simply as yet have not recognized them. Certainly, attempts to passively search for ETI has been going on since the 1960 when Francis D. Drake and his colleagues at the National Radio Astronomy Observatory listened for radio signals from two nearby stars (Project Ozma). Since then there have been more than 60 projects[11] that search for radio-transmissions in our galaxy that would have a tell-tale signature of intelligence, some of the better known of which operating today are the High Resolution Microwave Survey (HRMS), the Search for Extraterrestrial Radio Emissions from Nearby Developed Intelligent Population, operated by a group at UC Berkeley (SERENDIP), and the projects carried on by the Search for Extraterrestrial Intelligence (SETI) Institute. The consensus is that ETI transmitters would most likely choose radio waves because they are less susceptible to interstellar absorption and scattering than other frequencies.[12] The wavelengths preferentially searched for by most SETI projects were chosen according to a couple of reasonable criteria, ones that we assume that ETIs would also be aware of. As Francis Drake explains:

[B]oth Project Ozma and the Cocconi-Morrison paper identified the region around the hydrogen line as a primary hunting ground for interstellar signals. We are still covering that same ground today. The region has come to be known as the "waterhole" because it is bounded on one end by the hydrogen atom, H, which emits a natural radio signal with a wavelength of 21 centimeters, and on the other by the hydroxyl radical, or OH molecule, which emits a signal with a wavelength of 18 centimeters. In chemistry, H plus OH equals H20, or water....We suspect that water is very important to life elsewhere in the universe...What's more, the electromagnetic waterhole occupies a very quiet region, containing the least possible extraneous noise from the Galaxy (and the Earth's atmosphere).[13]

Despite certain difficulties that have to be overcome in order to transmit waves across the galaxy, such as those posed by noise and refraction,[14] still there seems to be a general consensus in the literature that such transmission is at least close to being in our power, and could reasonably be expected to be in the power of a more advanced civilization.[15] Given that SETI is still relatively young,[16] it would be a little premature to conclude that ETIs are unlikely to be out there on the grounds that no ETI message has been detected as of yet.[17]

Another defense of ETI existence in face of the Fermi Paradox consists in maintaining that ETIs could talk to us if they wanted to, but they do not want to for various reasons. Perhaps, the ETIs have contacted so many other intelligent civilizations they are bored with space communication and/or travel. Or perhaps they have no interest in speaking to a race as technologically inferior to them as ours is—like people who can't be bothered speaking with children. These reasons may seem adequate to those who think that there is nothing special about the human race (Carl Sagan, for example). But if we indeed we are special because the reconciliation of all things was accomplished by one of us, there is reason to seek us out. ETIs would, of course, have to be aware of this reason, if it was to motivate them to search for us. They could know about us through a revelation from God. And fallen ETIs, even without a divine revelation, could suspect or hope that a race like ours existed for the same reasons that motivate some earthlings to seek for ETI life, namely, so as to discover a solution to the problems of war, crime, and exploitation. It is true that unfallen ETIs in the absence of a divine revelation concerning our existence might have little motive to seek for a life form such as ours. However, it is unlikely that God would leave unfallen ETIs in ignorance about the central event that has taken place in the universe. Thus, from a Christian standpoint, lack of interest in the human race does not provide a likely explanation for why ETIs have not contacted us.[18]

A final argument against the Fermi Paradox is that they have arrived. I set no store on accounts that contact has taken place. If ETIs are so intelligent as to have figured out to get there, then they certainly could figure out a means of protecting themselves from bad-willed humans who might want to capture them or harm them in some way, and thus there would be no reason for them to be afraid of showing themselves to the general public. Even if they came here with the purpose of staking out another home for themselves, only to be unpleasantly surprised to find us here, I think it unlikely that they would not try to establish some type of relationship with us. After all, intelligent beings naturally desire to know, and so once the ETIs had gotten over their initial chagrin, curiosity was bound to get the better of them, leading them to attempt to communicate with the rational beings they found on earth who were different from themselves—if only for a limited time before they headed off to search for an empty planet.

The Fermi Paradox, despite leading to the same conclusion that I am headed for, does not add much, if anything, to my conviction—too much speculation is involved.[19] Perhaps the space travel which would bring the ETIs to earth is ruled out by exorbitant cost, or by cost the ETI population is unwillingly to bear. Perhaps accidents in space resulting in ETI deaths account for a loss of enthusiasm in further implementation of space programs. ETIs may have adopted the safer and more affordable route of sending out some kind of electro-magnetic signal. Given that it has not even been sixty years since various SETI programs have tried to detect such signals, their failure to date to do so provides but a very weak reason for suspicion that future efforts will likewise be unsuccessful.

CHAPTER 11

Philosophical Arguments concerning ETI

I could not think to touch the heavens with my two arms.

—Sappho

So much for mistakes made in extrapolations. Another area of doubtful arguments remaining to be explored centers (yes, again) around contingency and necessity, but this time viewed from a more purely philosophical perspective. Historically philosophers have allied views on chance, design, and necessity with views on theism and atheism, and the manner in which they have done so subsequently influenced their view on whether there exists many inhabited worlds or only one. Plainly chance, necessity, design, theism and atheism are not topics to be discussed in depth here. My goal is simply to show how they have been related to the question of ETI existence, and to raise some questions and to point out some shortcomings in the manner in which these things have been interrelated. I am hardly the first to do so. As Crowe notes: "After the rediscovery in the fifteenth century of Lucretius's poem, a host of authors from Gassendi to Newton and Kant investigated whether or not Epicurean atomism, evolutionism, pluralism, and atheism were detachable from each other."[1]

Long ago, Aristotle divided the potential explanations for natural phenomena into two categories: chance versus action for an end.[2] Between these two explanations of natural phenomena, theists opt for purpose and design, whereas atheists find the blind forces, chance and necessity an adequate and more economical substitute for design. What is curious is that some of those who reject chance, affirm design, and are theists come to opposite conclusions on ETI existence (Davies vs. Aquinas).

Equally curious is that some of those who affirm chance, deny God's existence (or at least the existence of a God that orders all material things to man), also come to opposite conclusions on the ETI issue (e.g., Gould vs. Epicurus). The net result is that theists will in some cases agree with atheists on ETI, though, of course, they arrive at their conclusion by different means. One could take this as a sign that there is no connection between one's position on ETI and one's position on the other matters mentioned. People do, however, claim that there is some sort of a connection, and so something needs to be said, though again, it will be rather sketchy due to the difficulty of these issues.

It is not hard to see how the radical contingentism of Gould leads to viewing man as a "cosmic accident." There is no orderly procession leading to man as the pinnacle of life, and he may just as well have never appeared. Certainly the position that the human species arose by mere chance, and was in no-wise intended, is incompatible with the view of a divine creator who has made all things for man.[3] However, in another account, a radically contingent universe is allied with many ETI inhabited planets. Atomists such as Lucretius and Epicurus posited that the random motion of the infinite atoms in an infinite universe moving for an infinite time would eventually result in every possible combination, some of which would be planets populated with people like ourselves. They were explicit in their rejection of any deity, and in their affirmation that the atoms could do the work that the gods did in explaining the world around us:[4]

> Furthermore, where would the gods derive a scheme
> For making things, how would they understand
> What men were to be like, so gods could know,
> Or only imagine, how to fashion them?
> Or how would they comprehend the principles
> Of primal bodies, what was possible
> Through changed arrangement, unless nature gave
> A model for creation? Atoms move
> In many ways, since infinite time began,
> Are driven by collisions, are borne on
> By their own weight; in every kind of way
> Meet or combine, try every possible,
> Every conceivable pattern, so no wonder
> They fell into arrangements, into modes
> Like those whereby the sum of things preserves

> Its system by renewal.
> But suppose
> That I were ignorant and did not know
> What atoms are, I'd still make bold claim
> To state, from my observance of the ways
> Of heaven, and from many other things:
> This world of ours was not prepared for us
> By any god. Too much is wrong with it.[5]

How can it be that thinkers who both espouse contingency and deny a divine mind intending man and ordering things to him end up with different views on ETI? Perhaps the difference lies in the atomists' claim that there is *infinite* random change. For finite random change rarely produces anything. If one attempts to hit a target sentence by purely random means, the odds against one doing so are astronomical. However, if infinite combinations are possible, then astronomical odds will eventually be met, or so we are told.[6] Contingency operating in a finite universe will come up with a given combination on the rare occasion, and all the more rarely when it depends upon chance heaped upon chance. It is possible to miss an opportunity that will never rise again if indeed things are as the biologist E. O. Wilson describes them:

> Each species is the product of mutations and recombinations too complex to be grasped by unaided intuition. It was sculpted and burnished by an astronomical number of events in natural selection, which killed off or otherwise blocked from reproduction the vast majority of its member organisms before they completed their lifespans....Such is the ultimate and cryptic truth of every kind of organism....The flower in the crannied wall—it is a miracle....Every kind of organism has reached this moment in time by threading one needle after another, throwing up brilliant artifices to survive and reproduce against nearly impossible odds.[7]

It is within this perspective that Gould's idea that *Homo sapiens* is a cosmic fluke has plausibility.

In an infinite universe, however, such opportunities arise an infinite number of times, and eventually every combination is come up with, and that many times over (or so it is claimed). While Gould's view of contingency regards chance operating within constraints set by the laws of nature, the atomists' view is one of utter chaos. In the words of Lucretius:

> Now I'll describe how the chaos motes,
> The turbulent atoms, met, somehow to form
> The basic order of the earth, the sky....
> Never suppose the atoms had a plan,
> Nor with a wise intelligence imposed
> An order on themselves, nor in some pact
> Agreed what movements each should generate.
> No, it was all fortuitous....[8]

It may be the case that the atomists' view is ultimately untenable, but here is not the place to argue the matter. The point is that two atheistic explanations (or at least non-theistic explanations) of natural things lead to different views on whether ETI exists or not.

Another player in the chance-design debates that is interrelated with the theist-atheist positions that in turn bear upon the ETI question is necessity. Commitment to necessity as being the ruling factor in nature comes in many forms. For example, convergentism attributes necessity to the evolutionary process to some degree or another. While convergentists generally do not see the development of the various life-forms to unfold with the sort of determinism found in the ontogeny of individuals (e.g., a human zygote normally undergoes a programmed series of changes over a period of approximately nine months), they do expect certain biological features to eventually appear with time. Some convergentists hold that it was inevitable that things such as wings and eyes arise in the earth's evolutionary history, without making the further claims that life inevitably arises on planets throughout the universe, and inevitably complexifies to a human level of intelligence. It is not clear how a convergentist position such as that of Conway Morris (who holds that the human race might be the only intelligent species around) stands vis-a-vis theism versus atheism.[9]

Other biological convergentists take a far more radical position on necessity. In the words of Paul Davies:[10]

> My discussion centers on the notion of biological determinism: given the right conditions, life inevitably will form after a sufficiently long time, and once life gets started, it will very probably progress toward intelligence.[11]

Davies, who favors the notion that necessity is the dominant feature in explaining the natural world, ties this notion to the Epicurean contingent world view:

> Belief in the plurality of worlds was also adopted by the Roman poet and philosopher Lucretius. Also an atomist, Lucretius repeated Epicurus' argument, that given an infinity of atoms, there is no obvious hindrance to the formation of other worlds: "when abundant matter is ready, when space is to hand, and no thing hinders," then other worlds will naturally form. Here in antiquity was the essence of an argument that lies at the heart of modern SETI research. Given an abundance of matter and the uniformity of nature, the same physical processes that led to the formation of the Earth and solar system should be repeated elsewhere. And, given the appropriate conditions elsewhere, life and consciousness should emerge on other worlds in roughly the same manner as they have emerged here.[12]

This line of argument was criticized earlier insofar as there are not as yet adequate grounds from which one can extrapolate whether life is common or not. What we are trying to see here is what, if any, are the allegiances between necessity, atheism-theism, and belief in many ETI inhabited worlds. Paradoxically, positing infinite matter, space, time, and motion in the radically contingent Epicurean scheme supposedly leads to the necessary formation of multiple well-ordered biospheres inhabited by rational beings. Davies distances himself somewhat from the Epicurean picture of an infinity of atoms colliding with one another, emphasizing rather the "abundance of matter and the uniformity of nature." It is ironic that after having given the nod to the Epicureans who are convinced that mankind needs to be purged of belief in gods and recognize atomism as the rational explanation for things, Davies goes on to maintain that if it were established that there was a multitude of inhabited planets in the universe that this would provide better support for theism than if intelligent life only arose once:

> I think both Monod and Gould are absolutely right to perceive bleak atheism in the scenario that life and intelligence are freak accidents, unique in the cosmos. But the flip side is also true. If it turns out that life does emerge as an automatic and natural part

of an ingeniously biofriendly universe, then atheism would seem less compelling and something like design more plausible.[13]

The Epicurean view again explicitly denies any rhyme or reason in the formation of the cosmos, which of course entails the denial of an ordering intelligence behind the cosmos. Davies excises these aspects of Epicureanism, retaining only the abundance of matter and the uniformity of nature[14] to explain the way things are. Thus, it appears that adopting the view that necessity plays the dominant role in the evolution of intelligent life is not tied to a world-view embracing a Cosmic Designer, at least not in an obvious and indisputable way. The lack of such a link between necessity and theism (at least in the strong sense of the word) is also apparent in the view of those who see the universe's unfolding over time as something necessary, while failing to posit a Designer separate from the universe who is responsible for the plan according to which the universe necessarily unfolds. Some proponents of process philosophy adopt this view. For example, Errol Harris holds that:

> The whole which contemporary physics has revealed...necessarily involves the generation of its own observation by intelligent beings, in whose minds it brings itself to consciousness....If God is conceived as the absolute universal principle of order manifesting itself in and as the universe, and transcending all finite phases, the argument from design, as proof of his existence, can be justified in this, its modern form, without requiring any inference from a contrived plan to a Supreme Architect....[15]

Davies's view on necessity, which emphasizes the uniformity of nature, then stands alongside both the Epicurean view that employs an infinite universe, radical contingency and necessity as a replacement for God, and the view of necessity articulated by certain process philosophers. It is thus plain that there is no neat and obvious connection between embracing necessity and espousing atheism or theism, at least not with a theism compatible with Christianity. Davies may in fact be a pantheist, as Harris is, but Davies's take on necessity, unlike Harris's is compatible with a God who is other than the universe and who made all things for man. (Once again, the dominance of law that Davies supposes does not say anything one way or the other about the likelihood of intelligent life arising in the universe.)

Another puzzle remains as to why Davies who is favorable to theism (or at least to design) and who rejects chance as providing the chief explanation of the natural world goes from there to hold that the universe is teeming with life, while Aquinas, who also subscribes to theism, and who also rejects chance as providing the chief explanation of the natural world, nonetheless rejects the view that there are many worlds.

First, a clarification is in order as to Aquinas's position on chance, theism, and the multiplicity of worlds. Benjamin Wiker appears to be enunciating Aquinas's position when he argues against the kind of position Davies holds:

> Christians should not be cowed by the materialists' logic of probability, which had its birth in Epicurus and Lucretius. The logic runs thus: Our sun is a star; since the number of stars is so vast, sheer probability demands that there must be other inhabited planets beyond our solar system. But probability does not demand any such thing, unless we think (with Epicurus) that the universe is governed by chance....[16]

Aquinas himself says:

> For, the world is said to be one by a unity of order, according as certain things are ordered to other things. Everything, however, that is from God has an order to everything else and to God himself.... Whence, it is necessary that all things belong to one world. And therefore those who did not hold the cause of the world to be some ordering wisdom, but held it was chance, were able to posit many worlds; such as Democritus who said that this world was made from the collision of atoms, and infinite other worlds as well.[17]

As we saw earlier the word "world" for Aquinas almost always means "universe," and this is the case here. However, the case he makes against many universes is one that I have been adapting throughout to argue against many earthlike planets as well, again on the grounds that the supposed intelligent races on some of these planets would be incapable of communicating with others, due to the expansion of the universe. The partisans of many worlds are relegated to the camp of those who hold that the universe was a product of chance due to the fact that the many worlds are unable to form an interactive whole. While I think that the interconnectivity argument is a pretty strong argument, I regard it as only a probable argument for two reasons. First, a doubt remains as to whether there may not be some possible means of communication that would eventually unite the different worlds, despite the rapid expansion of the universe. The second reason for questioning the interconnectivity argument is that the inference from lack of order to lack of an orderer worthy of the name is arguably not entirely airtight.

Even if it were known for sure that communication to all (supposedly) inhabited parts of the universe is impossible, a case could still be made that some lack of connection among the intelligent beings in the universe is not incompatible with an orderer, on the grounds that it results from what Aquinas terms the "necessity of the matter."[18] Matter that an agent chooses as well suited to an end often comes with unavoidable and unwanted side effects e.g., iron is a suitable material for making a blade, but it also rusts. Thus, if many, rather than all, intelligent groups would establish a connection with some of the other groups, the lack of perfect interconnection need not be taken to indicate lack of intelligence on the part of the creator, but can be construed as an unwanted side-effect of having the production of many intelligent life forms occur in the sort of evolving material universe that is ours. However when this argument is examined more closely, it does not seem to have much weight, because God not only makes things out of matter, he has made the very nature of matter. God made matter to have the characteristics it has in order to achieve his goals. If it is correct that a well-ordered universe requires the interaction of its highest parts, then God will create matter of such a sort that this end can be achieved.[19] At most, then, there seems to be room for the odd group of intelligent material beings ending up separated from the rest, as this might occur due to chance, which is part and parcel of the natural world.

Aquinas appears to take the interconnection argument as eliminating for sure the existence of many universes. He thinks that *only* those who did not hold the cause of the world to be some ordering wisdom could countenance there being many universes. Albert, on the other hand, regards this sort of argument as having "little more strength than dialectical proofs by way of sign."[20] Certainly the law-like character of nature, from whence the many worlds issue, according to the views of the biological determinists, seems to argue for the rule of some ordering wisdom, rather than against it.

There is a noteworthy difference in approach between the arguments of Thomistic inspiration regarding the existence of inhabited worlds and Davies's argument. Davies's argument looks to the efficient causality available,[21] whereas the Thomistic arguments look to the final cause (in addition to which many of them rely on things known by faith, e.g., the singular wonder of the Incarnation).

More specifically, it appears to Davies that if God is going to make use of natural agents as secondary causes, he must rely on those natural agents that act in a necessary and law-like manner to ensure that the desired outcome, human-type life, be realized. The other option would be leave things to chance, in which case there would be a risk that human-type life not come about. And if a human-type life form did arise by luck, it seems to Davies hard to believe that it could have been aimed at. As scientist Eugene Mallove puts it:

> The universe would seem fantastically imbalanced to have "accidentally" originated life on but one very receding planet. Scarcely admitted by the advocates of a universe filled with life is the almost essential concomitant theory: the "plan" to make dead matter quicken is inherent in the laws of physics. It is almost a truism that if one believes in the prevalence of life in the universe, then one must also believe that the laws of physics *imply* and in a sense "mandate" life.[22]

The Thomistic arguments regarding the multiplicity of worlds approach the question from the point of view of the type of goal an intelligent agent would aim at, and not from the point of view of the means such an agent would use to achieve that goal. A single unique world seems the only appropriate goal for an intelligent agent when one considers the two alternatives to be pointless redundancy vs. one unique masterpiece.[23] I think that Aquinas is not concerned with efficient causality the way Davies is when it comes to the question of many worlds because Aquinas does not have Davies's evolutionary perspective. Aquinas's universe comes close to being one which is essentially the same as when God formed it out of nothing during the first six periods of creation: the same kinds of elements, plants, animals that we see today were the kinds that were there since the initial creation. This is something of a caricature of Aquinas's position, which is somewhat more dynamic than it might first seem (e.g., he does not find unreasonable Augustine's notion that in the initial creation there were some things which were only present in seeds, as it were, from which they would develop at some later point in time[24]). Still, the universe has essentially the character of something directly designed and realized by God, in a way similar to a sculptor who forms an exemplar for a statue in his mind, and then goes ahead to directly realize his design. Thus, there is no apparent tension between this type of efficient causality and the resultant universe containing one unique world inhabited by beings made in God's image.

Davies has evidence that both the non-living and living parts of nature developed over long periods of time, rather than being all there practically from the very beginning. And so it seems to him that if God and not chance is the efficient cause ultimately responsible for the production of intelligent life, that the only non-miraculous option at God's disposal for producing intelligent life is natural causes acting in a law-like fashion. Thus, while Davies is to be criticized for never considering that a thing may be one of a kind, not because it is the product of a freak accident, but because it is intended to be a one-of-a-kind masterpiece, still one cannot blame him for wondering how something can be part of a divine plan and not come about in a necessary, law-like fashion (a question that does not arise for Aquinas with his non-evolving universe).

The biological determinist envisages a theistic universe as a huge laboratory with multiple incubators churning out life here and there on a regular basis, without considering the alternative that God wanted to produce at the pinnacle of material creation one unique work of art.[25] Aquinas on the other hand insists upon the sort of goal intelligent agents aim at (a unique, non-redundant masterpiece; an interactive whole), while offering no explanation for how this goal can be achieved in an evolving universe (an understandable omission given that he had no reason to think that evolution occurred).

I am not totally devoid of sympathy for the biological determinist's point of view. My gut feeling, inspired by, but hardly justified by the rapidity that life arose on earth, and by the harsh conditions it can endure, is that there are plenty of bacteria-like organisms out there.[26] I do not think that if this were so that it would detract from God's ordering wisdom. Aristotle in speaking of the good of the universe, after noting that it lies in part in the order of its parts, comments:

> And all things are ordered together somehow, but not all alike—
> both fishes and fowls and plants; and the world is not such that

one thing has nothing to do with another, but they are connected. For all are ordered together to one end, but it is as in a house, where the freemen are least at liberty to act at random, but all things or most things are already ordained for them, while the slaves and the animals do little for the common good, and for the most part live at random; for this is the sort of principle that constitutes the natures of each.[27]

If Aristotle is right about finality in the universe, then it is not surprising that bacteria spring up here and there in the universe, but not human-like beings. For if the beings most tied up with the good of the universe, namely, rational beings, appeared in the random manner of bacteria, it would detract from the universe's goodness, and cast doubt on the wisdom of its maker.

I also do not think that affirming necessity or uniformity in nature, as Davies does, amounts to a denial of purposeful agency in the production of things, as the passage from Aquinas tying belief in many worlds to the view that chance rules supreme seems to suggest it must. For as Aristotle observes:

> The current view places what is of necessity in the process of production, just as if one were to suppose that the wall of a house necessarily comes to be because what is heavy is naturally carried downwards and what is light to the top, wherefore the stones and foundations take the lowest place, with earth above because it is lighter, and wood at the top of all as being the lightest. Whereas, though the wall does not come to be without these, it is not due to these, except as its material cause: it comes to be for the sake of sheltering and guarding certain things. Similarly in all other things which involve production for an end; the product cannot come to be without things which have a necessary nature, but it is not due to these (except as its material); it comes to be for an end. For instance, why is a saw such as it is? To effect so-and-so and for the sake of so-and-so. This end, however, cannot be realized unless the saw is made of iron. It is, therefore, necessary for it to be of iron, if we are to have a saw and perform the operation of sawing.[28]

Aristotle could hardly make it clearer that intelligent agents make use of features of natural things that are necessary in order to achieve their goals, and hence that necessity be operative in a particular phenomenon does not as such exclude the presence of intelligent agency as well.

Some will argue that Davies's attempt to preserve a role for divine causality in the evolution of life by attributing to God the law-like nature of the universe is a non-starter, the claim being that it is impossible to determine the initial conditions in such a manner as to insure that one gets anything at all, much less planets and then inhabited planets. Without examining this position, I will simply note that it provokes us to consider that chance may have played a greater role in us being here than both Davies and Aquinas are inclined to think. Even if Davies is right, and causes acting according to law predominate in the universe, this does not mean that chance cannot be an important cause on occasion. Admitting that a chance event, such as an asteroid striking the earth, had a powerful impact on the future evolution of life forms on earth does not constitute a denial that events in nature for the most part occur with a certain regularity. And to entertain the position that the origin of intelligent life requires an extraordinary amount of luck is not to deny the importance of law. If the universe from the very beginning turns out to be far more radically contingent than was previously thought, this is not adequate reason for denying that life arose in accord with physical and chemical laws and would do so again if like conditions obtained, and that even if luck is required to get those conditions.

Biological determinists tend to worry that if one attributes an important role in the evolution of intelligent life to chance, one is then compelled to regard such life as a freak accident. However, chance events do not escape from divine causality, and indeed God can use chance events to achieve his goals. Perhaps the necessity of law that biological determinists invoke is not enough, and God relies on chance as well to achieve his goal. Aquinas, for his part, is so leery of according any haphazardness in the result of God's activity that he ends up distancing himself from chance, despite it being a natural means that God could use to achieve the goal of producing one unique rational species. This is somewhat surprising given that Aquinas takes pains to show that chance and divine providence are not opposed. Indeed he goes so far as to say that: "It would be contrary to the notion of providence…if there were no chance happenings."[29] Elsewhere he shows that "nothing prevents things that happen by fortune or chance from being traced back to…the divine intellect."[30] Aquinas also maintains that God's total control over everything that is and happens does not preclude that he act through secondary causes that are contingent.[31] Unqualified biological determinism is thus not the only way to bring God back into the picture. It may turn out that a built-in tendency towards life in nature is a necessary, but not a sufficient condition for its origin in our universe.

I do not intend here to adjudicate between Davies's and Aquinas's views as to whether one world or many is a better indication of design and a Designer. I'm not sure I can for one, and then even if I could, the matters of chance, necessity, finality, and design deserve treatment in their own right.

I hope that this section has shed a little light on whether affirming the existence of many inhabited worlds necessarily commits one to rejecting theism (were this to be so, belief in ETI and Christianity would be incompatible). We have seen that there is not a neat tie between pluralism and atheism (as mediated through views on chance, necessity, and action for an end),[32] for at least one atheistic viewpoint is compatible with intelligent life having arisen only once. Similarly, there is no neat tie between pluralism and theism, for at least one theistic viewpoint favors the uniqueness of intelligent life. I have tried to show how those espousing the same initial view on theism/atheism arrive at different positions regarding ETI, without attempting to fully resolve any incoherencies there might be in their viewpoints. It should at least be clear that when it comes to efficient causality, affirmation of the presence of necessary law uniformly productive (or unproductive) of life everywhere in the universe does not necessarily entail a denial of final causality, since agents realize their ends by making use of necessary properties found in nature. Nor does attributing a role in the production of intelligent material life forms to the accidental efficient cause, chance, entail a denial of final causality, since chance does not elude God's direction. When it comes to final causality, it is questionable for a number of reasons whether arguments given concerning the type of goal that intelligent agents would aim at (namely, a unique, non-redundant, interactive whole) demonstratively exclude the possibility of more than one human-type species. But doubtlessly the debates among those who try to link views on ETI existence to theism or atheism will remain with us for a long time.

Turning, now to another type of teleological argument, one arguing in favor of ETI: In the past, it was not uncommon for proponents of ETI to point to the vastness of space and/or the supposed large number of earth-like planets, and argue that there would be no point for the universe to be so large and so full of planets, if there were not also many intelligent life forms out there.[33] This view lost popularity when it was realized that:

> In order to create the building blocks of life—carbon, nitrogen, oxygen and phosphorus—the simple elements of hydrogen and helium which were synthesized in the primordial inferno of the Big Bang must be cooked at a more moderate temperature and for a much longer time than is available in the early universe. The furnaces that are available are the interiors of stars. There, hydrogen and helium are burnt into the heavier life-supporting elements by exothermic nuclear reactions. When stars die, the resulting explosions which we see as supernovae, can disperse these elements through space and they become incorporated into planets and, ultimately, into ourselves. This stellar alchemy takes over ten billion years to complete. Hence, for there to be enough time to construct the constituents of living beings, the Universe must be at least ten billion years old and therefore, as a consequence of its expansion, at least ten billion light years in extent. We should not be surprised to observe that the universe is so large. No astronomer could exist in one that was significantly smaller. The Universe needs to be as big as it is in order to evolve just a single carbon-based life-form.[34]

In other words, the large size of the universe would not be overkill, even if a goal of the universe was to produce a single intelligent life form, because it takes a universe that large in order to do so. The size of the universe, then, does not tell us one way or the other whether the goal of the universe is one intelligent race or many, assuming the universe has intelligent life as its goal.

Before the Anthropic Principle was discovered another response to the "all-that-wasted-space" argument in favor of ETI was formulated by William Whewell.[35] Whewell maintains that "a single case of success among many of failure is exactly the order of nature in the production of life,"[36] and in light of this principle concludes that there would be nothing unusual about only one planet in the universe bringing forth intelligent life. Whewell establishes his general principle inductively, looking to cases such as ova in animals: "The female is stocked with innumerable ovules, capable of becoming living things: of which incomparably the greatest number end as they began, mere ovules..."[37] Sir Arthur Eddington, much later, gives essentially the same argument. Basing himself on instances of "profligacy" in nature, such as the enormous number of acorns produced in order that one oak grow, Eddington suggests that "if indeed [Nature] has no greater aim than to provide a home for her greatest experiment, Man, it would be just like her methods to scatter a million stars whereof one might haply achieve her purpose."[38] The "her greatest experiment, Man," is somewhat question-begging in our context. However, if one puts in the place of it simply "intelligent life," then this rebuttal of the objection that nature would never wastefully leave hoards of planets uninhabited is not without a certain persuasiveness.[39]

Whewell's and Eddington's argument is not ordered to establishing that earth is in fact the only planet inhabited by intelligent life, but is only intended as a response to those who reject such a claim on the grounds that it implies that nature acts in vain. Another response can be formulated looking to God's nature rather than simply to the workings of nature. God is the ultimate artist, and his works cannot be lacking in beauty. It could not be other than the case that: "The heavens declare the glory of God, the vault of heaven proclaims his handiwork" (Ps. 19). For his first miracle, the Word Incarnate did not change water into wine merely adequate for wedding guests who had already drunk quite a bit, he made the best wine. Thus, whether God created the universe to be inhabited by one intelligent material species or by many, it would have to be magnificent.

In addition to befitting the wisdom and power of God, the splendor of the heavens also serves a useful purpose vis-à-vis man, for certainly the heavens are one of the things *par excellence* that St. Paul is referring to when he says: "Ever since God created the world his everlasting power and deity—however invisible—have been there for the mind to see in the things he has made" (Rom. 1:20, 21).[40] It is fitting that a loving God, after having made man with a mind that rises to intelligible things starting from sense experience, would provide the senses of man with things apt to lead him to knowledge of his Creator. So even if it is just us, it befits both God's creative wisdom and his concern for his rational creatures that the heavens be as immense and beautiful as they are.

Yet another way of gaining perspective on "all that wasted space" is to realize that a single human individual in the state of grace is more valuable than the entire material universe.[41] In this perspective, it would not be a waste to produce an entire universe for a single good human being.

Thus far we have seen that the main problem in determining whether ETI life is improbable or probable is our ignorance on virtually every score concerning the necessary and sufficient conditions for its developments. We are ignorant to a greater or lesser extent of how earthlike planets form, how stringent the requirements for a life-sustaining planet are, how life originates, how it evolves to complex levels, and how easily it evolves to human-like levels. Thus, any extrapolations made concerning the likelihood or unlikelihood of ETI life are highly speculative.

The alternate approach to arguing in favor of ETI existence on the basis of scientific extrapolations is to argue for it theoretically by looking to theistic and teleological concerns. These arguments were also shown to be inconclusive. If we are the only intelligent species in the material universe, this does not exclude the possibility that the mind behind the universe intended us as a unique work of its art. The value of a single masterpiece may trump the attractiveness of mass-produced ETI life everywhere. And the number of stars in the universe do not represent waste, if our star turns out to be the only one providing life with an energy source, any more than millions of spores yielding one mushroom are waste. The theistic and teleological arguments given in support of ETI existence do stem from legitimate concerns, however, despite their inconclusiveness.

Chapter 12

Fallacious Arguments for ETI Existence

> The greatness of man is great in that he knows himself to be miserable. A tree does not know itself to be miserable. It is then by being miserable that one knows oneself to be miserable; but it is also by being great that one knows that one is miserable.
>
> —Pascal, *Pensées*

There is another group of arguments that some advocates of ETI existence offer that are entirely worthless. Given that there are no compelling reasons to think that ETIs exist, it is not surprising that a number of ETI proponents would resort to rhetoric, and slip into fallacious reasoning. I intend to briefly list some of the more common mistakes.[1]

Appealing to authority is a weak, but sometimes legitimate, form of argument. For example, studies have shown that drinking red wine in moderation is beneficial to one's health. Plainly, however, that some expert says that something is so does not make it so. Thus, it is clearly a mistake to use an appeal to authority as a substitute for direct evidence for a position, as if the two were equivalent. This type of error is prevalent in the only book written in the last century specifically on the topic of Catholicism and ETI, Kenneth Delano's *Many Worlds, One God*. Delano spends page after page[2] citing the testimony of scientists and others who think that ETI life is likely, while generally omitting any reasons the experts might give for this view.

A fallacy that most authors avoid, but does comes up now and again, is the appeal to ignorance. The "argument" runs along these lines: "You do not have sufficient grounds to rule out that ETIs exist; therefore they do exist." However, the simple fact that an opponent cannot provide an adequate argument for his position does not permit one to conclude that he is wrong.

A particularly pathetic logical fallacy, and one that is frequently used by ETI proponents, is a form of personal attack which is sometimes referred to as "circumstantial ad hominem." What this fallacy amounts to is instead of addressing the argument that one's opponent is proposing—which is obviously what one should be doing—one simply dismisses the argument on the grounds that the opponent stands to gain something if his conclusion is accepted. The typical form the argument takes is something like this: "You maintain that ETI does not exist, for if it did exist then you stand to lose, since your species would no longer be unique in the universe. Therefore your argument concluding that ETI life does not exist is incorrect." Delano employs this sort of argument:

> With the jealousy of a spoiled only child, the human race is upset by the suggestion that it may have to share its cosmic domicile with others. To make their instinctive reaction seem less like childish resentment, many think of themselves as being "Defenders of the Faith" in denying the possibility of intelligent beings existing on other worlds.[3]

Now, instead of attributing bad motives to one's opponent, and using that as an excuse to dismiss his argument, one should evaluate his argument, and provide reasons for rejecting it. Even if the person was ultimately rejecting ETI life because it would be a blow to his ego if his species was not number one in material creation, this is not a reason to ignore any arguments that he has given. Sad to say, this gross fallacy is probably the one most frequently committed. Rabbi Barry Friedman asserts: "It would be an incredible conceit of egotism to think we're the only form of life."[4] Physicist Russell Stannard claims: "that although, for all we know, intelligent life in the cosmos might be unique to planet Earth, that smacks of arrogance...."[5]

Another common fallacy is begging the question. This often takes the form of first proposing that ETIs exist, then assuming that they have characteristics that would make their existence incompatible with Christianity, from which it is then concluded that Christianity is false or at least to be put into doubt. For example, the physicist Paul Davies reasons:

...it is hard to see how the world's great religions could continue in anything like their present form should an alien message be received....If they practiced anything remotely like a religion, we should surely soon wish to abandon our own and be converted to theirs.[6]

Another example of such tactics is found on the part of Robert Jastrow:

> [It has been suggested that] as Judeo-Christian values were superior to those of paganism, with its human sacrifice and other pernicious practices, advanced extraterrestrial life-forms may have a form of monotheism superior to Judeo-Christian beliefs. Does this not create problems for the traditional Judeo-Christian view of the Deity as being very much concerned with the affairs of the particular race of intelligent beings that exists on our planet?[7]

In both these cases it is simply assumed that Christianity is likely to be inferior to anything ETIs might believe. Possible ETI existence is not being used as grounds to reject Christianity—Christianity has been rejected in advance.

Delano presents another argument that borders on begging the question: "That we are the sum and substance of the capabilities of the cosmos is something so preposterous as to be exquisitely comic."[8] The implicit conclusion, of course, is that ETI exists. One could say that this statement does no more than imply that we are not the only intelligent life form simply because it is absurd to think that we are the only intelligent life form. However, given that there is some obvious reason for thinking it strange that we are the only intelligent life form in the cosmos, it is fairer to look at the tacit premise or premises. Delano goes on to say: "Our pretentious illusions may appear just as ridiculous to more advanced stellar societies as the claims of the Yanomanö Indians...are to us." While it would constitute a personal attack to dismiss a person's claim to excellence on the ground that the person was conceited, it is not a personal attack to ask whether in fact his claim has merit. Thus, it is a fair question whether taking the position that ETI does not exist, or is unlikely to exist, implies a mistaken estimation of the eminence of the human race in the cosmos.

I think that what sometimes underlies doubts about the status of our race is the paradoxical smallness and greatness of man, about which Pascal spoke so eloquently. Humans on the whole are moral mediocrities, in addition to which most lack very penetrating intellects, and fail to acquire any great learning. On the other hand, we, unlike the rest of creation on earth, have the capacity to understand the whats and whys of things in the material universe. Our ability to contain the entire universe in our minds was one reason why the Greeks called man a "microcosm." This is not to say that we are necessarily the brightest of lights in the material universe when it comes to intelligence, but that we represent a remarkable advance over the non-rational animals. Whence Aristotle says: "[R]eason…alone is divine. For its activity shares nothing with the activity of the body."[9] The Greeks were not alone in their estimation of human capabilities. The biologist Christian De Duve, in response to the question "what is the meaning of the universe?," asserts that "[it] is found in the structure of the universe, which happens to be such as to produce thought by way of life and mind. Thought, in turn, is a faculty whereby the universe can reflect upon itself, discover its own structure, and apprehend such immanent entities as truth, beauty, goodness, and love."[10] It is natural for human beings, as material beings, to be impressed by the sheer vastness of the heavens and number of the stars. The author of Psalm 8 expresses the sentiment of wonder that the sight of the heavens commonly elicits: "What is man that you are mindful of him?" However, when all is said and done, the stars are just big balls of fire, whereas we are beings who are not only able to see the stars, but in addition can reflect on their worth.

Christianity, looking at man from a supernatural standpoint, also recognizes his smallness and greatness. The smallness of humanity comes from sin, both original sin and personal sin. The greatness of humanity comes from a free gift of God:

> "God fashioned man with his own hands [that is, the Son and the Holy Spirit] and impressed his own form on the flesh he had fashioned, in such a way that even what was visible might bear the divine form." Disfigured by sin and death, man remains, "in the image of God," in the image of the Son, but is deprived "of the glory of God," of his "likeness." The promise made to Abraham inaugurates the economy of salvation, at the culmination of which the Son himself will assume that "image" and

restore it in the Father's "likeness" by giving it again its Glory, the Spirit who is "the giver of life."[11]

The economy of salvation consists in Christ's restoration of the disfigured "image of God," first by his own incarnation as man, and then by his grace which enables Christians to live Christ-like lives, "to become true images of the Son" (Rom. 8:29).[12] Again, one human being in the state of grace is of more value than the entire material universe—and this is Christ's work.

A person could concede that humans are of greater value than the material universe, but still find hard to believe that God would create this immense and beautiful universe for but a single mediocre species. This objection is reminiscent of and related to an objection against the Incarnation, namely, that it does not befit divine majesty to be united to the least of intellectual creatures. It is very astonishing and mysterious that "the Son of God became man, that we might become God."[13] Given that the original creation is ordered to the New Creation wrought by Christ, it is not surprising that the original creation shares in this mystery. It does so to a lesser degree, to the extent that in the hierarchy of nature, human nature surpasses the rest of material creation in dignity, whereas it is only through a supernatural gift of God that human nature can be raised in some sense to the level of the divine. It is a source of amazement to look at the myriad stars in the sky and think that only one planet around one sun harbors intelligent life. But it is not inherently absurd that this be the case. God can certainly order the universe this way. And indeed, as I have been arguing, Scripture and Church teaching indicate that he has ordered the universe this way.[14] Ultimately it is the Faith, and not some a priori conviction that the human race is all so wonderful, that leads me to the conclusion that we are alone.

Part IV

How Would Church Teaching be Affected if Contact were Made?

Chapter 13

Would Adjustments to Catholic Teaching Have to be Made if ETI was Discovered?

Christians have to ask themselves (and skeptics will certainly ask them), What can the cosmic significance possibly be of the localized, terrestrial event of the existence of the historical Jesus? Does not the mere possibility of extraterrestrial life render nonsensical all the superlative claims made by the Christian church about his significance? Would ET, Alpha-Arcturians, Martians, et al., need an incarnation and all it is supposed to accomplish, as much as *Homo sapiens* on planet Earth? Only a contemporary theology that can cope convincingly with such questions can hope to be credible today.

—Arthur Peacocke, *Many Worlds*

I would be most amazed if some form of contact took place, to put it mildly. It would certainly be interesting from a philosophical and sociological viewpoint to learn about their moral values, religion(s), and cosmological beliefs, and from a scientific viewpoint to examine their physiology. But what impact would it have on the Catholic faith? Robert Jastrow claims that:

> If and when the communication with advanced life occurs, I believe these implications will have a transforming effect on Western religion, requiring far greater adjustments in theological thought than those prompted by the discovery that the Earth revolves around the Sun or even the evidence in the fossil record that seems to link humans to simpler forms of life.[1]

Would the needed readjustment indeed be more radical? To answer this question one would first need to examine what readjustment was needed in the other two cases. Without embarking on an extensive analysis of the effects the Copernican Revolution and evolutionary theory had on Christianity, something others have devoted entire books to, we can look very briefly at the general impact these scientific teachings had on Christianity.

It is typical for problems to arise when science comes into apparent conflict with what the Bible teaches. Heliocentrism is, of course, a case in point. As Pierre de Cazre explains in a letter (1592) to Gassendi:

> Ponder less on what you yourself perhaps think than on what will be the thoughts of the majority of others who carried away by your authority or your reasons, become persuaded that the terrestrial globe moves among the planets. They will conclude first that, if the earth is doubtless one of the planets and also has inhabitants, then it is well to believe that inhabitants exist on the other planets and are not lacking in the fixed stars, that they are even of a superior nature and in proportion as the other stars surpass the earth in size and perfection. This will raise doubts about Genesis which says that the earth was made before the stars and that they were created on the fourth day to illuminate the earth and measure the seasons and years. Then in turn the entire economy of the Word incarnate and of scriptural truth will be rendered suspect.[2]

Genesis, if looked at as science, contains a number of other inaccuracies, in addition to the one noted by de Cazre, i.e., that the formation of the earth preceded the formation of all of the stars. For example, Genesis says that "trees bearing fruit with their seed inside" (Gen. 1:12) were created before birds and reptiles (Gen. 1:20, 24). And yet in the fossil record angiosperms appear much later than birds and reptiles.

The same sort of problem arises with evolution. If man evolved from a non-human animal ancestor, then it seems that God could not have made him from dust as Genesis states. Faced with these seemingly contradictory statements, some people will reject Scripture, while others reject what science teaches.

The mistake of both these camps lies in failing to realize that the purpose of Scripture is not to give a scientific account of certain features of the world, but rather to teach us what we need to know about God and how to get to him so that we can save our souls. Even when one understands this general principle, it sometimes takes an effort to discern in Scripture what is the teaching of salvation, and what pertains to a manner of speaking geared to make the story of salvation comprehensible to the listener.

The task of discerning what Scripture means to say is made all the more difficult by the fact that we naturally seek to form a world view encompassing all of our knowledge. Thus, when Scripture appears to be telling us something which in fact is a matter for science to treat of, we tend to take it at face value, for it appears to complete our vision of the world, something we are desirous to do. The more we lack knowledge about scientific matters, the more inclined we are to fill in the gaps in our knowledge with what we read in Scripture. Books in the Bible written in the figurative manner of Genesis, rather than as an historical account, are apt to feed this tendency.[3] The basic points conveyed by Genesis could be summed up in a relatively limited number of propositions that would fill a paragraph or two. It is easier, however, for human beings to grasp abstract truths when they are attached to a concrete story. Indeed, abstract truths must be attached to some concrete image, though not necessarily a story, for as Aristotle pointed out long ago, thinking depends upon imagining.[4] When such truths are conveyed by a Biblical story, there is a risk that people incorporate elements into their faith which were not intended as part of the meaning of the story, being rather means by which the author adapted the truths to the audience.[5] A modern day Genesis story would perhaps make reference to things like DNA and the Big Bang, but back then these things would mean nothing to people who thought themselves to live in a world where a vault separated rainwater from the lakes and oceans. And if a modern day Genesis story did make mention of the Big Bang, this would not mean it was to be taken as the true scientific explanation, any more than that the affirmation in Genesis concerning the vault of the firmament constituted a true scientific explanation when interpreted in light of the scientific world view of that day.[6]

The more scientific knowledge we have, the less likely we are to fail to recognize that certain statements in Scripture are not meant to be taken as the scientific statements that they appear to be on first sight. For example, when Scripture says that the sun stood still (Jos. 10:13[7]), Christians should have recognized that it was not trying to teach us about the movements of the heavenly bodies, but rather was expressing in a manner comprehensible to the audience that a miracle had taken place. Still, their mistake is to some extent understandable inasmuch as it is harder to distinguish science from what is proposed for our salvation when one lacks a command of the relevant scientific knowledge than when one possesses it. When people are unable to identify what is and is not a scientific issue, upon being told things such as that Scripture does not necessarily mean that God created man directly from dust, their reaction is that next they will be told that Christ was not born of the virgin Mary, and did not rise from the dead. These are the type of people who would be liable to lose their faith if scientific evidence too compelling for them to reject was discovered that appeared to contradict what Scripture said.

There is another more subtle problem for people's faith that scientific knowledge can feed into, and that is the temptation to redefine elements of the faith in function of science in a manner which is contrary to the faith. For example, some theologians in light of evolution reason that since the first people must have been more animal-like than modern man, the Fall was not a fall from a preternatural state (i.e., in which man did not have to struggle to nourish himself, was not subject to death, and did not have his freedom of choice impaired by unruly emotions such as lust[8]), but was a failure to move up, i.e., turn away from animal-like behavior centered on survival and reproduction,[9] to pursue the good of reason. Anticipating the unorthodox views that would be developed, as well as recognizing that not all the evidence was in, the Church cautioned the faithful against being overhasty in embracing evolution, but at the same time did not reject the view as contrary to the faith. It did insist that part of Genesis could be understood only in one way, namely the line which indicates that the human soul comes directly from God:

> ...the Teaching Authority of the Church does not forbid that, in conformity with the present state of human sciences and sacred theology, research and discussions, on the part of men experienced in both fields, take place with regard to the doctrine of evolution, in as far as it inquires into the origin of the human body as coming from pre-existent and living matter—for the Catholic faith obliges us to hold that souls are immediately created by God. However this must be done in such a way that the reasons for both opinions, that is, those favorable and those unfavorable to evolution, be weighed and judged with the necessary seriousness, moderation and measure, and provided that all

are prepared to submit to the judgment of the Church, to whom Christ has given the mission of interpreting authentically the Sacred Scriptures and of defending the dogmas of faith. Some however rashly transgress this liberty of discussion, when they act as if the origin of the human body from pre-existing and living matter were already completely certain and proved by the facts which have been discovered up to now and by reasoning on those facts, and as if there were nothing in the sources of divine revelation which demands the greatest moderation and caution in this question.[10]

Evidence eventually accumulated from several areas of biology making it beyond reasonable doubt that evolution has taken place (I am not speaking here of the theories proposed to explain how evolution took place, which is a separate matter).[11] But this caused no change in the Catholic faith. The modalities of the production of the human species were a matter of faith when it comes to production of the human soul, which the Catholic Church teaches is directly created by God. As for the human body, although the Church teaches that its ultimate source is God,[12] the modalities by which God produced this body are not an object of faith, but rather are a matter for science to study.

Admittedly, before evolution had been proposed as a theory, the faithful simply understood the human body to be created directly by God. This is again due to our natural tendency to want a complete picture of things. Where there is no scientific evidence we tend to fill in scientific details about creation from Scripture. For example, when Aquinas poses the question of "whether the human body is immediately produced by God,"[13] he cites Genesis's statement "God created man from the earth" as settling the matter. Aquinas did also offer an argument drawn from natural philosophy, based on the notion that like comes from like—something not possible in Adam's case, as he had no human ancestor. But in any case, the belief that God made the human body directly from dust was never an official teaching of the Church.

How do heliocentrism, evolution, and ETI existence compare as to the adjustments in theological thought they provoke, if they did or do indeed provoke adjustments in it? In the case of the motion of sun and earth, it was fairly plainly a scientific matter that was at stake, and it was unfortunate that Church officials treated it as if it were a matter for heresy. Recognizing that the heliocentric theory was correct, and that Galileo was wrongly condemned, something the Church later did,[14] required no adjustment to the faith. The passage about the sun standing still retained the same basic meaning it had been understood to have before, namely, it was a miracle. The difference is that now it is recognized that the miracle would be for the earth to stand still. However, to have stated it thus would have made no sense for people whose world view was geocentric. Where adjustment was needed was in the attitude of certain of the faithful, including members of the hierarchy, who had as yet failed to realize that Scripture teaches how to go to heaven, not how the heavens go.[15] It was certainly the hierarchy's job to delimit where the faith began and science ended. Their failure to do a good job of it was probably more responsible for people losing their faith, than the change from the geocentric to heliocentric world view was.

Of course heliocentrism elicited speculation about ETI which in turn was perceived by some as incompatible with the faith in ways that we have been discussing. Historically, however, the main conflict in the Galileo case concerned heliocentrism and stemmed from a failure to distinguish what faith can tell us from what science can tell us.[16]

The case of evolution was much more complex. There was not just the problem that what was being proposed appeared to contradict what the Bible said when taken at face value. Even if one recognizes that it pertains to science to describe the details of the origins of the human body, evolution leaves the faithful with a few sticky questions: How does the preternatural state of our first parents fit with their having just evolved from primate ancestors? Did the human race have many parents, or only one set of first parents? Can a believer accept the mechanisms proposed to explain evolution, random variation and natural selection? These questions, in addition to the problem of how to interpret Genesis, led a sizable number of people to pit faith against science, with the result that quite a few people retreated into fundamentalism, while a fair number went in the opposite direction and rejected theism, and thus Christianity as well. While I think this opposition is needless, for again it is not Sacred Scripture's purpose to explain the modalities of the production of the human body, it is the case that to deal adequately with all the facets of the impact of evolution on Catholicism is a lot more difficult than to deal with the shift from geocentrism to heliocentrism. This is why the Church came out with statements indicating to the faithful where the faith left off, and science began. It clarified which issues were open to question (namely, the details as to the manner in which the human body was produced) and which were not open to question (namely, God is the ultimate cause of the body, and he is the creator of the human soul; that the human race is descended from a single pair of parents[17]). The Church had never explicitly denied that the body may not have been directly formed by God from earth; prior to the evidence for evolution it had no real reason to consider that possibility.

In the case of ETI, the conflict does not lie chiefly in a confusion about what the Church can teach us and what science can tell us. Rather, it lies in the apparent incompatibilities between hypothetical ETI existence (something many scientists argue is probable, but is plainly something that can only be established empirically) and what the Catholic faith teaches about the role of Christ in the universe and about our place in it, basing itself, of course, in large part on Scripture. In other words, it is not the case here that the Church is making pronouncements about scientific matters concerning which it has no authority. The Church is not infringing on the territory of science when it affirms that Scripture tells us about the role of Our Lord Jesus Christ in the cosmos and about our place therein, for such things pertain to our salvation. Nor is science overstepping its limits in trying to estimate the likelihood of ETI existence (at least so long as it does not pretend to explain the origin of the human soul or of the intellect[18]). Science rightfully seeks to understand how life arose here and evolved to the level of man, and whether and how this may have happened elsewhere. (Of course not all scientists are inclined to think that ETI life exists; as we have seen many do not.) The problem lies elsewhere, in an apparent conflict Paine complains of:

> Though it is not a direct article of the Christian system that this world that we inhabit is the whole of the habitable creation, yet it is so worked up therewith from what is called the Mosaic account of the Creation, the story of Eve and the apple, and the counterpart of that story—the death of the Son of God, that to believe otherwise, that is, to believe that God created a plurality of worlds at least as numerous as what we call stars, renders the Christian system of faith at once a little ridiculous.... The two beliefs cannot be held together in the same mind; and he who thinks that he believes in both has thought but little of either.[19]

What Paine is saying is that Christianity gives the distinct impression that the Fall and the Redemption form a complete story that is *the* story of the universe, one which leaves no room for ETI existence, at least not in the mind of anyone who thinks about it. This sounds very much like what I have been arguing. However, I think that Paine is mistaken in holding that Christian belief is completely incompatible with ETI existence. ETI existence is certainly possible from the point of view of God's power, and as I endeavored to show in section two, there is no statement in Scripture or official church teaching that says that ETIs do not exist or that humans are the only rational animal in the universe (as Paine himself notes). Nor does it follow as a necessary conclusion from Scripture or any article of faith that they do not exist (at least not the unfallen). Paine's mistake, which I think is one of the big mistakes made by those who see opposition between Christianity with ETI existence, is to think that if the conclusion of the probable arguments against ETI existence was shown to be false by the discovery of such beings, this would necessarily show that some Christian belief is false. This mistake may be due to a failure to understand the nature of probable arguments or to properly identify the weak link or links in the probable arguments given or to a combination of the two. Thus, I next intend to discuss briefly the nature of probable arguments, and then go on to show that if the conclusion of my probable arguments proves false, the fault never lies in any premise derived from the faith.

A probable argument is one that leads a person to adopt one of two contradictory positions, while not being sufficiently cogent to remove from his mind the fear or doubt that the other position may in fact be true.[20] Now, arguments arrive at false conclusions for two main reasons. Either the form of the argument is deficient, and thus the conclusion does not necessarily follow, or one or more of the premises the argument is based on is false. I do not intend here to systematically treat every specific flaw that arguments can contain, but only to give some examples of such, for the purposes of making clear that there are a number of ways that my arguments may be flawed without the faith being impugned as a consequence.

A probable argument that generalizes starting from cases may suffer from the flaw of being based on an insufficient number of cases. Also, generalizations that have been arrived at inductively often do not apply to every specific case falling under that generalization, for some cases may be exceptions. Arguments by sign (arguments from effect to cause) may have a defective logical form, e.g., as would be the case if one inferred from the dried-up condition of a lawn that there had been a drought, for there may be other causes that could account for it, e.g., people having neglected to do the watering. It is especially easy to be taken in by a faulty argument by sign when one lacks complete information about an event, something which is certainly true in the case we are examining, concerning as it does what God has wrought in the universe. The long and the short of it is that there are many ways for my probable arguments to turn out to be defective that in no way impugn the faith, but either stem from flaws in the form of reasoning or from faulty premises that do not have the faith as their source. And this is want I intend now to go on to show. For if a defect in these arguments could be traced back to a faulty premise supplied by the faith, then Paine would be correct in his contention that embracing belief in both Christianity and ETI existence involves absurdity. In effect, what I will next do is show in a somewhat different way from Part I that ETI existence is possible (at least in an unfallen state) on the assumption that Christianity is true.

I will begin by analyzing the six probable arguments against ETI existence that presupposed that the Incarnation took place only one time. Five of them pertain to fallen ETIs, and five to the unfallen.

The first argument was that if the Word became incarnate one sole time, then it is fitting that the race that the Word took unto himself also be special. Since what is unique as being the one and only has nothing more special than it (that is, in the respect that it is unique—a thing special in one way is not necessarily special in every way), it was fitting that the human species be unique, as being the one and only rational material species. This argument is an argument by fittingness. Arguments by fittingness are less likely to miss the mark when one knows what God has in fact done, reasoning after the fact as to why it is appropriate that he has done so.[21] For example, Scripture tells us that God sent Christ in the fullness of time, and so starting from that fact, theologians seek out reasons why it was good that Christ did not come right after the Fall, nor in the last days, but at the time he did come.[22] In the case of ETIs, we do not know what God has done. So we are in the same situation that we are in regard to Limbo, the existence of which is unknown to us, and about which we can only speculate from what we do know from Scripture or Church teaching. In such cases, there may be arguments of fittingness leading to opposite conclusions, and it is often hard to judge which sort of fittingness has more weight. In our case, some would argue that it befits God to create more of higher things, and this outweighs the fittingness that man be unique, whereas others would maintain the contrary. However, even if the former is true, and we did not turn out to be unique as being the only rational animal in the universe, we would still be unique in that we are the species whom the Word united in his person for the purposes of redemption. The faith teaches the latter, and not the former, so there is no conflict between the faith and ETI here.

The second argument was that if the Incarnation was to profit all of creation, the nature that was most appropriately assumed was one that links spiritual and material realms. Given that the human race was created to serve this purpose, there is no need for a second human-like species, and thus God would not create something that in effect is redundant. It could be argued, however, that especially an unfallen ETI race would not be redundant, and that even a fallen ETI race redeemed through Christ could be seen as offering a different variation on the salvation story. Again, the potential problem with my argument lies not in its foundation in the faith (that mankind, like all things, were created for Christ who is the central figure in the plan for the universe, being the one through whom all creation is perfected), but in determining with certitude what counts for redundant.

The third argument is based on the way in which so many details of the Incarnation and Passion were specially adapted for human benefit, for this makes it implausible that Incarnation and Passion were also ordered to the benefit of some other rational being. The conclusion that many of the benefits of the Incarnation and Passion accruing to the human race would not fall to the lot of ETIs is arrived at, first, by considering the Scriptural passages and philosophical concepts (e.g., equality allows for more intimate friendship) that indicate the variety of benefits humans derive from the Incarnation and Passion, and then by establishing that these benefits would not accrue to ETIs. (This argument appears to be the one that Thomas Paine had in mind.) The weak point in the argument is that the Incarnation and Passion could still also apply to an ETI race, despite it not fitting that race with the same nicety that it fits the human race. This is especially true of unfallen ETIs who would not even need the same sort of care that fallen humans were so desperately in want of.

The fourth argument is based on Hebrews 2:14 which seems to says that Christ intended to belong to the same stock as all those he was to save, so that he could save them. Although unfallen ETIs are not affected by this passage, fallen ETIs do seem to be eliminated by it. My interpretation of this passage, however, has never been presented by the Church as being her own. Thus, so long as the Church does not make a pronouncement confirming my interpretation, the appearance of fallen ETIs would not affect the Church's credibility.

It is worth noting that it is extremely rare that the Church pronounces on a specific verse of Scripture:

> ...in the immense matter contained in the Sacred Books—legislative, historical, sapiential and prophetical—there are but few texts whose sense has been defined by the authority of the Church, nor are those more numerous about which the teaching of the Holy Fathers is unanimous. There remain therefore many things, and of the greatest importance, in the discussion and exposition of which the skill and genius of Catholic commentators may and ought to be freely exercised, so that each may contribute his part to the advantage of all, to the continued progress of the sacred doctrine and to the defense and honor of the Church.[23]

The fifth argument concludes that ETIs do not exist because they would be unable to interact with us and/or with many of the other intelligent races there might be. I think that the general metaphysical notion the argument is based on is sound, namely, that the universe should exhibit the greatest possible order, one form of which is realized through the interactions of its parts. And the principle seems quite applicable to the case of ETI races. While this is a philosophical, and not a theological argument, it does fit quite well with what Scripture says about God's wisdom. Consider Ps. 104 which begins by describing the interactions among things in the world:

> You made the moon to tell the seasons, the sun knows when to set: you bring darkness on, night falls, all the forest animals come out: savage lions roaring for their prey, claiming their food from God. The sun rises, they retire, going back to lie down in their lairs, and man goes out to work, and to labor until dusk.

At the end of this description of the order God has established in nature, the psalmist exclaims: "Yahweh, what variety you have created, arranging everything so wisely!" Thus, Scripture too seems to be saying that it is a characteristic of wisdom to order a variety of things in such a manner that they form an interactive whole.[24]

The weak point in the interactivity argument lies not in its general premise, but in its application to ETIs. One cannot entirely rule out that we will one day communicate with each other via some faster-than-light means of communication which is as yet to be discovered. Nor can we rule out the possibility that communication via radio waves will eventually connect together all rational species, because it may prove to be the case that all or most intelligent life forms are close enough to each other for such means to be adequate, despite what the principle of mediocrity would first lead one to believe.

The sixth argument is based on the notion that the intellects of beings who possess a material intelligent nature have a greater admixture of potency than do the intellects of pure intelligences (the angels), and whence such beings are even more likely to fall than the angels were. This seems to be a fairly strong dialectical argument, based on a general understanding of the natures of created intellects. However, the faith does not require us to agree with either the premises or with the conclusion of this philosophical argument. (As for the inductive argument to the conclusion that every intelligent kind contains individuals who fall: This argument starts from an enumeration of instances of intelligent kinds containing members which fell, namely, the angels, some of whom fell, and then the human race, the first parents of which fell—this is an even weaker argument from the standpoint of logic.)

I think that the improbability of a second incarnation is the main problem with ETI scenarios that presuppose a second incarnation. I am not going to reiterate my arguments that aim at showing that a second incarnation is unlikely, because in any case, the Church has never made any pronouncement on this matter, nor does tradition contain any constant teaching on it. Other problems with ETI scenarios involving a second incarnation overlap with those posed on the supposition of one incarnation, with the exception of one additional problem: Fallen ETIs would have a faith that was confusing. However, God in his wisdom may judge such a faith sufficiently intelligible, although it might not seem so to us.

It takes a certain amount of effort to see that the weak link in the probable arguments that I have given is not any truth of the faith, but is to be found elsewhere, either in the other premises that enter into these arguments, or in weakness in the form of argumentation, or in the interpretations of Scripture that I have proposed. Thus, it is somewhat understandable that people pit Christianity against ETI existence, as if the two were mutually exclusive. However, my above analysis, combined with my earlier dismantling of arguments opposing Christianity and ETI existence on the grounds that the centrality of Christ and human specialness are incompatible with ETI existence, indicate that there is no necessary opposition between the two. Consequently *the discovery of ETIs would entail no adjustment to any teaching of the faith*, contrary to what is often claimed. At most it would entail addition, in the sense that the faith would recognize these rational beings as potential members of the one Church of which Christ is the head. If the ETIs were fallen, a question would arise as to whether they should be baptized. And if there was evidence that a second incarnation had taken place, this would constitute a theological matter that would fall to the Church to pronounce on.

ETI discovery would entail a change in world view, similar to what happened when it was realized that the earth moves around the sun, and when evidence in favor of the evolution of the human body rolled in. We would learn the answer to the question of whether we are the only intelligent material being (a question the Church has never pronounced upon). Doubtlessly, the wonder and awe that we experience in contemplating the great chain of being as it is presently known to us would be increased, if yet another intelligent link was discovered.

The relative ease with which people are taken in by arguments turning on the centrality of Christ and/or human specialness, compounded by the ease with which one can mistake a probable argument against ETI existence for being a certain argument are indicative that the intellectual subtleties of the ETI debate are equal if not greater than those involved in evolution. Looked at from this point of view, it seems likely that if contact were ever made, people would lose their faith to the same or to a greater extent than they did in the case of the evolution debate, despite this not giving them any reason whatsoever for doing so. On the other hand, ETI does not pose the same problem to those of fundamentalist disposition that evolution did. One might also ask whether in this day and age truth matters as much to the average believer as it did in the past. A certain number of believers, influenced by the skepticism and relativism prevalent in our day, may have adopted a "flexible attitude" towards truth, and this combined with ignorance of Catholic doctrine, may prevent them from even being able to rise to the level of asking the question Paine asked himself about the compatibility of belief in Christianity and in ETI existence. Believers such as these are not specially liable to lose what faith they have if contact were made.

Chapter 14

Do ETI Proponents Have an anti-Christian Agenda?

> The time is sure to come when, far from being content with sound teaching, people will be avid for the latest novelty and collect themselves a whole series of teachers according to their own tastes; and then, instead of listening to the truth, they will turn to myths.
>
> —2 Timothy 4:3

In my introduction I note that there is no shortage of authors who use the possibility of ETI existence as a reason to discard Christianity. I have endeavored to show that their reasoning is unsound. One might ask the further questions of whether some of the ETI proponents do not have an anti-Christian agenda, and thus whether Christians would not do well to distance themselves from such people. Stanley Jaki minces no words when expressing his view on the matter:

> Fashionable speculation on ETI, nay brave assertions of its factuality, are so many rigged testimonials in a courtroom set up to banish God from the realm of the living, to pre-empt purpose of all its significance, and to assure the rule of meaninglessness.... Only a few advocates of ETI speak their minds openly on what they consider to be the supreme fallout from an eventual detection of ETI. Such an outcome, so they believe, would be the final rebuttal of supernatural revelation, the ultimate unveiling as sheer myths of such tenets as Fall, Incarnation, and Resurrection.[1]

I find this claim extreme, though not entirely unfounded. On the one hand, a number of theologians who are not at all interested in giving up their faith endorse the likelihood of ETI existence. Other advocates of ETI may be persuaded by scientific reasoning such as that summarized in the Drake equation, without reflecting on what impact ETI discovery would have on their faith one way or the other. Many websites on ETI make no reference to religion.

Leaving aside the question of ETI proponents' motives, it is easy to see that some of the arguments pitting Christianity against ETI existence are patently lacking in depth. This is particularly true of the personal attacks and the question-begging that are not infrequently indulged in. It does become tiresome to read "arguments" such as that of Jill Tarter:

> At a minimum, this inferred result [their longevity] is likely to have a great deal to say about religions throughout the universe. In my opinion, it will mean that the detected, long-lived extraterrestrial either never had, or have outgrown, organized religion.[2]

In a similar question-begging manner, Willem B. Drees presents us with a dichotomy that suggests that belief in the child of Bethlehem might be opposed to being loving:

> But that is not to say that extraterrestrials are to be conformed to traditional theological schemes; Bethlehem does not have to be the center of the universe. It is more important to be open-minded, loving, responsible.[3]

Reasoning that appeals to ETI existence in order to show that Christianity is to be discarded, while at the same time supposing that Christianity has no special value does give the impression of a "rigged testimonial" against Christianity. That people accept or reject Christianity is certainly a matter of free choice. But there are objective criteria which must be respected if an argument is to avoid being sophistical.

On the other hand, perhaps Christian authors should shoulder some of the blame for the shabby reasoning that is paraded before the public's eyes.[4] To the extent that relatively little has been said by Christian authors on the subject of extraterrestrial life, it is understandable that people are readily persuaded by the arguments that are in circulation, many of which suggest that ETI existence should be deposited in the balance against Christianity. Exacerbating the problem is the fact that many, and perhaps most, Christians who have spoken on the issue offer generic answers that gloss over apparent points of conflict. The science fiction writer, Robert Sawyer, after participating at a week-long meeting of the Pontifical Academy of Science on ETI, criticized the response of one of the members of the Vatican Observatory on this very score:

> It was basically a spiritual as opposed to an explicitly Christian reply, and it amounts to nothing more than saying that in this whole vast universe, sure, there might be other intelligences. The hard response would be to deal with the issue in explicitly Christian terms....[5]

I may have given the wrong response, but I have certainly given a hard response based on Scripture and Church doctrine, or at least as hard a response as I dare, given that the Catholic Church has made no pronouncement on the matter. In light of Scripture and Church teaching, the view that I think most likely on the question of the compatibility between Christianity and ETI existence is that Christianity is compatible with the existence of unfallen ETIs, but not with fallen ones. As for whether unfallen ETIs actually exist, this seems to me unlikely, but not impossible, in light of the faith.

If the Church pronounced on the compatibility issue it could take three possible positions: 1) that Catholics can believe that fallen and unfallen ETIs might exist; 2) that Catholics can believe that unfallen ETIs might exist, but not fallen ones; 3) that Catholics must deny that ETIs in any condition exist. If the Church adopted either 1) or 2), then there would be no need for me to revise my position. (To say that Catholics are permitted to believe that unfallen ETIs might exist, is plainly not to say that they have to believe this, and thus such a pronouncement would not demand any revision of my probable arguments against unfallen ETI.) It is only if the Church officially adopted 3) that I would have to retract my view that Christian belief does not necessarily exclude every form of belief in ETI existence, and concede that Paine was right in saying the two beliefs are incompatible.

Chapter 15

What Might the Catholic Church Say on the ETI Question?

I saw that in the right hand of the One sitting on the throne there was a scroll that had writing on back and front and was sealed with seven seals. Then I saw a powerful angel who called with a loud voice, "Is there anything worthy to open the scroll and break the seals of it?" But there was no one, in heaven or on the earth or under the earth, who was able to open the scroll and read it....The Lamb came forward to take the scroll from the right hand of the One sitting on the throne, and when he took it, the four animals prostrated themselves before him and with them the twenty-four elders.... They sang a new hymn:

"You are worthy to take the scroll and break the seals of it, because you were sacrificed...."

In my vision, I heard the sound of an immense number of angels gathered around the throne and the animals and the elders; there were ten thousand times ten thousand of them and thousands upon thousands, shouting, "The Lamb that was sacrificed is worthy to be given power, riches, wisdom, strength, honor, glory and blessing." Then I heard all the living things in creation—everything that lives in the air, and on the ground, and under the ground, and in the sea crying, "To the One who is sitting on the throne, and to the Lamb, be all praise, honor, glory and power, for ever and ever."

—Revelation 5: 1-3, 7-14

I think that the Roman Catholic Church may very well come out with some sort of statement on ETI, due to the high level of public interest in the subject[1] accompanied by the confusion that reigns in the minds of some of the faithful and potential faithful.[2] The Church's pronouncement would most likely be similar to *Humani Generis*'s statement on evolution in that central doctrines touching upon the issue would be reaffirmed and the area left open to inquiry would be delineated. Like *Humani Generis* it will most likely advise the faithful to exercise caution, lest they be taken in by speculations that conflict with the faith, and lest they make precipitous judgments, for this is contrary to respect for truth (all truth comes from God).

I think that in the case of ETI the Church is likely to reaffirm the following:

First, that the import of Christ and his mission of salvation extends not only to humankind, but to the entire universe. On this score, I disagree with Thomas O'Meara, O.P. who holds that:

> Our species on earth is the subject of the biblical narratives.... Nor is there any reason to think that the "economy of salvation," a phrase of Greek theologians, is anything other than a divine enterprise for our terrestrial race, the people in and for which it is enacted. It is superficial and arrogant to assert that the Christian or Jewish revelation of a wisdom plan for salvation history on earth is about other creatures. Faith affirms that the Logos has been incarnate on a planet located, in past Ptolemaic astronomy, in a small, closed system. The Logos, the second person of the divine Trinity, indeed has a universal domination, but Jesus, Messiah and Savior, has a relationship to terrestrials existing within one history of sin and grace.[3]

First, Scripture does tell the story of another intelligent life form, namely, the angels. It tells us that certain angels fell,[4] while others did not.[5] It also tells us that God never assumed an angelic nature.[6] It is true that what Scripture tells us is told us for our salvation: The Old and New Testaments teach "that truth which God, for the sake of our salvation,[7] wished to see confided to the Sacred Scriptures."[8] It would be arrogant to assert that one knows better than God what is or is not to the purpose to tell us. And, in fact, in addition to telling us certain things about the angels, he has also chosen to tell us certain things about the relation of Christ to the universe. The Church has traditionally seen the role that Christ plays in the universe as having a cosmic importance, and not just importance to us, as can be seen from the following passages from the *CCC*:

Creation is the foundation of "all God's saving plans," the "beginning of the history of salvation" that culminates in Christ. Conversely, the mystery of Christ casts conclusive light on the mystery of creation and reveals the end for which "in the beginning God created the heavens and the earth": from the beginning, God envisaged the glory of the new creation in Christ.[9]

"Christ died and lived again, that he might be Lord both of the dead and of the living." [Rom. 14:9] Christ's Ascension into heaven signifies his participation, in his humanity, in God's power and authority. Jesus Christ is Lord: he possesses all power in heaven and on earth. He is "far above all rule and authority and power and dominion," for the Father "has put all things under his feet." [Ep. 1:20-22] Christ is Lord *of the cosmos* and of history. In him human history and *indeed all creation* are "set forth" and transcendently fulfilled. [Ep. 1:10, cf. Ep. 4:10][10] (Emphasis mine)

The *CCC* explicitly affirms that the "economy of salvation" or "the economy of the Word Incarnate" is more than "a divine enterprise for our terrestrial race:"

In the Symbol of the faith the Church confesses the mystery of the Holy Trinity and of the plan of God's "good pleasure" for all creation: the Father accomplishes the "mystery of his will" by giving his beloved Son and the Holy Spirit for the salvation of the world and for the glory of his name. Such is the mystery of Christ, revealed and fulfilled in history according to the wisely ordered plan that St. Paul calls the "plan of the mystery" and the patristic tradition will call the "economy of the Word incarnate" or the "economy of salvation."[11]

The Congregation for the Doctrine of the Faith in its Declaration, *Dominus Iesus* also affirms that the salvific value of Christ's acts extends beyond humanity, and that there is only one economy of salvation:

There is only one salvific economy of the One and Triune God, realized in the mystery of the incarnation, death, and resurrection of the Son of God, actualized with the cooperation of the Holy Spirit, and extended in its salvific value to all humanity and to the entire universe: "No one, therefore, can enter into communion with God except through Christ, by the working of the Holy Spirit".[12]

The Eucharist, as well, bespeaks the cosmic character of Christ's salvific sacrifice. John Paul II makes this point in his encyclical letter *Ecclesia De Eucharistia*:

> This varied scenario of celebrations of the Eucharist has given me a powerful experience of its universal and, so to speak, cosmic character. Yes, cosmic! Because even when it is celebrated on the humble altar of a country church, the Eucharist is always in some way celebrated on the altar of the world. It unites heaven and earth. It embraces and permeates all creation. The Son of God became man in order to restore all creation, in one supreme act of praise, to the One who made it from nothing. He, the Eternal High Priest who by the blood of his Cross entered the eternal sanctuary, thus gives back to the Creator and Father all creation redeemed. He does so through the priestly ministry of the Church, to the glory of the Most Holy Trinity. Truly this is the *mysterium fidei* which is accomplished in the Eucharist: the world which came forth from the hands of God the Creator now returns to him redeemed by Christ.[13]

Christ's Incarnation, Passion, and Resurrection on Earth are not happenings with solely terrestrial import. The *CCC*, *Dominus Iesus*, and *Ecclesia De Eucharistia* base themselves solidly on Scripture in their claim that the plan for the entire universe, and not just for the inhabitants of earth, centers on Christ and his salvific mission. The scriptural passages that these documents refer to include Ep. 1:8-10, Ep. 3:9-12, Ep. 4:10, Col. 1:18-20. Since these passages (with the exception of Ep. 4:10[14]) have already been quoted in chapter six (in the context of arguing against a second Incarnation), to avoid repetition, I ask the reader to refer back to chapter six or directly to the New Testament. It is important to note that the Catholic Church throughout the ages has understood these passages to indicate that God's plan for the entire universe hinges on Christ, and the redemption he wrought for us—it is not a matter here of my merely personal interpretations.

Scripture also makes clear that our Savior Jesus has universal dominion *as man*, and not just, as O'Meara would have it, "a relationship to terrestrials existing within one history of sin and grace."

> His state was divine, yet he did not cling to his equality with God, but emptied himself to assume the condition of a slave, and became as men are; and being as all men are, he was humbler yet, even to accepting death, death on a cross. But God raised him high and gave him the name which is above all other names, so that all beings in the heavens, on the earth and in the underworld, should bend at the name of Jesus and that every tongue should acclaim Jesus Christ as Lord, to the glory of God the Father. (Ph. 2:6-11)

Christ's universal dominion as man is also affirmed by Heb. 2:8, 9:

> "You have put him in command of everything." Well then, if he has "put him in command of everything," he [God] has left nothing which is not under his command. At present it is true, we are not able to see that "everything has been put under his command," but we do see in Jesus one who was "for a short while made lower than the angels and is now crowned with glory and splendor" because he submitted to death....

The *CCC* (#668, quoted earlier) maintains that Christ in his humanity possesses "all power in heaven and on earth," relying in part on Ep. 1:22 which reads:

> He [God] has put all things under his feet, and made him, as ruler of everything, the head of the Church; which is his body, the fullness of him who fills the whole creation.

The Eucharist, in a less obvious way, also constitutes an affirmation of the unlimited compass of Christ's rule as man. Christ is physically present under the appearance of bread in every tabernacle in the world. If Mass were said on the Moon, or Mars, or in any other location in the universe, Christ would be present there, body, soul, humanity, and divinity.

It is thus not surprising that the Church has always spoken of all of creation as being ordered to the new creation in Christ, and has always maintained that Christ both as God and Man is Lord of all and Head of the Church to whom all the blessed belong. It has not done so because of some sort of anthropocentric obsession, but because this is what God reveals to us in Scripture to be the case. Again, the fact that Scripture is ordered to human salvation does not dictate to God what he can and cannot tell us about how his plan for us fits into his greater plan for the universe as a whole, nor what he can tell us about Christ our Redeemer (as for instance that Christ is "head of every Sovereignty and Power" [Col. 2:10]). It amazes me how ready some theologians are to discard biblically based traditional teachings concerning the cosmic Christ to accommodate beings that are not even known to exist.[15]

What I have tried to show is that the Church's teaching concerning the cosmic Christ does not logically entail the rejection of ETI life. Even the hypothesis of other incarnations of the Word does not make it necessary to deny that it is through Christ's work of Redemption that the universe is brought to perfection. Those things which are attributed to an assumed nature in virtue of its assumption by the Word would not be multiplied by other assumptions of a same or different nature. Thus, the Word's ETI incarnation would be Lord of all, just as Christ is Lord of all, for the Word would not become an additional Lord with each nature that he assumed. Those things which are not attributed to an assumed nature in virtue of its assumption by the Word, but which are proper to it (e.g., the number of fingers) can be attributed to another assumed nature in virtue of the unity conferred on these natures in the person of the Word. However, they are not attributed to the other nature as belonging properly to it. So again, one can say that a man made the stars, because the Second Person, who is both God and Man, made the stars, but one cannot say that he did so as man. Similarly, if the Word assumed an ETI nature, and if it was proper to an ETI nature to have seven fingers, then one could say that a man, Christ, had seven fingers; however, this would not be true of Christ in his human nature, but in his ETI nature. The centrality of Christ in the plan for the universe is compatible both with the attributes which would belong to the ETI incarnation in virtue of the union of this nature with the Word, and with the attributes proper to the ETI nature, albeit activities founded upon the latter sort of attribute do appear to dilute Christ's central role (e.g., if an ETI incarnation used his seventh finger to heal a sick ETI, it does not seem that one could attribute this healing to Christ in his human nature).

What are we to make, then, out of the Jesuit Christopher J. Corbally's assertion that "while Christ is the First and the Last Word (the Alpha and the Omega) spoken to humanity, he is not necessarily the only word spoken to the whole universe."[16] The dichotomy Corbally presents us with is ambiguous. If by saying that Christ "is not necessarily the only word spoken to the whole universe," Corbally means to indicate that perhaps one could rightly deny that Christ is the word spoken to the whole universe, then what he says is false, insofar as the entire universe is perfected through Christ, who is Lord of all that is. If Corbally means to say that the Word's incarnation on earth does not exclude the Word's incarnation on other planets, then what he says is true, but he certainly could have worded his statement more carefully.

While Christ's salvific act extends to all of creation, this does not necessarily mean that it extends to other fallen beings—they would have to exist for this to be the case. I again have argued against the existence of fallen ETIs based on Heb. 2:14 which seems to say that the reason why Christ shared the in same flesh and blood that we humans have, was so that he could free all who lived in the fear of death—ETI redemption does not fit in with Christ's stated rationale for sharing our flesh and blood. However, I do not think that the Church is going to endorse this position or indeed make any pronouncement on whether Christ's Redemption extends to other intelligent material beings or not. For the existence of these other beings is merely hypothetical, in addition to which their existence cannot be of importance to our salvation, for then Scripture or Tradition would have told us about them. The Church might, however, reiterate that Christ's sacrifice is infinite in its saving power.

After speaking about the central role Christ plays in creation, the Church is likely to reaffirm what human specialness consists in. We, unlike other material beings on earth, are created in the image of God. It is a consequence of our rational nature that we have dominion over other things that are not created in God's image. These things would be true even if other intelligent material beings existed who were also created in the image of God and to whom material things would consequently also be ordered. I do not think that the Church will address the question of whether we are the only material being created in the image of God. Rather, I suspect that the Church will leave this matter open to speculation, partly because there is no basis in tradition to settle the matter, and partly because finally it makes no difference to our salvation whether we believe that other material rational beings exist or not.

Another form of specialness that the Church is liable to mention lies in the special favor that God showed man when the second person of the Trinity became incarnate as man and died for our salvation. Looking at the Incarnation alone, certainly man is special to the extent that we are recipients of an extraordinary blessing that was freely bestowed upon us. From a comparative point of view as well, the Incarnation makes us special, inasmuch as there are other intelligent beings in whose nature the Word did not become incarnate: "For it was not the angels that he took to himself; he took to himself descent from Abraham" (Heb. 2:16, 17). Perhaps we are also special because God united only our nature to himself, but I do not think that the Church will pronounce on this matter because there is no tradition to draw on (the Fathers and Doctors who wrote about the Incarnation had no real reason to ask themselves whether it only occurred once). If there were a second incarnation, we would not be special in the sense of favored above all others. Whether we are special because we are the only ones to profit from Christ's redemption, amounts to the question of whether Christ is a universal savior of more than one type of fallen being or not. As noted above, the Church is not in the habit of making statements about beings that are not mentioned in Scripture or Tradition, and are not even known to exist.

We are also special inasmuch as the ultimate destiny of the universe is achieved through man, namely, through Christ the Redeemer, and in a secondary way through the just human beings who accept the graces Christ gained by his sacrifice on the cross. If people wish to speculate that the human race is the one sheep that got lost amongst many others who did not, and it was the only one in need of a Good Shepherd to rescue it, doing so entails no necessary conflict with Church teaching or Scripture. Though this view does not lack a certain appeal, the one argument in favor of this view (taken from the notion of plenitude) is outweighed by the several arguments against it (and especially by the argument against the existence of a multitude of unfallen races).

A third thing that the Church is likely to reiterate as relevant to the ETI question is that all the blessed belong to one Church (or kingdom[17]) of which Christ is the head. There is one blessed company, not two, composed of angels and men contemplating the glory of God. This company is the Church Triumphant, which has as its sole head, Jesus Christ.[18] These statements leave understood that any other beings ordered to supernatural happiness would end up together with the angels and with us in the same Church under Christ as head. (It seems that Catholic proponents of ETI existence would draw better support for their cause by emphasizing the cosmic dimensions of the Church instead of downplaying them.)

Fourthly, I think that the Church would reiterate that the entire human race has descended from one set of first parents. These parents are responsible for the fall of man by their sin, a sin which is passed on to their biological offspring ("original sin"). These teachings would in nowise be affected by the existence of intelligent life elsewhere in the universe. Reaffirming this is less necessary now than it was in the past when people more readily might think that extraterrestrials were somehow of Adam's race, be it as offspring or as progenitors, instead of having evolved on their own. Nonetheless it is important that no confusion be left on this score.[19]

Fifthly, the faithful need to be reminded that Revelation is complete, and no new message is going to come to us from any source, terrestrial or other. This is necessary because it is not uncommon for ETI proponents to affirm that:

> This powerful theme of alien beings acting as a conduit to the Ultimate...touches a deep chord in the human psyche. The attraction seems to be that by contacting superior beings in the sky, humans will be given access to privileged knowledge, and that the resulting broadening of our horizons will in some sense bring us a step closer to God.[20]

The *CCC* clearly maintains that there will be no new public revelation:

> The Christian economy, therefore, since it is the new and definitive Covenant, will never pass away; and no new public revelation is to be expected before the glorious manifestation of our Lord Jesus Christ.[21]

The *CCC* statement is based on Gal. 1:8:

> I am astonished at the promptness with which you have turned away from the one who called you and have decided to follow a different version of the Good News. Not that there can be more than one Good News; it is merely that some troublemakers among you want to change the Good News of Christ; and let me

warn you that if anyone preaches a version of the Good News different from the one we have already preached to you, whether it be ourselves or an angel from heaven, he is to be condemned.

Plainly, a Catholic cannot countenance the notion that ETIs bring us some new spiritual message improving upon Christ's revelation.[22]

Finally, the Church is likely to tell the faithful so long as the above points are safeguarded, they are free to speculate as to whether ETI exists or not, for it is possible to adopt either viewpoint without necessarily denying any article of faith. However, caution will be most likely be advised, as there are certain scenarios which cannot be accepted without compromising the faith (such as that Christ died and rose more than once), and others that the faith renders at least highly questionable.

So I rest my case that, on the assumption that Christianity is true, ETI existence is possible, but not probable. I have argued both that one *can* hold that ETI exists without implicitly rejecting part of Christian message, and that one *can* reject the probable arguments that I have given against ETI existence without prejudice to the faith. At the same time, the probable arguments that I have given against ETI existence, on the assumption that Christianity is true, certainly outweigh the probable arguments for. (The chief argument for is taken from the notion that God should make more of better things; the fact that there are a tremendous number of stars proves nothing.)

The majority of my arguments against the probability of ETI existence were derived by looking to the central role that Christ, the Word Incarnate, plays in the history of the universe or by looking to the wisdom of God in creation. The only one of my main arguments that did not do so was the dialectical argument against the existence of unfallen ETIs that was based on a consideration of an inherent weakness in the nature of material rational beings. The interactivity argument looked to the wisdom of God through which created beings have a causal order to each other. The other four out of six main arguments against ETI existence have centered on Christ.[23] Two of them looked to the fact that human nature was originally created in view of the future Incarnation of the Word, while a third looked to what Scripture tells us concerning Christ's desire in regard to his salvific death. A fourth argument did appeal to the special relationship that humans have to God, namely, to the fact that the details of the Incarnation, Passion, and Resurrection, which are the central events in the universe, are so tailored to man that it is difficult to envisage that some other material rational being would also be part of this story. Ultimately, however, even this argument against ETI drawn from human specialness ultimately centers on Christ. For God intended from the very first to send his Son into the world, and it was part of his plan for the world to create man in his image and put him to the test, knowing from the very outset that man would fall and be in need of redemption.[24]

Christians then should not be cowed by unwarranted accusations that the rejection of the existence of ETI amounts to arrogance. Moreover, they should keep in mind that all of the scientific and philosophical arguments in favor of ETI existence are at best weak, and in most cases flawed. In the final analysis, Christians should be wary of jumping on the ETI bandwagon, lest it come at the expense of denying Christ's central role in the universe, or denigrating Divine Wisdom, or repudiating the place human beings have in creation as known to the believer through Revelation.

Epilogue

Upon telling a friend that a lot of people think that ETIs exist, and that speculation about whether their arrival will spell the demise of Christianity is becoming more and more common, she quipped: "Are they lonely?" In some cases, at least, ETI proponents appear to be searching for someone or something. Paul Davies is not the only one to note that belief in ETIs "stems in part...from a need to find a wider context for our lives than this earthly existence provides."[1] Barrow and Tipler, quoting Fred Hoyle, also remark: "one strongly suspects a psychological motivation common to both beliefs [i.e., ETIs and UFOs], namely, 'the expectation that we are going to be saved from ourselves by some miraculous interstellar intervention....'"[2]

I, as Roman Catholic, believe that what people are looking for is a relationship with our Lord and Savior, Jesus Christ. I could not put this more eloquently that David Wilkinson[3] does in his book *Alone in the Universe?*, and so I shall close with his words:

> The need in a cosmic context for companionship, for purpose, for self-understanding, for reassurance and for help to make things better are all real. They are an expression of men and women made in the image of the Creator of the Universe, yet feeling alienated from God and from their true selves. The Christian faith gives answers to these questions. We are not alone. The God who made the Universe wants to be in relationship with us. There is a purpose to our existence. We are created as an act of extravagant love by God. We can understand ourselves by reference to and experience of that love. That same love is a source of security, and out of that love God came in Jesus to offer salvation here and now....This invitation is to make personal contact. This involves making a commitment on the basis of trust. This commitment is demanding. On God's side it is forgiveness, companionship and his own power given to the

life of the Christian. On our side it means opening up our lives to be changed, and following God's way of self-giving love....'Therefore go and make disciples of all nations, baptizing them in the name of the Father and of the Son and of the Holy Spirit, and teaching them to obey everything I have commanded you. And surely I am with you always, to the very end of the age.' We are not alone in the universe.[4]

Endnotes

Introduction

1. I was reticent to use the abbreviation, ETI (Extraterrestrial Intelligence) because it is reminiscent of "pure intelligences," whereas the beings of interest here have bodies. IET (Intelligent Extraterrestrials) would have better suited my purposes. However, I will respect common usage. When ETI is used as an adjective, it should be understood to mean "intelligent extraterrestrial."

2. Robert Jastrow, "A Cosmic Perspective on Human Existence," in *God for the 21st Century*, ed. Russell Stannard (Philadelphia: Templeton Foundation Press, 2000), 63.

3. Thomas Paine, *The Age of Reason* (Buffalo, NY: Prometheus Books, 1984), 52.

4. Steven Dick, "Cosmotheology: Theological Implications of the New Universe," in *Many Worlds: The New Universe, Extraterrestrial Life & the Theological Implications*, ed. Steven Dick (Philadelphia: Templeton Foundation Press, 2000), 202.

5. Paul Davies, *Are We Alone?* (New York: Basic Books, 1995), 54, 55.

6. Robert Jastrow, "A Cosmic Perspective on Human Existence," in *God for the 21st Century*, 62.

7. See Stanley Jaki, *Cosmos and Creator* (Chicago: Regnery Gateway, 1980), 118.

8. Kenneth J. Delano, *Many Worlds, One God* (Hicksville, New York: New York Exposition Press, 1977).

9. See Steven J. Dick, *Life on Other Worlds The 20th-Century Extraterrestrial Life Debate* (Cambridge: Cambridge University Press, 1998), 250.

10. See Pius XII, *Divino Afflante Spiritu* (Boston: The Daughters of St. Paul, c1943), #28: "[T]he Catholic exegete will find invaluable help in

an assiduous study of those works, in which the Holy Fathers, the Doctors of the Church and the renowned interpreters of past ages have explained the Sacred Books. For, although sometimes less instructed in profane learning and in the knowledge of languages than the scripture scholars of our time, nevertheless by reason of the office assigned to them by God in the Church, they are distinguished by a certain subtle insight into heavenly things and by a marvelous keenness of intellect, which enables them to penetrate to the very innermost meaning of the divine word and bring to light all that can help to elucidate the teaching of Christ and promote holiness of life."

11 See David Wilkenson, *Alone in the Universe* (Crowborough, East Sussex, Great Britain: Monarch Publications, 1997), 143: "Third, belief in extraterrestrial intelligence expresses that we want to find out about ourselves. Humans do that fundamentally in relationship. Science fiction has used this device on many occasions. Star Trek reflected the Martian culture of the 1960s, exploring themes such as racism through encounters with 'aliens'. We want to find out about aliens because we want to find out about ourselves." This theme has also been elaborated on by Alfred Karcher of Iowa State University in a talk given September 2000 at the Center for Theology and the Natural Sciences conference held at Iowa State University: "This is what I believe to be the root of our fondness for aliens. It is not that they tell us what *they* are, it is that they tell *us* that we are human."

12 *Rare Earth* (2000), a book arguing that complex life is uncommon in the universe, had hardly been out a year when *Life Everywhere* (2001) appeared in print arguing just the opposite.

13 See John Paul II, *Fides et Ratio* (Washington, D.C.: United States Catholic Conference, 1998), #63, 94: "[I]t has seemed to me urgent to re-emphasize with this Encyclical Letter the Church's intense interest in philosophy—indeed the intimate bond which ties theological work to the philosophical search for truth." The entire chapter six is devoted to explaining philosophy's contribution to theology.

14 See Ted Peters, "Exo-Theology: Speculations on Extraterrestrial Life," in *The Gods Have Landed*, ed. James R. Lewis (Albany: State University of New York Press, 1995), 197-200. The section is subtitled: "Fundamentalist Literature: UFOs as Chariots of Satan."

15 Aquinas is hard put to find any point to an angel being united to a physical body, since angels have no need of bodies. He finally says that

such a being would be "united to the body as form not for the sake of intellectual operation, but for the sake of the execution of its active power, according to which it is able to attain to likeness to God as to causality, by [causing] the motion of the heavens" (*Quaestio Disputata de Anima* in *Quaestiones Disputatae*, vol. 2, ed. P. Bazzi [Turin: Marietti, 1965], unicus, art. 8, ad 3). See Marie I. George, "Aquinas on Intelligent Extra-Terrestrial Life," *The Thomist*, 65.2 (April 2001), 239-258.

16 See Aquinas, *Summa Theologiae*, ed. Instituti Studiorum Medievalium Ottaviensis (Ottawa: Commissio Piana, 1953), I, q. 84, art. 6, sc: "As the Philosopher shows in Bk. I of the *Metaphysics* and at the end of the *Posterior Analytics*, the beginning of our [intellectual] knowledge is from sensation." (Hereafter cited as *ST*.)

17 See *ST* I, q. 55, art. 2: "[L]ower intellectual substances, namely, human souls, have an intellective power that is not complete by nature; it is completed in them successively, through this that they receive intelligible species from things. The intellectual potency in higher spiritual substances, i.e., in angels are naturally complete through connatural intelligible species, insofar as they have connatural intelligible species for understanding all those things which they are naturally able to know....Lower spiritual substances, namely, [human] souls, have their being in proximity to the body, insofar as they are forms of bodies; and therefore, from this mode of being itself, it belongs to them that their intellectual perfection is attained from bodies and through bodies; otherwise it would be in vain that they were united to bodies."

18 Allen Tough, *Crucial Questions about the Future* (Lanham, Maryland: University of America Press, 1991), 91. The part Tough quotes is taken from Francis Drake.

19 Ernan McMullin notes that, in accord with a view popular among some philosophers of mind, ETIs may possibly have a mind which is purely material, with the matter in question operating at the highest level capable to it; such a mind does not survive the death of the body. See Ernan McMullin, "Life and Intelligence Far from Earth: Formulating Theological Issues," in *Many Worlds*, 170. The fact that our ideas are universal, unchanging and immaterial speaks against this view, but it would take me too far from my main purpose to elaborate on the argument here.

20 I would not deny that animals possess practical intelligence in the sense that they have the ability to recognize appropriate means to an end. However, they, unlike beings that are intelligent in the narrow sense of the word, never determine the appropriate means to an end by the application of universal principles. See Marie I. George, "Thomas Aquinas Meets Nim Chimpsky," *The Aquinas Review*, 10 (2003), 1-50.

21 See Jaki, *Cosmos and Creator*, 124-25: "[P]rojects [for the detection of ETI are] based on the philosophy...that intellects are a mere epiphenomenon of biochemical diversification and therefore thrive in every nook and cranny of the universe. Only a theist, for whom intellects are a special creation of God, can look at the question of ETI as a truly open question which cannot be prejudged scientifically."

22 *Catechism of the Catholic Church* (Bloomingdale, Ohio: Apostolate for Family Consecration, 1994), #356, 357. Hereafter cited as *CCC*. See *ST* III, q. 27, art. 2: [O]nly the rational creature can contract fault...."

23 See John Paul II, "Theories of Evolution," Address to the Pontifical Academy of Sciences, October 22, 1996, *First Things* 71 (March 1997), #5, 28: "Consequently, theories of evolution which, in accordance with the philosophies inspiring them, consider the spirit as emerging from the forces of living matter or as mere epiphenomenon of this matter are incompatible with the truth about man. Nor are they able to ground the dignity of man."

24 *CCC* # 363 and #366.

25 See *ST* I, q. 12, art. 4, ad 3 where Aquinas, while discussing the question of whether some created intellect can see the divine nature by its natural ability, maintains that: "the sense of sight, which is entirely material, in no manner can be raised to something immaterial. But our or the angelic intellect, because it is raised in some manner above matter according to nature, is able to be raised beyond its nature by grace to something higher [namely, to the knowledge of self-subsisting being, i.e., God]."

26 *CCC* #365.

27 Pius XII, *Humani Generis* (Boston: Daughters of St. Paul, 1950), #37, 15. The footnote refers us to Rom. 5:12-19. Rom. 5:17 reads: "If it is certain that death reigned over everyone as the consequence of one man's fall, it is even more certain that one man, Jesus Christ, will cause

everyone to reign in life who receives the free gift that he does not deserve, of being made righteous."

28 *The Council of Trent*, Session VI in *Dogmatic Canons and Decrees* (Rockford, Illinois: Tan Books and Publishers, Inc., 1977), chap. 1, 22.

29 *CCC* #404.

30 *CCC* #260 cites Acts 17:24 in affirming "Because of its common origin *the human race forms a unity*, for 'from one ancestor [God] made all nations to inhabit the whole earth.' The footnote refers us to Tob. 8:6: "It was you who created Adam, you who created Eve his wife to be his help and support; and from these two the human race was born."

Chapter 1—The Son of Man and ETI

1 See *CCC* #457.

2 See *CCC* #108: "[T]he Christian faith is not a 'religion of the book'."

3 Thomas Aquinas gives several philosophical arguments that there can be only one human species, e.g., "[G]ranted, there is not some kind of living thing that possesses intellect among mortal living things, other than the human species. For since the intellect does not have a corporeal organ, those that possess intellect are not able to be diversified according to the diverse physical make-up (complexionem) of organs, as the species of sensitive beings are diversified according to diverse make-ups (complexiones), by which they are related in diverse ways to the operations of sensation" (*In Aristotelis Librum De Anima Commentarium* [Italy: Marietti, 1959], #293, 294). Aquinas appears to be concerned with the philosophical, and not the biological, notion of "species." I will examine this matter in chapter five.

4 Translations of the Bible are taken from *The Jerusalem Bible*, ed. Alexander Jones (Garden City, NY: 1966).

5 See Michael J. Crowe, *The Extraterrestrial Life Debate 1750-1900: The Idea of a Plurality of Worlds from Kant to Lowell* (New York: Cambridge University Press, 1986), 413.

6 See Crowe, *The ET Life Debate 1750-1900*, 303. Note that I do not intend to consider scriptural references to putative ETIs unless they are accompanied by some indication that what is being spoken about are ETIs, and not other beings such as angels or the celestial bodies. For example, there is no reason to take "all the stars of the morning

were singing for joy" (Jb. 38:7) to refer to ETIs, in addition to which other more parsimonious interpretations are available. Similarly, while I acknowledge that the Genesis passage concerning the Nephilim lacks an obvious interpretation (there may be interpretations offered by Church Fathers or Doctors that I am unaware of), at the same time it does not speak in any clear way of ETIs either ("The Nephilim were on the earth at that time [and even afterward] when the sons of God resorted to the daughters of man, and had children by them. These are the heroes of days gone by, the famous men" [Gen. 6:4].)

7   See William Whewell who cites Ps. 8 at the very beginning of his book *Of the Plurality of Worlds*, ed. Michael Ruse (Chicago: The University of Chicago Press, 2001), rpt. 1853 edition.

8   C. S. Lewis is to be thanked here for one of the more systematic considerations of the possibile relations between Christ and ETIs. See C. S. Lewis, "Religion and Rocketry," in *Fern-Seed and Elephants*, ed. Walter Hooper (London: Fontana, 1975).

9   Pius XII, *Humani Generis*, (Boston: Daughters of St. Paul, c1950), #26.

10 *Scriptum super Sententiis*, (Paris: Lethielleux, 1956), Bk. II, dist. 4, q. 1, art. 3. (Hereafter cited as *Sent*.)

11 II *Sent*. dist. 4, q. 1, art. 3, sed contra 3.

12 II *Sent*. dist. 29, q. 1, art. 2. Note that Aquinas understands things to depend *solely* on the will of God (or on the *simple* will of God), when there is no necessity that God will them. There are other things that depend on the will of God, such as God's love of himself and God's love of creation, which could not be otherwise.

13 See *ST* I, q. 95, art. 1. The children of Adam and Eve children also would have been created in grace, if Adam had not sinned, given that "original justice...was an accident of the nature of the species, not as caused by the principles of the species, but as a certain divine gift given to the whole nature" (*ST* I, q. 100, art. 1). See also II *Sent*., dist. 20, q. 2, art. 3.

14 See Aquinas, *Quaestiones Disputatae de Potentia* in *Quaestiones Disputatae*, vol. 2, ed. P. Bazzi et al. (Turin: Marietti, 1965), q. 5, arts. 3 and 4. In art. 3, Aquinas argues that God can annihilate things. In art. 4, Aquinas reasons that God does not in fact do so: "God wants creatures to exist for the sake of his goodness, namely, so that they represent it and imitate it according to their mode, which certainly

comes about insofar as they have being from him, and subsist in their natures."

15 *CCC* #1261. There is a theory that the unbaptized children will be given the exercise of free will and presented with one choice, somewhat in the manner of the angels, and on the basis of that choice will merit eternal life or eternal damnation. I used to find this theory far-fetched. However, it does preserve the value of baptizing infants (since they would have the advantage of being assured of beatitude), affords all rational beings a chance at supernatural happiness, and allows all the good to be gathered together in one Church Triumphant of which Christ is the head.

16 The question of whether unbaptized children are afflicted by the loss of supernatural happiness is subject to debate. Even Aquinas gives different explanations of why they do not suffer. For example, in *Quaestiones Disputatae de Malo* q. 5, art. 2 he says that it exceeds natural knowledge to know that the perfect good for which man was made is the beatific vision (this is only known to us by faith), and thus since these children lack faith, they have no idea what they are missing. Yet this explanation seems to conflict with what he says in other places, e.g., in *ST* I-II, q. 3, art. 8, Aquinas maintains that the desire to know the ultimate cause in itself is natural to man, and thus that "it is required for perfect happiness that the intellect arrive at the essence itself of the first cause." Thus knowledge of the supernatural ultimate end seems to fall under the unbaptized children's natural knowledge. This question is part of the greater debate concerning the possibility of a purely natural end for man.

17 See II *Sent.*, dist. 33, q. 2, art. 2: "Every human being having the use of free will is proportioned to obtaining eternal life, because he can prepare himself for grace, through which eternal life is merited; and therefore if such people fail to obtain it, this will be a very great sorrow for them because they lost something which could have been theirs."

18 Whether in a different order of providence God would have created man with a purely natural end is one of the topics that was part of the "mid-century crisis at the time of *Humani generis*, and of persistent controversy since" (Steven A. Long, "On the Possibility of a Purely Natural End for Man," *The Thomist* 64 [January 2000], 213). In addition to Long's article, some other recent work on the subject includes Denis Bradley's *Aquinas on the Twofold Human Good* (Washington, D. C.:

The Catholic University of America, 1997) and Peter A. Pagan-Aguiar's "Human Finality," *The Thomist* 64 (July 2000), 375-400.

19 See II *Sent.*, dist. 5, q. 2, art. 2.

20 II *Sent.*, d. 33, q. 2, art. 2.

21 See *ST* I, q. 100, art. 2.

22 *CCC* #760.

23 *CCC* #336.

24 *ST* III, q. 8, art. 4. See also *ST* I, q. 108, art. 8: "Nevertheless certain held that not all of the saved were assumed into the orders of the angels, but only those who were virgins or who were perfect; others held that the saved constituted their own order, as divided against the entire society of the angels. But this is contrary to Augustine, who says in *De Civitate Dei* (Bk. 12) that there will not be two societies of men and of angels, but one; because beatitude consists in adhering to the one God."

25 See *Dominus Iesus*, Congregation for the Doctrine of the Faith (Manchester, UK: Catholic Truth Society, 2000), #18, 15. See also John Paul II, *Redemptoris missio* (Washington, D.C.: United States Catholic Conference, 1990), #14-20, 26-36 and especially #18, 31: "The kingdom cannot be detached either from Christ or from the Church."

26 See Crowe who recounts the view of Jean Terrasson: "Admitting that Christ's terrestrial incarnation and redemption have sufficient merit for the entire universe, he nonetheless suggests that because Christ has a role both as savior and as teacher, his incarnation as teacher on sinless planets is fully appropriate" (*The ET Life Debate 1750-1900*, 135).

27 *ST* III, q. 3, art. 7 ("On Whether One Divine Person is Able to Assume Two Human Natures").

28 See Crowe, *The ET Life Debate 1750-1900*, 135: "At another point [Terrasson] counters the claim that Scripture explicitly states that there is but one Lord by interpreting it as applying only to the divine part of Christ's nature."

29 Aquinas notes that the manner in which the Father gave this name, "Lord," to a man is through the grace of union, by which Christ would be at the same time God and man. The incarnation was not a reward

for Christ's passion, but preceded it. However, sometimes in Scripture something is said to happen, when it becomes known. Christ's divinity was much more manifest after the resurrection. Therefore, the Father does not give Christ the name "Lord" as if Christ did not have it from the time of his incarnation, but he is said to give it when Christ comes to be commonly venerated as Lord. See Thomas Aquinas, *Super Epistolas S. Pauli*, ed. P. Raphaelis Cai, O.P., vol. 2 (Rome: Marietti, 1953), ad Philippenses #70, 71.

[30] *Summa Contra Gentiles*, ed. C. Pera, O.P. et al. (Turin: Marietti, 1961), Bk. IV, chap. 34. (Hereafter cited as *SCG*.)

[31] To be "lord" and to be "head" are closely related, but not exactly the same thing. One is called "Lord" in virtue of one's power, whereas one is denominated "head" by likeness to certain features of a bodily head. These features include perfection (the head is the seat of all five senses), sublimity (the head is the highest member), influence (in a certain manner sensation and motion flow to the other parts of the body from the head), governance (the head directs the members in virtue of being the seat of both the interior and exterior senses), and conformity of nature with the other members. See Thomas Aquinas, *Super Epistolas S. Pauli*, ed. P. Raphaelis Cai, O.P., vol. 1 (Rome: Marietti, 1953), I Ad Corinthios, #587 and *Quaestiones Disputatae de Veritate*, in *Quaestiones Disputatae*, vol. I, ed. Raymond M. Spiazzi, O.P. (Turin: Marietti, 1964), q. 29, art. 4

[32] I disagree with Gottfried Nebe who maintains that the angels are not part of the Body of Christ (the Church). Nebe holds that in Col. 2:10 "Christ [is] a ruler over the cosmic powers...the term 'head' [is used here] to mean 'chief, highest, supreme' and so on. We do not seem to have here the specific image of the head of a body with various parts...." ("Christ, The Body of Christ and Cosmic Powers in Paul's Letters and the New Testament as a Whole," in *Politics and Theopolitics in the Bible and Postbiblical Literature*, eds. Henning Reventlow, Yair Hoffman and Benjamin Uffenheimer [Sheffield, England: Sheffield Academic Press, 1994], 115). Four of Aquinas's criteria for why a person would be called a "head" (mentioned in the previous note) clearly apply to Christ in his relation to the angels. Also, it is traditional to refer to angels as saints, e.g., St. Michael the Archangel. This indicates that angels are thought to be part of the communion of saints—which would seem to be the same thing as Christ's mystical body.

33 *Quaestiones Disputatae de Veritate*, q. 29, art. 4. The question addressed is: "Whether it belongs to Christ according to his human nature to be the head of grace."

34 *Ibid.*, ad 3.

35 Duns Scotus, *Summa Theologica*, vol. 5, ed. Hieronymus de Montefortino (Rome: Typographia Sallustiana, 1903), q. 8, art. 4.

36 See *ST* III, q. 70, art. 4 ("Whether Circumcision Conferred Justifying Grace"): "[I]n circumcision grace is conferred as to every effect of grace; nevertheless otherwise than in baptism. For in baptism, grace is conferred from the power (virtute) of baptism itself, a power which baptism possesses insofar as it is an instrument of the already accomplished passion of Christ. In circumcision, however, grace is conferred not by the power of the circumcision, but in virtue of faith in the passion of Christ, of which circumcision was the sign; namely, so that a person who received circumcision professed that he embraces such faith, either an adult for himself, or someone else for children. Whence too the Apostle says, Rom. 4:11, that 'Abraham received the sign of circumcision, a gage of the justice of faith;' namely, because the justice was from the faith signified, not from the circumcision which signified it. And because baptism operates instrumentally in virtue of the passion of Christ, whereas circumcision does not, therefore baptism imprints a character incorporating man into Christ, and confers grace more abundantly than circumcision; for greater is the effect of a thing when it is already present than when it exists in hope."

37 One might wonder why the Fathers of the Old Testament had to await Christ's death and resurrection in order to enter into the kingdom of heaven, given that they were justified by their faith. Aquinas maintains that: "When a person was circumcised, original sin was taken away on the part of the person; an impediment to entering the kingdom of heaven nevertheless remained on the part of the whole nature, which was removed though the passion of Christ. And therefore even a person who was baptized before the passion of Christ did not gain entry into the kingdom. And also circumcision, if it would have taken place after the passion of Christ, would have given entry into the kingdom" (*ST* III, q. 70, art. 4, ad 4).

38 *ST* III, q. 62, art. 6. Note that this position concords with the definition of the dogma of the Immaculate Conception: "definimus, doctrinam, quae tenet, beatissimam Virginem Mariam in primo

instanti suae conceptionis fuisse singulari omnipotentis Dei gratia et privilegio, intuitu meritorum Christi Iesu Salavatoris humani generis, ab omni originalis culpae labe praeservatam immunem...." (Pius IX, "Ineffabilis Deus" quoted in Denzinger, #2803). Pope Pius IX declares here that the Virgin Mary was preserved from original sin "by a singular grace and privilege of the almighty God, in view of the merits of Jesus Christ," and not that she was preserved in the said way by a grace coming from Jesus as man.

39 See Thomas Aquinas, *Super Epistolas S. Pauli*, ed. P. Raphaelis Cai, O.P., vol. 2 (Rome: Marietti, 1953), ad Colossenses, #100: "And therefore he says: 'Who is the head of every sovereignty and power,' insofar as he [Christ] is their king and Lord, not through conformity of nature, for in this manner he is head of men."

40 Questions which pertain to the hypostatic union are of the greatest difficulty, and I do not pretend to be able to resolve them. I note that Thomas Aquinas, on the related question of whether the Word would be two men if he assumed two human natures, gives two somewhat different answers. In the *Commentary on the Sentences* he says that "although Jesus and Peter [the name given to the Word in his supposed second incarnation] would be one supposit, nevertheless they would be called two men on account of the plurality of the natures assumed, but keeping the unity of the supposit, the diversity of natures would not impede that one would be predicated of the other, [i.e., it could be said that Jesus is Peter]; because the identity of supposit suffices for the truth of the predication" (III *Sent.*, dist. 1, q. 2, art. 5, ad 2). Yet in his later work, the *Summa Theologiae*, Aquinas maintains that: "The assumed nature, however, as to something stands in the manner of a vestment, granted that there is not a likeness on all points, as was said above. And therefore if a divine person would assume two human natures, he would be called one man having two human natures on account of the unity of the supposit" (*ST* III, q. 3, art. 7, ad 2). Our hypothetical case, unlike the one Aquinas takes up, involves two different natures, and so Aquinas's latter solution, even if correct, does not seem applicable. I bring it up chiefly to show the difficulty of such considerations.

41 See *CCC* #280.

42 Aquinas, *Super Epistolas S. Pauli*, I *Cor.*, #92. See *SCG* IV, chap. 55: "For the union in the person is made in such a manner that what is

proper to both natures, namely the divine and the human, remain... and therefore when Christ suffers even death and the other things which pertain to his humanity, his divinity remains impassible; although on account of the unity of the person, we may say that God suffered and died; an example of which in a certain manner appears in our case, because when our flesh dies, the soul remains immortal." See also *SCG* IV, chap. 48: "What is proper to the person of Christ, however, is not enunciated by reason of his human nature, unless with some addition expressed or understood."

43 *CCC* #464. The Latin version reads: "Eventus unicus and prorsus singularis Incarnationis Filii Dei non significat Iesum Christum esse partim Deum et partium hominem.... Ille factus est vere Homo, vere permanens Deus."

44 See *ST* III, q. 27, art. 2.

45 The official version of the *CCC* is the Latin version. However, since the meanings of the Latin words "singularis" and "unicus" correspond very closely to the meanings of "singular" and "unique," and because distinguishing the meaning of these English words is useful for our discussion, I am giving only the English definitions of these two words (and only those that are relevant to our discussion): "singular 1 c: relating to a single instance 2: distinguished by superiority: EXCEPTIONAL 3: set apart or memorable as being out of the ordinary: UNUSUAL" (*Webster's New Collegiate Dictionary* [Springfield, Massachusetts: G. & C. Merriam Company, 1980]).

46 *Ibid.*: "unique 1 a: being the only one: SOLE b: producing only one result 2: being without a like or equal: UNEQUALED 3: very rare or uncommon: very unusual."

47 See *ST* III, q. 3, art. 5: "[A]ssumption involves two things: namely, the act itself of assuming and the term of the assumption. The principle of the act is divine power; the term is the person. Divine power, however, stands commonly and indifferently to all of the persons. Also, the common notion of personhood is also the same in the three persons, granted that the personal properties are different. Whenever a power stands indifferently to many, it can terminate its action at any one of them.,... Thus therefore divine power can unite human nature to the person of the Father or of the Holy Spirit, as it united it to the person of the Son."

48 See Ephesians 1:10: "...he would bring everything together under Christ, as head, everything in heaven and everything on earth." Aquinas, commenting upon this passage, says this: "*All things*, he [St. Paul] says, *which are in heaven*, i.e., the Angels—not that Christ died for the Angels, but by redeeming man, the fall of the Angels was repaired" (*Super Epistolas S. Pauli*, ed. P. Raphaelis Cai, vol. 2 [Rome: Marietti, 1953], ad Ephesios, #29).

49 See *CCC* #326: "The Scriptural expression 'heaven and earth' means all that exists, creation in its entirety. It also indicates the bond, deep within creation, that both unites heaven and earth and distinguishes the one from the other: 'the earth' is the world of men, while 'heaven' or 'the heavens' can designate both the firmament and God's own 'place'—'our Father in heaven' and consequently the 'heaven' too which is eschatological glory. Finally, 'heaven' refers to the saints and the 'place' of the spiritual creatures, the angels, who surround God."

50 Surprisingly few Christian authors take note of this passage from Scripture. John Jefferson Davis speaks of the importance of this passage at length in "Search for extraterrestrial intelligence and the Christian doctrine of redemption," in *Science and Christian Belief* 9.1 (April 1997), 21-34. Centuries earlier Beilby Porteus (1731-1808) also used this passage to support the view that any ETI in need of redemption would be redeemed through the cross of Christ. See Crowe, *The ET Life Debate 1750-1900*, 103.

51 See *Compendium Theologiae* in *Opuscula Theologica*, vol. 1, ed. Raymond A. Verardo, O.P. (Rome: Marietti, 1954), chap. 199: "...such is the condition of man while he lives in this mortal life that as he is not immobilely confirmed in the good, so neither is he immobilely obstinate in evil. Therefore, it pertains to the human condition that it is able to be purged from the infection of sin. It would not be fitting therefore that divine goodness set aside this ability completely unused; which would be the case if he had not procured a remedy for its reparation." See also *Quaestiones Disputatae de Malo* in *Quaestiones Disputatae*, vol. 2, ed. P. Bazzi et al. (Turin: Marietti, 1965), q. 5, art. 1, ad 1: "Man would have been made pointlessly and in vain if he was not able to attain happiness, as is the case of anything that cannot attain its ultimate end. Whence in order that man not be made pointlessly and in vain due to being born with original sin, God, from the beginning of humankind, proposed a remedy for man by which he would be

freed from this futility, namely, Jesus Christ as mediator between God and man, through faith in whom the impediment of original sin could be taken away."

52 See Paine, *The Age of Reason*, 59, 60. Paine rejects Christianity in favor of many inhabited worlds on the grounds that if there were a large number of human-like civilizations, Christ would thus be very busy traveling from world to world in an endless succession of deaths. This argument is based on the gratuitous assumption that Christ would have to die over and over. Paine fails to consider the alternative that Christ's death on Calvary was applied to all intelligent beings in need of redemption.

53 Quoted by Michael J. Crowe, *The ET Life Debate 1750-1900*, 103. See also, *ibid.*, 412: "Montignez in his fourth essay develops the thesis that although Christ came only to the earth, he is nonetheless Lord of the universe, and moreover 'the blood which flowed on Calvary has gushed out on the universality of creation...; has bathed not only our world, but all the worlds which roll in space....'" See also *ibid.*, 181 where Crowe quotes de Maistre: "If the inhabitants of the other planets are not like us guilty of sin, they have no need of the same remedy, and if, on the contrary, the same remedy is necessary for them, are the theologians of whom I speak then to fear that the power of the sacrifice which has saved us is unable to extend to the moon? The insight of Origen is much more penetrating and comprehensive when he writes: 'The altar was at Jerusalem, but the blood of the victim bathed the universe.'"

54 Abbé Joseph Émile Filachou, *De la pluralité des mondes*, quoted by Crowe in *The ET Life Debate 1750-1900*, 411.

55 *CCC* #772. It quotes Ep. 1:10.

56 Thomas Aquinas, *Super Epistolas S. Pauli*, ed. P. Raphaelis Cai, vol. 2, (Rome: Marietti, 1953), ad Hebraeos #130: "The Apostle makes three points [at Heb. 2:11]. First he shows that we depend on Christ. For the sanctified depend on the sanctifier—Christ, however, is the sanctifier....Therefore it is well said that we depend on him because he is the author and sanctifier, while he himself depends on the Father from whom he has it that he sanctifies, which is the second point. But all, namely, he who sanctifies and we who are sanctified, are from one, namely, from the Father, which is the third point."

57 *Ibid.* #131.

58 III *Sent.*, q. 2, art. 2, qla. 2.

59 Tt. 1:14 says something quite similar to Heb. 2:14: "He sacrificed himself for us in order to set us free from all wickedness and to purify a people so that it could be his very own...." One could say, however, that Christ's wanting to purify a people so that it could be his very own does not exclude that he purify other peoples by his sacrifice, or alternately that ETI peoples who were purified would henceforth form one people with us, as the Gentiles were united to the Jews through the cross of Christ (see Ep. 2:15). It still may be the case that understanding Tt. 1:14 to say the same thing as Heb. 2:14 is a better interpretation.

60 A well-known dictum of Gregory Nazianzus which might seem applicable to the Christianity-ETI debate is: "That which is not assumed is not redeemed;" or more accurately: "That which was not assumed is not healed; but that which is united to God is saved (to gar aproslepton, atherapeuton ho de henotai to theô, touto kai sozetai)" (W. H. Kent, "Atonement" in the *Catholic Encyclopedia*, eds. Charles G. Herbermann, Edward A. Pace, Condé B. Pallen, Thomas J. Shahan, John J. Wynne [New York: The Encyclopedia Press, Inc., 1908], vol. 2, 55). However, it is a matter of fittingness, not of absolute necessity that a person of the Trinity assume the nature of a fallen race for the purpose of redeeming it. God could save fallen beings in another manner, but this is the one most in keeping with his wisdom and justice. See *ST* III, q. 31, art. 1: "Christ assumed human nature so that he might purge it from corruption. Human nature would not have been in need of purgation unless it was infected through the original fault which came down from Adam. And therefore it was fitting that he assumed flesh from matter derived from Adam, so that this very nature through assumption could be cured."

61 The Latin uses the word "debuit" which has a range of meanings similar to "ought" in English, some of which imply stronger obligation or necessity than others. The Greek employs "opheile," a word weaker than the English "essential." "Opheile" means useful, advantageous, beneficial. One can maintain that it is fitting that the one who saves be of the same race as the saved, without saying that it is the only way an intelligent race can be saved.

62 See Phm. 10: "I am appealing to you for a child of mine, whose father I became while wearing these chains."

63 *ST* I, q. 33, art. 4.

Chapter 2—Something Wrong with Being Special?

1 John Paul II, *Evangelium Vitae* (Washington, D.C.: United States Catholic Conference, 1995), #53, 22.

2 See *SCG* III, chap. 111: "Oportet tamen aliquam rationem providentiae specialem observari circa intellectuales et rationales naturas prae aliis creaturis...."

3 Two examples of Christianity-ETI arguments turning on the notion of "special" are found in notes 31 and 38 below.

4 Arthur C. Clarke quoted by Kendrick Frazier in *Extraterrestrial Intelligence: The First Encounter*, ed. James L. Christian (Buffalo, New York: 1976), 74.

5 See *ST* I, q. 93, art. 3: "[W]e can speak about the image of God in two ways. First, as to what is first considered in the notion of image, which is the intellectual nature. And in this way the image of God is more present in angels than in human beings, because the intellectual nature is more perfect in them."

6 *Gaudium et Spes* in *The Documents of Vatican II*, ed. Walter M. Abbott, S.J. (New York: The American Press, 1966), #12, 210.

7 See *CCC* #364 and #366.

8 *SCG* III, chap. 111.

9 *SCG* III, chap. 112: "First, the very knowledge belonging to an intellectual nature, according as it has control over its act [domina sui actus], calls for the care of providence by which it is provided for for its own sake; the condition of others, which do not have control over their acts, indicates that care is not to be shown them for their own sakes. For what only acts when moved by another has the notion of an instrument; what acts of itself has the notion of a principal agent. Instruments are not desired for their own sake, but as useful to the principal agent; whence it is necessary that all diligence shown in activities concerning instruments be referred to the principal agent as to an end. The care shown the principal agent, be it by himself or by another, insofar as he is principal agent, is for his own sake. Therefore intellectual creatures are governed by God as cared for for their own sakes, other creatures as ordered to rational creatures....When we say

that intellectual substances are ordered by divine providence for their own sakes, we do not understand this to mean that they are not further ordered to God and to the perfection of the universe. For they are said to be cared for for their own sakes because the goods which are dispensed in view of divine providence are not given to them for the sake of the utility of another; the things which are given to them, yield to their use by divine ordinance."

10 Aristotle argues in the *Politics* that nature "has made all animals for the sake of man" (1256b22).

11 See *Gaudium et Spes* in *The Documents of Vatican II*, #12: "According to the almost unanimous opinion of believers and unbelievers alike, all things *on earth* should be related to man as their center and crown." (emphasis mine)

12 Filachou, *De la pluralité des mondes*, quoted by Crowe in *The ET Life Debate 1750-1900*, 411.

13 *CCC* #358.

14 *CCC* #331.

15 II *Sent.* dist. 1, q. 2, art. 3, ad 3. See also II *Sent.*, dist. 1, text of Peter Lombard, 7, 8: "For all things are ours, as the Apostle says, namely, the superior and the equal and the inferior. Superior things are ours for the completion of our joy (perfruendum), as the triune God; equals are for living together with, namely, angels; which even if they are in a certain manner our superiors, in the future will be our equals; who even in a certain manner are ours because they are for our use as the things of lords are said to belong to the servants, not by way of dominion, but because they are at their disposal to be used. And in certain passages of Scripture the angels themselves are said to serve us when they are sent to minister to us for our sakes."

16 See *ST* I, q. 20, art. 4, ad 2: "Speaking about human nature in general [as opposed to the human nature assume by the Word] in comparison to the angelic nature, equality is found according to the order of grace and glory, since same be the 'measure of man and of angel,' as it is said in Apoc. 21:17; nevertheless in such a manner that certain angels are preferred to certain men, and certain men to certain angels."

17 See *ST* I, q. 23, art. 6, ad 1: "God would not permit some to fall unless he would raise up others, according to Jb. 34:24: 'He crushes innumerably many, and puts others in their place.' For in this manner, men

will be substituted in the place of the fallen angels...." See also *ST* I, 108, art. 8 ("Whether Humans will be Assumed into the Orders of Angels"): "And therefore through the gift of grace men are able to merit so much glory that they might be equal to the angels according to the individual grades of the angels."

18 See *ST* I, q. 20, art. 4, ad 2: "But as to the condition of nature, the angel is better than man. Therefore, God did not assume human nature because he loved man more absolutely speaking, but because man was in greater need. Just as good paterfamilias gives something precious to a sick servant that he does not give to his healthy son."

19 See *ST* I, q. 96, art. 2: "All things are in man in a certain manner; and therefore according to the manner in which he rules these things in himself, according to this same manner it belongs to him to rule over other things....Reason, however, in man has the place of ruler and not of a subject of rule. Whence man in his original state does not rule the angels; and thus when it is said [that man has dominion over] every creature, it is understood: every creature that is not in the image of God."

20 *CCC* #1042. The passage it quotes is *Lumen Gentium*, #48.

21 Christ was also the judge of the angels only as the Word of God since this judgment took place at the world's beginning. See *ST* III, q. 59, art. 6c and ad 1.

22 "Devil" in *The Catholic Encyclopedia*, vol. 4, 765.

23 Francisco Suarez, *De Angelis*, vol. 2, ed. D. M. André (Paris: Ludovicum Vivès, 1861), Bk. VII, c. 13, #30, 890.

24 Ibid., Bk. VII, c. 13, #32, 891. According to Suarez the fallen angels desired that God be united to their nature through a hypostatic union. Thus when it was revealed that God would unite himself to human nature and not to an angelic nature, the angels out of excessive self-love chose to regard the divine plan with repugnance: "Lucifer did not conform his will to the divine will, but desired for himself what God did not want to give him" (ibid., #10, 884).

25 It is hard to state what the exact relationship is between Christ and the saints of the Old Testament. Bonaventure describes the situation thus: "To the one who objects that that which does not have being cannot influence (influere-literally, "flow into") another, it ought to be said that this is true of influence through the mode of an efficient principle

(principii effectivi). This is not true as to influence through the mode of merit, however; for it suffices that it exist in the faith and love of the believer, and even through this that while it is believed and loved, the one believing and loving is vivified by it, and while it is also promised, from the divine promise itself the strictness of severity is in some manner placated, that he [God] may show his benevolence" (*Sententiarum* III, dist. 13, q. 3, ad 5 in *Opera Omnia*, ed. A. C. Peltier, vol. 4 [Paris: Ludovicus Vivès, 1865]).

26 See *CCC* #280: "Creation is the foundation of 'all God's saving plans,' the 'beginning of the history of salvation' that culminates in Christ. Conversely, the mystery of Christ casts conclusive light on the mystery of creation and reveals the end for which 'in the beginning God created the heavens and the earth': from the beginning, God envisaged the glory of the new creation in Christ."

27 See *ST* I, q. 73, art. 1: "The ultimate perfection, however, which is the end of the entire universe, is the perfect happiness of the saints which will be at the ultimate completion of the ages."

28 See Mk. 7:26-28: "Now the woman was a pagan…and she begged him to cast the devil out of her daughter. And he said to her, 'The children should be fed first, because it is not fair to take the children's food and throw it to the house of dogs.'" See also Rom., c. 11 which recounts that the Jews are the chosen people, while the Gentiles have been as grafted onto the tree of salvation.

29 Robert Jastrow, "A Cosmic Perspective on Human Existence," in *God for the 21st Century*, 62, 63.

30 Whewell, *Of the Plurality of Worlds*, 44, 45.

31 A number of authors point out that even human beings can have a special relationship with more than one person, e.g., David Wilkinson notes: "Even relationships at the same level can be unique and special. We have a unique relationship with our son which is very special indeed. However, that is not to say that we do not have an equally special but different relationship with our daughter" (*Alone in the Universe?*, 123). On the other hand, Aristotle rejects Plato's communal notion according to which each parent was to regard every child in one's society as one's own, on the grounds that it would dilute affection between parent and child. However, God is not subject to

the limitations of the human heart, and can have any number of special relationships with individuals or with races.

32 Montignez quoted by Michael J. Crowe, *The ET Life Debate 1750-1900*, 412.

33 See *CCC* #441: "In the Old Testament, 'son of God' is a title given to the angels, the Chosen People, the children of Israel, and their kings. It signifies an adoptive sonship that establishes a relationship of particular intimacy between God and his creature."

34 This passage is found in the Vulgate, but not in the Jerusalem Bible.

35 It is not uncommon for ETI advocates to generate a straw man argument by attributing to their opponents the view that humans are collectively remarkably selfless and learned. I discuss this sort of argument in c. 12 which is devoted to examining common fallacies committed in discussions of ETI and Christianity.

36 If the Word became incarnate a second time, it could be said that the first cause of the completion of the universe's destiny is the God-ETI, because of the unity of the two natures in one person; it could not, however, be said that this completion was due to the God-ETI in his ETI nature.

37 It is commonly held that heliocentrism caused the earth to be viewed of lesser importance than it was in the geocentric world view, by displacing it from the center of the universe. However, strong evidence to the contrary is found in the fact that Aristotelian cosmology had enjoyed a virtually unchallenged reign up until Galileo's day.

In Aristotelian cosmology, the center of the universe was not a noble and superior place. Rather it was where the heavy elements, such as earth, naturally accumulated, and also where generation and corruption occurred. It was the seemingly incorruptible heavenly bodies, moving in the heavens with an apparently unchanging and perfect motion, that were regarded as wonderful and divine, and *not* the stationary earth that was in the center of them all (see *De Caelo*, Bk. 1, chaps. 2 and 3 *On the Parts of Animals*, Bk. 1, chap. 5). It was not until Copernicus that the Aristotelian view received any serious challenge. In Galileo's own day Copernicus was not well received, and presumably the Aristotelian view of the earth still prevailed. Thus, as Dennis Danielson observes, Pico della Mirandola (1463-1494) referred to the earth as "the excrementary and filthy parts of the lower world," and Galileo acknowledged that the heliocentric view was in disaccord with the Aristotelian cosmology dominant in his day which regarded the earth as the "sump where the universe's filth and ephemera collect" (Danielson is quoted by Thomas E. Phillips, "Cosmologists: Scientific tools can lead to Christian revelations," *Research News*, October 2003, 11). Another piece of evidence against the notion that it was common for Christian thinkers before the Copernican revolution to place special importance on the supposedly central location of the earth is that a search of "center" and "central" in the CD-ROM version of *The Early Church Fathers* (Salem, Oregon: Harmony Media, Inc.) did not turn up a single passage to that effect. Nor have I ever seen a single Church figure quoted to that effect. The position I adopt here is developed at length by Dennis Danielson in a lecture entitled: "Copernicus and the Tale of the Pale Blue Dot" (www.english.ubc.ca/~ddaniels/), and by Guillermo Gonzalez and Jay W. Richards in chap. 12, "The Revisionist History of the Copernican Revolution," in The Privileged Planet (Washington, DC: Regnery Publishing Company, 2004). Note that those Christian thinkers who adopted the Aristotelian view were not logically constrained to regard the earth as bad, but only as less perfect than the heavenly bodies. (See *CCC* #299: "On many occasions the Church has had to defend the goodness of creation, including that of the physical world.")

38 Careful examination of the ways in which the faith does and does not hold humans to be special reveal how vague statements such as that of Paul Davies completely miss their mark: "Four hundred years ago, the Roman Catholic church burned Giordano Bruno at the stake for heresy. Among other things, he proposed the existence of an infinite number of inhabited worlds. Since this ran counter to the doctrine of man as God's supreme and special creation, Bruno was undermining a key tenet of the Christian faith at that time" (back cover of Dick, *Many Worlds*).

39 *CCC* #331.

Chapter 3—The Bible's Silence on ETI

1 Melanchthon's view as expressed by Steven J. Dick, *Plurality of Worlds* (Cambridge: Cambridge University Press, 1982), 88, 89.

2 See Aquinas, *De Quaestiones Disputatae de Potentia* in *Quaestiones Disputatae*, vol. 2, ed. P. Bazzi (Turin: Marietti, 1965), q. 6, art. 6.

3 Roland Puccetti, *Persons: a study of possible moral agents in the universe* (New York: Herder and Herder, 1969), 125, 126.
4 *Dei Verbum* in *The Documents of Vatican II*, #6.
5 Ibid., #11.
6 See *CCC* #82: "[T]he Church, to whom the transmission and interpretation of Revelation is entrusted, 'does not derive her certainty about all revealed truths from the holy Scriptures alone. Both Scripture and Tradition must be accepted and honored with equal sentiments of devotion and reverence'" (*Dei Verbum* #9).
7 See Dick, *Plurality of Worlds*, 99, where Dick quotes John Wilkins: "The lack of mention of other worlds in Genesis no more denied other worlds than its silence about planets denied their existence; 'tis besides the scope of the holy Ghost either in the new Testament or in the old, to reveale any thing unto us concerning the secrets of Philosophy.'...the negative authority of Scripture did not hold 'in those things which are not the fundamentalls of Religion.'"
8 While some argued that animate stars do not exist because no mention of them was made at the last judgment, Aquinas does not find this adequate reason to deny their existence. See Aquinas, *De Quaestiones Disputatae de Potentia*, q. 6, art. 6.
9 *CCC* #328.

Chapter 4—What Church Documents and Tradition Say about ETI

1 See "Fourth Session, April 8, 1546," in *Council of Trent*, ed. and trans. J. Waterworth (London: Dolman, 1848), 19, 20: "It decrees, that no one, relying on his own skill, shall,—in matters of faith, and of morals pertaining to the edification of Christine doctrine,—wresting the sacred Scripture to his own senses, presume to interpret the said sacred Scripture contrary to the sense which holy mother Church...hath held and doth hold; or even contrary to the unanimous consent of the Fathers...."
2 To my knowledge none of the later Doctors of the Church address the issue.
3 *The ET Life Debate 1750-1900*, 337. See *Rambler*, no. 38, 130 in *The Wellesley Index to Victorian Periodicals*, vol. 2, ed. Walter E. Houghton (Toronto: University of Toronto Press, 1972).

4 See Albertus Magnus, *De Caelo et Mundo*, in *Opera Omnia*, vol. 5 (Aedibus Aschendorff: Monasterii Westfalorum, 1971), 68.
5 Ibid., 68.
6 Ibid., 69.
7 Ibid., 69.
8 Ibid., 72.
9 See Aquinas, *In Duodecim Libros Metaphysicorum Aristotelis Expositio*, ed. Raymond M. Spiazzi, O.P. (Rome: Marietti, 1950), #2656-2663.
10 *ST* I, q. 47, art. 3.
11 Origen, *De Principiis*, 341. It is sometimes claimed that when Origen speaks of another world he understands it to be a kind of purgatory, and not part of a series of worlds. (See Thomas F. O'Meara, "Christian Theology and Extraterrestrial Intelligent Life," in *Theological Studies* 60 [1999] 9, footnote #15.) I disagree with this view because the *De Principiis* text gives as the reason for why there had to be other worlds that otherwise one would have to say that God was inactive before he made our world—it is not a matter of a human need for purgation or successive purgations.
12 See Origen, *De Principiis*, Bk. II, chap. 4, in *Fathers of the Third Century*, vol. 4, ed. A. Cleveland Coxe (Grand Rapids, Michigan: Wm. B. Eerdmans Publishing Company, 1985), 272: "It seems to me impossible for a world to be restored for the second time, with the same order and with the same amount of births, and deaths, and actions; but that a diversity of worlds may exist with changes of no unimportant kind...."
13 See Augustine, *The City of God* (New York: The Modern Library, 1950), Bk. XI, chap. 5 and Bk. XII, chaps. 11-13, 17.
14 See *ibid.*, Bk. XII, chap. 14, 395: "Of the creation of the human race in time, and how this was effected without any new design or change of purpose on God's part," and chap. 17, 398: "What defense is made by sound faith regarding God's unchangeable counsel and will, against the reasonings of those who hold that the works of God are eternally repeated in revolving cycles that restore all things as they were."
15 Augustine, *The City of God*, Bk. XI, chap. 23, 368-370.

16 Jerome, *Apology against the Books of Rufinus*, in *Saint Jerome Dogmatic and Polemical Works*, trans. John N. Hritzu (Washington, D.C.: The Catholic University Press, 1965), Bk. II, no. 12, 123.

17 Jerome, Letter 124, "To Avitus" in *Nicene and Post-Nicene Fathers*, vol. 6, eds. Philip Schaff and Henry Wace (Wm. B. Eerdmans Publishing Co., 1986), #5, 240).

18 Ibid.

19 See ibid., #3, 239: "Moreover, the very demons and rulers of darkness in any world (mundo) or worlds (mundis), if they are willing to turn to better things, may become human beings and so come back to their first beginning."

20 Jeromes quotes Origen as saying: "worlds vary with the sins that cause them, and those are exploded theories which maintain that all the worlds are alike" (ibid. #5, 240).

21 Hippolytus of Rome, *The Refutation of All Heresies*, in *Fathers of the Third Century*, vol. 5, ed. A. Cleveland Coxe, (Grand Rapids, Michigan: Wm. B. Eerdmans Publishing Company, 1965), Bk. I, chap. 11, 16.

22 Philastrius, *Sancti Filastrii episcopi Brixiensis Diversarvm hereseon liber* (Vindobonae, Austria: F. Tempsky, 1898), no. 86, 79.

23 John Chrysostom, *Homilies on First Corinthians*, vol. 12 of *Nicene and Post-Nicene Fathers*, ed. Philip Schaff (Grand Rapids, Michigan: Wm. B. Eerdmans Publishing Company, 1988), Homily XVII, #3, p. 98.

24 See Athanasius, *Contra Gentes*, ed. and trans. Robert W. Thomson (Oxford: Clarendon Press, 1971), 109: "[N]ot because the creator is one is the world one, for God could have made other worlds. But because the created world is one, we must believe that its creator is also one."

25 See Saint Basil, *Exegetic Homilies*, trans. Agnes Clare Way, C.D.P. (Washington, D.C.: The Catholic University of America Press, 1963), Homily 3, 40: "For, although they see bubbles, not only one but many, produced by the same cause, they yet doubt as to whether the creative power is capable of bringing a greater number of heavens into existence. Whenever we look upon the transcending power of God, we consider that the strength and greatness of the heavens differ not at all from that of the curved spray which spurts up in the fountains."

26 See Bonaventure, *Sententiarum*, in *Opera Theologica Selecta*, vol. 1, ed. Leonardi M. Bello (Florence: Typographia Collegii S. Bonaventurae, 1934), Bk. I, dist. 44, art. 1, q. 4: "For he could make a hundred such worlds, and in addition make one enclosing them all, and make one in a higher place than another."

27 See Dick, *Plurality of Worlds*, chap. 4 : "The Heliocentric Theory, Scripture, and the Plurality of Earths."

28 *The Clementine Homilies*, in *Fathers of the Third and Fourth Centuries*, vol. 8, trans. Thomas Smith and James Donaldson (Wm. B. Eerdmans Publishing Company, 1986), Homily 2, chap. 15, 231.

29 St. Clement of Rome, *The Epistle to the Corinthians* in *The Epistles of St. Clement of Rome and St. Ignatius of Antioch*, trans. James A. Kleist (New York: Newman Press, 1946), #20, 22.

30 See Origen, *De Principiis*, Bk. II, chap. 3, para. 6, 273.

31 See ibid., chap. 3, "On the Beginning of the World, and its Causes, 274: "But from what Clement seems to indicate when he says, 'The ocean is impassable to men, and those worlds which are behind it,' speaking in plural number of the worlds which are behind it, which he intimates are administered and governed by the same providence of the Most High God, he appears to throw out to us some germs of that view by which the whole universe [universitas] of existing things, celestial and super-celestial, earthly and infernal, is generally called one perfect world [mundus], within which, or by which, other worlds, if any there are, must be supposed to be contained. For which reason he wished the globe of the sun or moon, and of the other bodies called planets, to be each termed worlds [mundos]." The Latin is taken from *Vier Bücher von den Prinzipien*, ed. Herwig Görgemanns and Heinrich Karpp (Darmstadt: Wissenschaftliche Buchgesellschaft, 1976), 318.

32 See *A Greek-English Lexicon*, vol. 1, eds. Henry Liddell and Robert Scott, trans. Henry Stuart and Roderick Mckenzie (Oxford: Clarendon Press, 1948), 45.

33 *A Greek-English Lexicon of the New Testament* (Grimm's Wilke's *Clavis Novi Testamenti*), trans. Joseph Thayer (New York: Harper & Brothers, 1893), 18.

34 John of Damascus, *The Orthodox Faith* in *Writings*, vol. 37, trans. Frederic H. Chase (New York: Fathers of the Church, Inc., 1958), Bk. II, chap. 1, 203, 204.

35 See Tt. 2:12, 13: "[W]e must be self-restrained and live good and religious lives here in this present world [nun aiôni]...."
36 Second Ecumenical Council (381) in *The Seven Ecumenical Councils*, vol. 14, eds. Philip Schaff and Henry Wace (Grand Rapids, Michigan: Eerdmans, 1986), 164. One also finds this sort of formulation in the Divine Liturgy of the Holy Apostle and Evangelist Mark which dates back to the second century: "O God of light, Father of life, Author of grace, Creator of worlds [poiêta aiônôn], Founder of knowledge, Giver of wisdom...." ("The Divine Liturgy of the Holy Apostle and Evangelist Mark, the Disciple of the Holy Peter," in *The Ante-Nicene Fathers*, vol. 7, ed. A. Cleveland Coxe [Wm. B. Eerdmans Publishing Company, 1985], 558). The Greek text is found in *Liturgiarum Orientalium collectio*, vol. 1, ed. Eusèbe Renaudot (England: Gregg International Publishers, 1970), 142.
37 The Greek text is taken from *Acta et Symbola Conciliorum quae saeculo quarto habita sunt*, ed. E. J. Jonkers (Leiden: E. J. Brill, 1954), 138.
38 Clement of Alexandria, *Stromata*, in *The Ante-Nicene Fathers*, vol. 2, ed. A. Cleveland Coxe (Wm. B. Eerdmans Publishing Company, 1986), Bk. V, chap. 12, 463.
39 Irenaeus, *Against Heresies*, in *The Ante-Nicene Fathers*, vol. 1, eds. Alexander Roberts and James Donaldson (Wm. B. Eerdmans Publishing Company, 1987), chap. 9, 369.
40 Ibid.
41 *Epistola XI Zachariae Papae ad Bonifacium Archiepiscopum* in the *Patrologia Latina*, vol. 89, 946-47. I came upon this reference in Guiseppe's Tanzella-Nitti "Extraterrestrial Life," in *Interdisciplinary Encyclopaedia of Religion and Science*, http://www.disf.org/en.
42 James F. Loughlin translates Pope Zachary's condemnation of Vergilius thus: "beneath the earth there was another world and other men, another sun and moon" ("Antipodes" in the *Catholic Encyclopedia*, vol. 1, 581-2). Note that "Vergilius" is an alternate spelling for Virgilius.
43 *The City of God*, Bk. XVI, chap. 9.
44 See Louglin, *op. cit*. Loughlin observes that there is no evidence that Vergilius was actually condemned and some evidence that he was not, as it appears that he was later made Archbishop of Salzburg.

45 I came across this text in Michael Malone's *A Layman's Look at Evolution* (Monrovia, California: Catholic Treasures, 1997), 8. The reference Malone provided unfortunately was inaccurate. My thanks to the anonymous referee who provided the correct reference (see following note).

46 *Enchiridion symbolorum: definitionum et declarationum de rebus fidei et morum*, ed. Heinrich Denzinger (Rome: Herder, 1963) #1363 (717c), 344: "Deum quoque alium mundum ab isto creasse, et in eius tempore multos alios viros et mulieres exstitisse, et per consequens Adam primum hominem non fuisse."

47 See Antoinette Mann Paterson, *The Infinite Worlds of Giordano Bruno* (Springfield, Illinois: Charles C. Thomas Publisher, 1970), 198: "Document XVII of Rome indicates that there were eight heretical propositions of which Bruno was accused on January 14, 1599. No statement of these eight propositions was ever made; nevertheless, Namer, working from the materials released by Mercati and from the analyses offered by Firpo, has reconstructed the eight propositions as follows:…'The second concerns the doctrine of the infinite universe and the innumerable worlds, which opposed the idea of creation in time. For Bruno confirms, in the course of these interrogations, that <whoever denies an infinite effect, denies infinite power.>'"

48 Giordano Bruno, *On the Infinite Universe and Worlds*, Third Dialogue, trans. Dorothea Waley Singer (New York: Henry Schuman, 1950), 323.

49 See Émile Namer, *Giordano Bruno* (Paris: Éditions Seghers, 1966), 29, 30. According to Namer's reconstruction of the eight propositions that Bruno was accused of on January 14, 1599 Bruno was *not* on trial for his views on *inhabited* planets.

Chapter 5—Plenitude or Redundancy?

1 See Arthur Lovejoy, The Great Chain of Being (Cambridge: Harvard University Press, 1936). See also Oliva Blanchette's *The Perfection of the Universe According to Aquinas: A Teleological Cosmology* (University Park, Pennsylvania: Pennsylvania State University Press, 1992).

2 *ST* I, q. 47, art. 1.

3   Aquinas, *Quaestiones Disputatae de Potentia* q. 6, art. 6. See also *ST* I, q. 50, art. 3: "[T]he perfection of the universe being what God chiefly intends in the creation of things, to the extent that some things are more perfect, to this extent they are created by God in greater abundance."

4   Ernan McMullin, "Life and Intelligence Far from Earth: Formulating Theological Issues," in *Many Worlds*, 163.

5   See *CCC* #310: "But why did God not create a world so perfect that no evil could exist in it? *With infinite power God could always create something better*." (emphasis mine)

6   II *Sent.* dist. 43, q. 1, art. 2. See also *ST* I, q. 7, art. 2, obj. 1: "The power of a thing is proportioned to its essence. Therefore if the essence of God is infinite, it is necessary that its power be infinite. Therefore it is able to produce an infinite effect, since the quantity of its virtue is known through its effect." Ibid., ad 1: "…it is contrary to the notion of 'made,' that the essence of a thing be its very being, because subsistent being is not created being; whence it is contrary to the notion of 'made' that it be simply speaking infinite. Therefore, granted that God has infinite power, nevertheless it is not possible to make something which is not made, for there would be contradictories simultaneously existing, so he is not able to make something infinite simply speaking."

7   *ST* I, q. 25, art. 6: "Whether God can make better things than those that he has made." See ibid., ad 3: "[T]hese particular things having been supposed, the universe cannot be better, on account of the most fitting order attributed to things by God, in whom the good of the universe consists. For if one of those things would be better, it would corrupt the proportion of order; just as if one string were stretched more than was fit, it would ruin the melody of the cithara. Nevertheless God could make other things, or add other things to those particular ones that are made; and thus that universe would be better."

8   *SCG* III, chap. 97. See also *SCG* I, chap. 81: "Therefore it ought to be considered why God may know things other than himself of necessity, but not will them of necessity, given that from understanding and willing himself, he understands and wills other things. There is a reason for this, however. For that the one understanding understand something is due to the intellect being a certain way; for that some-

thing is understood in act, is from this that a likeness of it is in the one understanding. But that the one willing will something is from this that the thing willed exists in a certain manner; for we will something, either because it is an end, or because it is ordered to an end. Divine perfection requires that all things exist in God so that they can be understood in him; divine goodness, however, does not require that other things exist of necessity which are ordered to him as to an end; and on account of this it is necessary that God know other things, but not, however, that he will them. Whence nor does he want all things which are able to have an order to his goodness; however, he knows all things which can have any sort of order to his essence, his essence being that through which he understands." See also *ST* I, q. 19, art. 3.

9 *ST* I, q. 112, art. 4, ad 2.

10 An order of angel is not the same thing as a genus of material living thing. However, given that an individual angel is its own species, an order of angels is closer to a genus of material living thing than to anything else. In any case, empirical examples show that in the realm of material living things there is no hard and fast rule regarding the numbers of species or of individuals.

11 *Quaestio Disputata de Spiritualibus Creaturis* in *Quaestiones Disputatae*, vol. 2, ed. P. Bazzi (Turin: Marietti, 1965), unicus 8, ad 10.

12 In the material world there appears to be another principle operative which may explain why in some cases there are more of inferior things, namely, need. For example, flies are inferior to great apes, but they are more needed in the balance of nature as food sources for other animals. For this reason it is not surprising that they exceed the great apes in number, both as to species and as to individuals.

13 One of the three passages where Aquinas argues that there can be only one species of rational animal is *Quaestio Disputata de Spiritualibus Creaturis*, unicus, art. 8, ad 10, cited in chap. 6, footnote 22. A second text is *In Aristotelis Librum De Anima Commentarium*, #293, 294 cited in chap. 1, footnote 3. The third text is *SCG* II, chap. 90 cited in the following footnote.

14 See *SCG* II, chap. 90: "For if it [an intellectual substance] were united to another body, either it would be united to a mixed body or to a simple body. It cannot however be united to a mixed body, because it is necessary that that body be of the most balanced make-up according

to its genus among the other mixed bodies, since we see that mixed bodies have nobler forms to the extent that they arrive at a more temperate mixture; and thus that body which has the most noble form, as an intellectual substance, would have to be of the most temperate mixture, if it is a mixed body; whence we even see that softness of flesh and goodness of touch which demonstrate balance of constitution are signs of a good intellect. The most balanced constitution is the constitution of the human body. It is necessary, therefore, that if an intellectual substance is united to some mixed body, it be of the same nature as the human body. The form of this being would be of the same nature as the human soul, if it be an intellectual substance. There would not therefore be a difference according to species between this animal and man."

15 See *ST* III, q. 5, art. 2: "For since the form of man is a certain natural thing, it requires a determinate matter, namely, flesh and bones, which must be put in the definition of man, as is plain from the Philosopher, *Metaphysics*, Bk. VII." Bones are needed so that man can stand erect and thus freely use his hands, and flesh in order to have a highly developed sense of touch.

16 Galileo, *Two New Sciences*, trans. Stillman Drake (Madison Wisconsin: The University of Wisconsin Press, 1974), 127, 128. Another example of physical constraints concerns the surface area of the lungs. If the surface of our lungs was not convoluted, blood would not be adequately oxygenated—as in fact happens in those with lung diseases such as emphysema that affect or destroy the alveoli which is where gas exchange takes place. A giant human, in whom the organs kept the same proportions, would have lungs lacking the necessary surface area, for surface area increases at a slower rate in comparison to the corresponding increase of volume.

17 See Puccetti, *Persons*, 90.

18 C. Owen Lovejoy, "Evolution of Man and Its Implications for General Principles of Evolution of Intelligent Life," in *Life in the Universe*, ed. John Billingham (Cambridge: The MIT Press, 1982), 326.

19 See Michael J. Denton, *Nature's Destiny: How the Laws of Biology Reveal Purpose in the Universe* (New York: The Free Press, 1998), chapter 12.

20 See *ibid.* 139, 140: "[I]magine ourselves...setting out to create life from scratch, being free to choose at every stage of the process the

most ideal materials and components available and being constrained only by the laws of physics. Playing the game is instructive, for it highlights one of the main arguments of the book, namely that the laws of nature are fit for only one specific type of life—that which exists on earth. To start the game we must choose an atom out of which to create life...we soon find that carbon is the most promising...as we continue we find, with increasing astonishment, that it is not a case of carbon will do, but that carbon atoms have all the properties we could desire....For life we need the carbon atom and water...we need all their chemical and physical properties precisely as they are. And for life anywhere in the cosmos it will be the same. For there is no alternative. So if there is in some distant galaxy another carbon-based biosphere as rich as our own, containing large active terrestrial organisms, they will, like us, inhale oxygen and exhale carbon dioxide and use the bicarbonate buffer system. No matter how many times we play the Demiurge, we will always be led via the same chain of mutual adaptations to the same unique solutions."

21 David Darling, *Life Everywhere* (New York: Basic Books, 2001), 128. See also ibid., 129-131, 144, 145.

22 See Denton, *Nature's Destiny*,130. See Darling, *Life Everywhere*, 130: "'When we get to some other planet and find life,' says [the biologist] Harold Morowitz of George Mason University..., 'I have no idea what that life will look like, but it will have the citric acid cycle.'"

23 See Robert Bieri, "Humanoids on Other Planets?" in *Philosophy of Biology*, ed. Michael Ruse (New York: Macmillan Publishing Co., 1989), 272: "I would like to present arguments...that if life has evolved on other planets in other solar systems and if some population has reached the level of conceptual thought, it is highly probably that the organisms so endowed will bear a strong resemblance to *Homo sapiens*." See also ibid., 276: "Could the conceptualizing organism have additional sense organs based on other parts of the electromagnetic spectrum besides the visual portion?...An acoustical ranging system similar to that of bat might be present, in which case the ears would be proportionately larger than ours. However, in this case the eyes might be reduced somewhat. On the other hand, any marked reduction in the visual sensors would be a serious impediment to the evolution of tools and the associated evolution of a large brain." Puccetti, relying in part on Bieri, is another author who argues that "intelligent extrater-

restrials everywhere will resemble *Homo sapiens* to a considerable extent" (*Persons*, 96; see also 90-98).

24 *ST* I, q. 47, art. 3, ad 2. See also *In Libros Aristotelis De Caelo et Mundo*, Bk. I, chap. 9, lec. 19, #197: "The world was made by God, but since the power of God is infinite it is not determined to this world alone; therefore it is not reasonable [to hold] that he cannot make other worlds as well. To respond to this, it should be said that if God would make other worlds, either he would make them like this world, or unlike. If they were entirely alike, they would be pointless: which does not pertain to his wisdom."

25 Paine, *The Age of Reason*, 59, 60.

26 One might ask why the multitude of human individuals does not constitute undesirable redundancy. This is because no human individual realizes the full potential of the human species due to differences in nature, nurture, and free choice (see *ST* I, q. 96, art. 3: Whether in the state of innocence all men would be equal). The human species in this respect differs from angelic species. Each angelic species is constituted by a sole member who fully realizes the potential of that species.

27 *Timaeus* 31a, b in *Timaeus, Critias, Cleitophon, Menexenus, Epistles*, trans. R.G. Bury (Cambridge: Harvard University Press, 1975).

28 C.S. Lewis, *Perelandra* (New York: Macmillan Publishing Co., 1944), 42, 43.

Chapter 6—Probable Arguments that Humans are Unique on the Supposition of One Incarnation: The Case of the Fallen ETIs

1 Dominic Caronna adopted this line of argument according to Christopher J. Corbally, S.J.: "he [Caronna] focuses on 'the unicity of God' (his term for describing unity, completeness, and absoluteness in God) to show that it would be absurd for the events of the bible, particularly the incarnation and redemption, to be repeated elsewhere in the universe. Since Christ is unique, so must human beings be the only intelligent life in the entire universe" ("Religious Implications from the Possibility of Ancient Martian Life," www.aaas.org/spp/DSPP/dbsr/resource/corbally.htm).

2 *SCG* IV, chap. 53.

3 Ibid.

4 Ibid.

5 Anselm, *Cur Deus Homo* in *St. Anselm: Basic Writings*, trans. S.N. Deane (La Salle, Illinois: The Open Court Publishing Company, 1974), 178, 179.

6 Ibid., 182. See *SCG* IV, chap. 53: "The faith is regarded by non-believers as stupidity because of the incarnation...non-believers apply themselves to fighting the incarnation, striving to show that what the Catholic faith preaches is not only impossible, but is also incongruous and does not befit divine goodness." Aquinas then goes to state more than a dozen reasons for thinking that the Incarnation is something that is unbefitting God. He responds to these objections in chapter 55.

7 See St. Leo the Great, "Sermon 26, Feast of the Nativity," in *St. Leo the Great: Sermons*, trans. Jane Freeland and Agnes Conway (Washington, D.C.: The Catholic University of America Press, 1996), 105-6: "That infancy, which the majesty of God's Son did not scorn, was eventually brought to perfect manhood.... It was precisely so that we might be able to become children of God that he was made the child of a human being. Had he not come down to us in this humility, none could come to him by any merit of their own"

8 St. Athanasius, *On the Incarnation*, ed. and trans. Penelope Lawson (New York: Macmillan, 1981). See ibid., 3: "...[we] must consider also the Word's becoming Man and His divine Appearing in our midst. That mystery the Jews traduce, the Greeks deride, but we adore; and your own love and devotion to the Word also will be the greater, because in His Manhood He seems of so little worth. For it is a fact that the more unbelievers pour scorn on Him, so much the more does He make His Godhead evident. The things which they, as men, rule out as impossible, He plainly shows to be possible; that which they deride as unfitting, His goodness makes most fit; and things which these wiseacres laugh at as 'human' He by His inherent might declares divine."

9 St. Bernard, "Homily for the Epiphany," in *Livre des jours*, 115.

10 St. Anselm, *Basic Writings*, 180.

11 *ST* III, q. 30, art. 2, ad 3. See also *SCG* IV, chap. 54: "If someone, however, diligently and piously considers the mystery of the incarnation he will find [in it] a profundity of wisdom such as exceeds all human understanding, in keeping with what the Apostle says: 'God's

foolishness is wiser than human wisdom.' Whence it happens that more and more wonderful reasons of this mystery are continually manifested to the one considering it."

12 See Crowe, *The ET Life Debate 1750-1900*, 162: "the French scholar Jean Milet...describes a 'religious bipolarity peculiar to Christianity [which was] especially evident when first-century Jews who worshiped a God 'whose name one did not even dare pronounce, whose face could not be seen without dying'...were asked to believe that this same God 'manifested himself in the form of a weak child in Bethlehem,...toiled on the roads of Judaea and Galilee,...[and]—as the height of improbability—was recognized under the disfigured features of the man put to death on Golgotha.' Milet suggests that 'a mental effort of such magnitude was an unparalleled demand....'"

13 *CCC* #668.

14 *CCC* #963 and #966.

15 Aquinas, *Compendium Theologium*, chap. 217: "It was necessary, however, that we take example from him [Christ] both as to the glory that we hope for and the virtue by which it is merited: in both cases the example would be less effective, if he [Christ] had assumed the nature of his body from elsewhere than other human beings assumed it. For the one who was to be persuaded that he may tolerate sufferings as Christ sustained them, [and] that he may hope to be resurrected as Christ rose from the dead, could put forth as an excuse the diverse condition of their bodies."

16 Unfallen ETIs would be less in need of a role model than fallen ones. Still, as will be discussed in more detail in chapter seven, unfallen ETIs are capable of falling, and thus they would profit from having a flawless role model.

17 See *Super Epistolas S. Pauli*, vol. 1, ed. P. Raphaelis Cai (Rome: Marietti, 1953), I ad Corinthios, #610: "woman is said to be the glory of man through a certain derivation.... 'For not' in the first establishment of things is 'man from woman,' namely as formed, 'but woman is from man.'" (1 Co. 11:8)

18 Up until a certain age Christ did live under the authority of Mary and Joseph (see Lk. 2:52); however, this was a temporary situation. Christ also respected civil authorities, but did so because he saw their authority as having "been given...from above" (Jn. 19:11).

19 It is interesting that Scripture speaks of human nature as the Word's vestment. The Latin text for Ph. 2:7 says of Jesus that "he was seen outfitted as man" (habitu inventus est ut homo). Aquinas points out that "human nature in Christ is assimilated to an outfit, i.e., a vestment, not insofar as the union of this nature is accidental, but insofar as the Word is seen in virtue of his human nature, as a man in virtue of his vestment" (*ST* III, q. 2, art. 6, ad 1).

20 *SCG* IV, chap. 54.

21 *SCG* IV, chap. 55.

22 See *Quaestio Disputata de Spiritualibus Creaturis*, unicus, art. 8, ad 10: "that there is only one species of rational animal, while there exist many species of irrational animal, arises from the fact that the rational animal is constituted from this that corporeal nature reaches the highest thing it can attain to, [namely], the nature of spiritual substance which [in turn] attains its lowest [grade]. There is only one highest grade, as well as lowest grade, of one nature...."

23 See *CCC* #355: "Man occupies a unique place in creation:...(II) in his own nature he unites the spiritual and material worlds...." One cannot be sure that "unique" here is to be understood to mean that no other being at all holds such a place. See also *Vatican Council I* in *Dogmatic Canons and Decrees* (Rockford, Illinois: Tan Books and Publishers, Inc., 1977), chap. 1, 219: "This one, only, true God, of His own goodness and almighty power...created out of nothing, from the beginning of time, both the spiritual and corporeal creature, to wit, the angelic and the mundane; and afterwards the human creature, as partaking, in a sense, of both, consisting of spirit and of body."

24 Heb. 2:10-18 speaks of Christ taking to himself "descent from Abraham" (Greek: spermatos Abraam; Latin: semen Abrahae). It does not say "descent from Adam." However, it is certainly not Church teaching that there is a temporal cut off line separating those descendants of Adam and Eve for whom Christ made atonement from those who did not, and thus a Catholic interpretation of Heb. 2:10-18 would not construe it to be indicating such. Aquinas notes that Paul in that passage is contrasting human nature with angelic nature, and chooses here to denote human nature by reference to descent from Abraham for the purpose of inspiring the Jews to a greater veneration of Christ, for they gloried in being descendants of Abraham. As Aquinas notes,

the genealogy of Christ in Matthew's gospel begins with Abraham, and the reason for this is that Abraham is the one with whom God made the covenant of which we are heirs—he is our "father in faith."

25 See *SCG* IV, chap. 54: "The order of divine justice so stands...that sin is not remitted by God without satisfaction. No one purely human, however, could make satisfaction for the sin of the entire human race (humani generis), because anyone who is purely human is something less than the entire ensemble of the human race. It was necessary, therefore, so that the human race could be freed from the sin common to it that someone would make satisfaction who would both be human, to whom the satisfaction pertained, and something beyond human, so that his merit would be sufficient for satisfying for the sin of the entire human race. As far as the order of beatitude, there is no one greater than man except for God; for angels, granted that they are superior as to the condition of their nature, are not nevertheless as to the order of the end, because they are made blessed in the same way as humans. It was therefore necessary that God become man in order to destroy the sin of the human race so that man might attain beatitude....and so the Apostle says: 'Therefore, just as condemnation came to all men through the fault of one man, so too the justification of life came to all men through the justice of one man' (Rom. 5:18)."

26 *SCG* IV, chap. 54 points out the further benefit of the *reliability* of Christ's example and moral counsel, for all men, no matter how good, can fail, whereas there is never anything defective in the God-Man's example and words.

27 See Heb. 4:15: "For it is not as if we had a high priest who was incapable of feeling our weaknesses with us; but we have one who has been tempted in every way that we are, though he is without sin." See also St. Hippolytus: "This *Man* we know to have been made out of the compound *of our humanity*. For if He were not of the same *nature with ourselves*, in vain does He ordain that we should imitate the Teacher" (*Refutation of All Heresies*, Bk. X, chap. 29, 152).

28 The benefits named in Heb. 2:10-18 are commented upon by St. Anselm (see *Cur Deus Homo fit*) as well as by Thomas Aquinas.

29 *SCG* Bk. IV, chap. 54.

30 Ibid.

31 Ibid.

32 Ibid.

33 Ibid.

34 Ibid.

35 Aquinas was of the opinion that not even a human being with a body derived elsewhere than from Adam's race would have made suitable reparation for the human race: "God could have formed Christ's body from clay, or from any other material, in the manner in which he formed the body of our first parents; but this would not have been fitting, because, as we hold, the reason why the Son of God assumed flesh was for the restoration of man. For if the victor over the devil and the conqueror of death (under the bondage of which the human race was held captive on account of the sin of the first parents) had assumed the body from elsewhere, the nature of the human race derived from the first parent, which was to be healed, would not have been sufficiently restored to its pristine honor. The works of God are perfect, and he led to perfection what he intended to repair, so that even more was added than had been subtracted, according to the words of the Apostle in Rom. 5. For the grace of God abounded through Christ to a greater extent than the fault of Adam did abound. It was therefore fitting that the Son of God assumed a body of the nature propagated by Adam" (*Compendium Theologium*, chap. 217).

36 See *CCC* #269: "He [God] is the Lord of the universe, whose order he established and which remains wholly subject to him and at his disposal. He is master of history, governing hearts and events in keeping with his will: 'It is always in your power to show great strength, and who can withstand the strength of your arm.'" See also *CCC* #303: "The witness of Scripture is unanimous that the solicitude of divine providence is concrete and immediate; God cares for all, from the least things to the great events of the world and its history. The sacred books powerfully affirm God's absolute sovereignty over the course of events: 'Our God is in the heavens; he does whatever he pleases.' And so it is with Christ, 'who opens and no one shall shut, who shuts and no one opens.'"

37 See Aristotle, *Poetics*, trans. Ingram Bywater in *The Basic Works of Aristotle*, ed. Richard McKeon (New York: Random House, 1968), chap. 8, 1451a31-35: "[I]n poetry, the story, as an imitation of action, must represent one action, a complete whole, with its several incidents

so closely connected that the transposal or withdrawal of any one of them will disjoin and dislocate the whole. For that which makes no perceptible difference by its presence or absence is no real part of the whole."

38 Pucetti, *Persons*, 135, 136. Pucetti is a philosopher. The astronomer George V. Coyne, S.J. (Director of the Vatican Observatory), attests to the scientific accuracy of Pucetti's statement (personal communication).

39 See J. Garriga and A. Vilenkin, "Testable anthropic predictions for dark energy," *Physical Review*, D67 (2003): "The anthropic approach to the cosmological constant problems (CCPs) predicts that the conditions for civilizations to emerge will be found mostly in galaxies that formed (or complete their formation) at a low redshift, $z \sim 1$."

40 See Kip Thorne, *Black Holes and Time Warps* (New York: Norton & Co., 1994) and Matt Visser, *Lorentzian Wormholes: from Einstein to Hawking* (New York: American Institute of Physics Press, 1995). See also, M. Visser, S. Kar, and N. Dadhich, "Traversable wormholes with arbitrarily small energy condition violations," *Physical Review Letters*, 90, 201102 (2003).

41 See *Quaestiones Disputatae de Malo*, q. 16, art. 12.

42 *In Duodecim Libros Metaphysicorum Aristotelis Expositio*, ed. Raymond M. Spiazzi, O.P. (Rome: Marietti, 1950), #2630.

43 *ST* I, q. 103, art. 4, ad 1. See also *SCG* III, chap. 69: "Moreover, to take away the order in created things is to take away what they have that is best; for individual things are good in themselves. At the same time all things are best for the sake of the order of the universe. For the whole is always better than the parts, and is the end of the parts. If, however, one take things' actions away from them, one takes away the order of things to each other. For there is no assembling of things which are diverse according to their natures in a unity of order, except through this that certain of them act and certain of them are acted upon."

44 *In Duodecim Libros Metaphysicorum Aristotelis Expositio*, #2661-63.

45 Albertus Magnus, *De Caelo et Mundo*, 69.

46 St. Paul elaborates on the unity of the body in 1 Co., chap. 12.

47 See *Quaestiones Disputatae de Potentia*, q. 3, art. 18 where Aquinas argues that the angels and the material universe were created at the

same time on the grounds that: "If, however, the angels would have been created separately, they would seem to be totally alien from the order of corporeal creatures, as if constituting of themselves another universe." See *ST* I, q. 61, art. 3: "Angels are a certain part of the universe; for they do not constitute one universe per se, but both they and corporeal creatures come together in the constitution of one universe. This is apparent from the order of one creature to another; for the order of things to one another is the good of the universe." See also, *CCC* #327: "The profession of faith of the Fourth Lateran Council (1215) affirms that God 'from the beginning of time made at once (simul) out of nothing both orders of creatures, the spiritual and the corporeal, that is, the angelic and the earthly, and then (deinde) the human creature, who as it were shares in both orders, being composed of spirit and body.'"

[48] See Gregory Nazianzen, *Theological Oration 28: On the Doctrine of God*, in *Faith Gives Fullness to Reasoning*, trans. Lionel Wickham and Frederick Williams (Leiden: E. J. Brill, 1991), 244: "As ministers of the divine will, powerful with inborn and acquired strength, they [the angels] range over the universe. They are quickly at hand to all in any place, so eager are they to serve, so agile is their being. Each has under him a different part of the Earth or the universe, which God alone, who defined their ranks, knows. They unify the whole, making all things obey the beck and call of him alone who fashioned them."

[49] See Peter Stravinskas, *The Bible and the Mass* (Mount Pocono, Pennsylvania: Newman House Press, 2000), 76: "Speaking of angels, we might here observe that all the anaphoras [of the Mass] feel compelled to allude to them. Their inclusion is a reminder that reality consists of something beyond the material universe (*CCC* #335). Further more, their activities are exemplary for us in certain key areas: their obedience to God ('stand before you to do your will'); contemplation of God ('they look upon your splendor'); and praise of God (which they do 'night and day')."

[50] *Super Epistolas S. Pauli*, ad Ephesios, #29. See also II *Sent.*, dist. 1, text of Peter Lombard, 7, 8: "By some Scripture is found [to say] that man was made for the sake of repairing the fall of the angels (angelicae ruinae); this is not to be understood as if man would not have been made if the angels had not sinned; but because this cause stands as one cause among the other causes that are the principal ones." See also

Bonaventure, *Sententiarum* III, dist. 13, q. 3, ad 3 in *Opera Omnia*: "there can be inflowing from Christ to the angels even according to human nature, albeit per accidens, because by flowing into and redeeming his members, Christ repairs the fall of the angels."

51 See *ST* I, q. 107, arts. 1-5.

52 See *ST* I, q. 106, arts. 1-4.

53 *Super Epistolas S. Pauli*, ad Hebraeos, #85-87.

54 God is certainly able to raise up priests among the ETIs. However, it would be a strange situation for the Bread of Life for unfallen ETIs, in whose flesh the Word also became Incarnate, to be the flesh and blood of a human. Similarly for a fallen race whose flesh Christ assumed, granted this would be less strange since at least they would be saved through the Sacred Humanity of the Word. The supposition of a single incarnation removes the incongruity which stems from ETIs knowing the Word in his ETI incarnation, while being fed with his body in his human incarnation. Still, it seems kind of odd that ETIs would be assimilated to the God-Man, which would be the case if they ate his flesh and drank his blood.

Chapter 7—Probable Arguments that Humans are Unique on the Supposition of One Incarnation: The Case of the Unfallen ETIs

1 Lewis, *Perelandra*, 144-45.

2 *CCC* #1066.

3 *CCC* #349.

4 See *ST* I, q. 95, art. 1.

5 See *ST* I-II, q. 89, art. 3: "And therefore it is necessary that there could be no moral disorder in man unless it began from this that what was highest in man would not subject itself to God...."

6 It is a fairly traditional view that one third of the angels fell. This view is based on Rev. 12:3, 4: "A huge red dragon [appeared]...its tail dragged a third of the stars from the sky and dropped them to the earth...." For a discussion of this point see Suarez, *De Angelis*, Bk. VII, chap. 17, #7, 917 and #20, 921.

7 I *Sent.*, dist. 39, q. 2, art. 2, ad 4.

8 Ibid.

9   See *ST* I, q. 95, art. 3.

10 See *ST* I, q. 50, art. 4.

11 *Quaestiones Disputatae de Malo*, q. 5, art. 4, ad 8. See also, *ST* I, q. 100, art. 2: "Whether children in the state of innocence would have been confirmed in justice." Here he argues that "a child at the time of its birth could not have more perfection than its parents in a state where reproduction took place. Parents, however, so long as they generated offspring, were not confirmed in original justice." See also, *Quodlibetum* 5, art. 1.

12 Aquinas, despite arguing in the *Commentary on the Sentences* that some individuals belonging to intelligent species eventually fall, presents us with a picture of an unfallen race in *ST* I, q. 96, art. 3 ("Whether human beings in the state of innocence were equal"). After pointing out that there would be inequalities as to age, he goes on to say "even according to the soul there would be diversity, both as to justice and as to science. For human beings do not operate from necessity, but from free will; for which reason, a man can apply his soul more or less to acting or willing or knowing. Whence, certain individuals can make more progress in justice and science than others....Nevertheless in those who were surpassed, there would be no defect or sin, neither in body, nor in the soul." Also, given some angels did not fall, and assuming that each angel is a species unto itself, perhaps, corresponding to the case of the angels, there could be material intelligent species that fell, and others that did not. But once again, material intelligent creatures are by nature more fallible than angels.

13 One could also argue against the existence of *many* unfallen races in the following manner: If there were more than a few unfallen races, it would be highly improbable that there would be no other fallen race besides ours. Thus, to the extent that the existence of fallen races is improbable, to that extent the existence of many unfallen races is improbable.

14 IV *Sent.*, dist. 48, q. 2, art. 4, obj. 5. See *Quaestiones Disputatae de Potentia*, q. 3, art. 18.

15 Augustine, *City of God*, Bk. XII, chap. 22, 405, 406.

Chapter 8—Probable Arguments that Humans are Unique on the Supposition of More than One Incarnation

1. Charles Davis argues that: "If we suppose other incarnations...Christ would retain His essential dignity as the God-man, but His work would lose its universal significance. We could no speak of His primacy in the same way....The Second Coming of Christ, for example, would not bring about the end of the world and transformation of all by itself but only as a subordinate factor in some higher scheme. We could not speak of the universal kingship of Christ as man....If we say our Christian faith allows the hypothesis of other incarnations in other rational natures elsewhere in this universe, then we are equivalently saying that the Christian view of the universe is not Christo-centric" ("The Place of Christ," *Clergy Review*, n.s., 45, 1960, 715). If Christ and the ETI incarnation are one and the same king, a second incarnation of the Word would not prevent one from speaking of the "universal kingship of Christ as man."

2. *ST* I, q. 47, art. 3.

Chapter 9—Weaknesses of Arguments in Favor of ETI Existence Derived from Science

1. One of the arguments that I give is not based on Christianity as such, but rather on a metaphysical notion, namely, that the parts of a well-ordered universe must be interactive.

2. See Dick, *Life on Other Worlds The 20th-Century Extraterrestrial Life Debate*, 268: "Despite all the problems of working in science at its limits, the charge of critics that exobiology had been marked by lack of progress is not sustainable. Compared to the beginning of the century, we now know that...not even organic molecules are to be found on Mars...." This was written in 1998. While it is true that the experiments performed by the Viking Landers at two different sites on Mars in 1976 indicated an absence of organic matter in the surface soil, as Monica M. Grady points out: "Although the surface of Mars is now apparently dry, and, as a result of oxidation by solar uv radiation, presumably devoid of organic compounds, we have no knowledge of what is present in the subsurface soil layers. There might be reservoirs of permafrost, or even liquid water trapped within pore spaces, giving rise to organisms like the cryptoendolithic bacteria of the Dry Valleys

of Antarctica. Residues from evaporating brines might host desiccated sulphur-loving micro-organisms" (*Astrobiology* [London: The Natural History Museum, 2001]), 59.

3   See Darling, *Life Everywhere*, 63, 64, 146, 151-153.

4   See ibid., 65.

5   See Charles W. Petit, "The icing on the red planet," *US News & World Report*, December 23, 2002, 54. NASA hopes to eventually send a probe to Mars capable of digging down to where there appears to be ice.

6   Freeman J. Dyson, *Origins of Life* (Cambridge: Cambridge University Press, 1999), 33, 34: "The second line of evidence for an early neutral atmosphere comes from the rarity of the inert gases remaining in the earth's atmosphere today. Neon is the seventh most abundant element in the universe and is abundant in the molecular clouds out of which the earth condenses. If any primitive reducing atmosphere had survived after the heavy bombardment stopped, it should have contained a large fraction of neon. Neon should have been about as abundant as nitrogen. When the hypothetical reducing atmosphere later became neutral or oxidizing, the neon would have remained. But today the ratio of neon to nitrogen in the atmosphere is one to sixty thousand."

7   See Darling, *Life Everywhere*, 30-31: "The slow accretion model of the Earth even allows for the possibility of reducing gases building up in the early atmosphere, so that Miller-type production of basic biochemicals comes back into the picture. The surface, sunlight guys are very much in business."

8   Darling, *Life Everywhere*, 30.

9   Ibid.

10 See Paul Davies, *The Fifth Miracle* (New York: Simon & Schuster, 1999), 159: "As late as 3.8 billion years ago, the Moon was hit by an object ninety kilometers in diameter, producing a colossal impact basin the size of the British Isles....Being that much bigger, Earth must have suffered dozens of collisions of this magnitude, as well as some that were even larger."

11 See Simon Conway Morris, *Life's Solution: Inevitable Humans in a Lonely Universe* (Cambridge: University of Cambridge Press, 2003), 18, 73, 74.

12 Francis Crick and L.E. Orgel are two of a number of scientists who hold that life most likely did not originate on earth, but was seeded from space. See Francis Crick, *Life Itself: its Origin and Nature* (New York: Simon and Schuster, c1981).

13 See Peter D. Ward and Donald Brownlee, *Rare Earth: Why Complex Life is Uncommon in the Universe* (New York: Copernicus, 2000), 74.

14 See ibid., 76-79. Note that until we discovered organisms that survive in extreme environments, we had no grounds to hypothesize that the first organisms may have originated in such environments, which appeared if anything to be hostile to life. However, the discovery of extremophiles in and of itself does not provide evidence as to whether the *first* organisms in fact originated under extreme conditions.

15 See Conway Morris, *Life's Solution*, 74.

16 See Darling, *Life Everywhere*, 13, 14.

17 See Ernan McMullin, "Persons in the Universe," *Zygon* 15.1 (March 1980) 69-89.

18 Frank W. Cousin's example is paraphrased by Crowe, *The ET Life Debate 1750-1900*, 553.

19 See Ernan McMullin "Life and Intelligence Far from Earth: Formulating Theological Issues," in *Many Worlds*, 166: "One has to be wary here of a fallacy induced by the contemplation of large numbers. It goes like this: out of a million planets (with conditions suitable for life, where life has developed,…), it is surely a 'conservative estimate' to suppose that 1 percent, at least, of those will (go on to develop life, will progress toward intelligent life…). And, lo! that gives us 10,000 candidates right away. But without a fair degree of knowledge of the necessary conditions involved in the process whose probability is being estimated, this kind of argument is logically treacherous."

20 See André Kukla, "SETI: On the Prospects and Pursuitworthiness of the Search for Extraterrestrial Intelligence," *Studies in History and Philosophy of Science*, 32.1 (2001) 39: "'In fact, there are billions of galaxies, each containing billions of stars. This is the single most important reason for optimism in the search for life. In a universe so vast, with stars as numerous as grains of sand, it is hard to imagine that the conditions for life have not arisen elsewhere. (McDonough, 1987, p. 59).' To call this an argument is to insult arguments. In fact, it's nothing more than a profession of one's faith that the number of stars

is large enough to overwhelm the smallness of the probability that there are ETIs associated with a randomly selected star. Certainly this conclusion doesn't follow from the admission that the probability of ETI is non-zero. For however many stars there may be, so long as the number is finite, there's going to be a non-zero probability for intelligent life that's so ultramicroscopically small that the net probability of ETI anywhere in the universe will still be as close to zero as makes no difference."

21 See Supplement to the *AMNH Natural History Magazine* (2002), "The Search for Life Are We Alone?": "Answers begin to emerge as we consider these newly revealed facts:...the processes that created our Sun and solar system—and ultimately allowed life to develop on Earth—are the same processes that have created every other star and planet in the Galaxy and continue to do so." See also Christian De Duve, *Vital Dust* (New York: Basic Books, 1995), 292: "In this organic cloud [containing carbon dust], which pervades the universe, life is almost bound to arise, in a molecular form not very different from its form on Earth, wherever physical conditions are similar to those that prevailed on our planet some four billion years ago....Life is either a reproducible, almost commonplace manifestation of matter, given certain conditions, or a miracle." Both these authors try to draw support from the regularity of nature, overlooking the fact that we do not know what the constraints for the appearance of life are, so as to be able to judge whether they are easily and frequently met in the universe.

22 There are definitely differences of opinion regarding the time frame in which various life forms arose. I am always giving the dates which are more favorable to the Life Everywhere school for the sake of the argument.

23 A commonly offered explanation or partial explanation for why it took animals, and especially large animals, so long to appear is the relative lack of oxygen in the atmosphere in Pre-Cambrian times.

24 There remains some controversy about whether the mass extinction of the Cretaceous was really caused by the meteorite; however, this view is widely accepted.

25 Stephen Jay Gould, *Wonderful Life The Burgess Shale and the Nature of History* (New York: Norton, 1989), 14.

26 See Gould, *Wonderful Life*, 288: "With so many Burgess possibilities of apparently equivalent anatomical promise—over twenty arthropod designs later decimated to four survivors, perhaps fifteen or more unique anatomies available for recruitment as major branches, or phyla, of life's tree—our modern pattern of anatomical disparity is thrown into the lap of contingency. The modern order was not guaranteed by basic laws (natural selection, mechanical superiority in anatomical design), or even by lower-level generalities of ecology or evolutionary theory. The modern order is largely a product of contingency."

27 Darling, *Life Everywhere*, 123.

28 Simon Conway Morris, *The Crucible of Creation* (Oxford: Oxford University Press, 1998), 200-202.

29 See Gould, *Wonderful Life*, 289: "Much about the basic form of multicellular organisms must be constrained by rules of construction and good design." See Darling, *Life Everywhere*, 123-127.

30 See Darling, *Life Everywhere*, 139.

31 Ernst Mayr, *Towards a New Philosophy of Biology* (Cambridge: Harvard University Press, 1988), 71.

32 See Barrow and Tipler, *The Anthropic Cosmological Principle*, 129: "No lineage in the entire plant kingdom has shown a significant increase in its ability to process information since the metazoan ancestors of the plants first appeared some 500-1000 million years ago. Such increase as has occurred—the ability to orient towards the light, the ability of certain plants such as the Venus fly-trap to react to tactile sensations, for instance—have developed so slowly that were the increase to be projected into the future at the rate inferred in the past, it would require many trillions of years for the information-processing ability to reach human level."

33 See Stanley Jaki, *Cosmos and Creator*, 118, 124, 125.

34 Ernst Mayr, *Towards a New Philosophy of Biology*, 71, 72. Note that Barrow and Tipler also uses this argument of Mayr's against those who claim that human-like intelligence is converged upon; see *The Anthropic Cosmological Principle*, 132.

35 Ibid., 72.

36 Ibid. Kukla objects that Mayr is guilty of extrapolating from a single case to the conclusion that the evolution of intelligent life is unlikely (see "SETI: On the Prospects and Pursuitworthiness of the Search for Extraterrestrial Intelligence," 41). While it is true that Mayr is looking solely to evolution of life on earth, and even conceding that life arose only once on earth, rather than independently many times, the variety of directions that the phyletic lines took do in some sense represent separate experiments. A similar point is made by Christopher B. Kaiser who elaborates on an observation made by Loren Eiseley. Eiseley pointed out that 300 million years ago all the continents formed one supercontinent, Pangaea. The breakup of Pangaea resulted in separate habitats which each could be regarded as the site of an experiment in evolutionary history, only one of which resulted in intelligent life. "As William Pollard later put it, we could even think of these separate habitats as if they were different planets, all of them with ideal conditions for the evolution of art-sci intelligence—in fact, all of them with the environmental conditions of earth. Unique and beautiful species evolved in all five habitats: Australia, Madagascar, South America, Southeast Asia, and Africa" ("Extraterrestrial Life and Extraterrestrial Intelligence," *Reformed Review* 51 [Winter 1997-98] 86-7). Kukla's rejoinder to this is that it is no more than a guess to say that the earth is hospitable to the evolution of intelligent life: "It could turn out that there's something about the terrestrial environment that *inhibits* the evolution of intelligence, as compared to other planetary environments which are suitable for life" (ibid.). Kukla is right in saying that it is a guess that the earth is hospitable in the said manner. One should note, though, that it is the more probable guess, as the alternative would be to hold to some scenario invoking luck, such as despite the inhibitory conditions of the earth, just the right mutation appeared at just the right moment to circumvent the factors on earth noxious to intelligent life.

37 Conway Morris offers us only the following vague reason for what could elicit increase in brain-size: "Large brains may therefore be favoured when the environment offers a special challenge" (*Life's Solution*, 249).

38 C. O. Lovejoy paraphrased by Barrow and Tipler in *The Anthropic Cosmological Principle*, 131.

39 Conway Morris, *Life's Solution*, 196.

40 Ibid., 260.

41 If Aquinas adopted an evolutionary perspective, he definitely would have seen the human species as converged upon: "Since anything whatsoever that is moved, insofar as it moves, tends toward divine likeness so that the thing may be perfect in itself, and anything is perfect when it comes to exist in act, it is necessary that the aim of anything that exists in potency be that it tend to act through motion. Therefore, to the extent that an act is posterior and more perfect, to that extent the appetite of matter is more chiefly conveyed towards it. Whence it is necessary that the appetite of matter, by which it desires form as the ultimate end of generation, tend towards the ultimate and most perfect act that matter is able to attain....[A] form more posterior and of greater dignity [than the form of man] is not found in generable and corruptible things. Therefore, the human soul is the ultimate grade of all of generation, and matter tends to this form as to an ultimate form" (*Summa Contra Gentiles*, Bk. III, chap. 22).

42 Crowe, *The ET Life Debate 1750-1900*, 552, 553.

43 See Darling, *Life Everywhere*, 164-167.

44 See Ward and Brownlee, *Rare Earth*, 50, 223-224. See also ibid., 234: "Unfortunately, there is no evidence on how common large moons are for warm terrestrial planets close to their parent stars."

45 See Kaiser, "Extraterrestrial Life and Extraterrestrial Intelligence," 83: "Actually, moons like ours are hard to come by. We know that the Moon could not have been formed directly as a spin-off from the early, molten Earth. Instead it was probably formed out of a blob of material ejected into space when a huge (larger-than-Mars) asteroid or comet struck Earth's surface at precisely the right angle. Computer models developed to work out the dynamics of such an ejection have shown that it is possible. But the required mass and speed of the meteorite and the necessary angle of impact make the probability of such a collision very low. In fact, the formation of our particular Earth-Moon system is something of a freak accident (a 'miracle,' if you prefer). Still, without the formation of the Moon, improbable as it is, Earth's behavior would have been as chaotic as Mars', and environmental conditions would not have remained stable enough to allow the evolution of more complex forms of life."

46 See Darling, *Life Everywhere*, 96-98.

47 See Ward and Brownlee, *Rare Earth*, 240: Jupiter also arguably plays an important role in regard to life on earth "[b]ecause it cleans our solar system of dangerous Earth orbit-crossing asteroids and comets." See Darling, *Life Everywhere*, 107 for a rebuttal of this position. See Bruce Jakosky, *The Search for Life on Other Planets* (Cambridge: Cambridge University Press, 1998), 116: "[I]n another solar system that did not have a Jupiter or Saturn, an Earth-like planet might be too heavily bombarded to sustain life."

48 See Conway Morris, *Life's Solution*, chap. 5, "Uniquely lucky? The strangeness of Earth," for an account of recent research indicating that that features of the earth that makes it conducive to life may well be unique to it. See also Gonzalez and Richards, *The Privileged Planet*.

49 Frank Drake and Dava Sobel, *Is Anyone Out There?*, 52

50 Jakosky, *The Search for Life on Other Planets*, 285.

51 See ibid. See also *Rare Earth* 274, 275 where the authors propose what they regard as a more realistic alternative to the Drake Equation, one which contains parameters which the Drake equation omits, parameters which decrease the likelihood that complex life exists elsewhere. See also Robert Naeye, "Are We Alone in the Universe? Evidence from a variety of scientific fields indicates that we might be the lonely inhabitants of a vast cosmic ocean," *Astronomy*, 24 (July 1996), 36-43.

Chapter 10—The Fermi Paradox

1 For a more complete discussion of the Fermi Paradox see Stephen Webb, *If the Universe is Teeming with Aliens, Where is Everybody? Fifty Solutions to Fermi's Paradox and the Problem of Extraterrestrial Life* (New York: Copernicus Books, 2002).

2 Ian Crawford, "Where Are They?," *Scientific American* (July 2000), 42.

3 Ward and Brownlee, *Rare Earth*, 164. See also Jakosky, *The Search for Life on Other Planets*, 270: "The Earth has lived through more than half and perhaps as much as 80% of its inhabitable lifetime."

4 See John D. Barrow and Frank J. Tipler, *The Anthropic Cosmological Principle* (Oxford: Oxford University Press, 1986), 79.

5 See ibid., 580.

6 Jakosky, *The Search for Life on Other Planets*, 285. Jakosky's estimate is based on velocities of 1-10% of the speed of light.

7   See Barrow and Tipler, *The Anthropic Cosmological Principle*, 581. This is Barrow and Tipler's estimate based on a velocity of $3 \times 10^{-4}c$.

8   If we go by the authority of Barrow and Tipler the time it would take to colonize a galaxy is "less than 300 million years" (*The Anthropic Cosmological Principle*, 577). The astronomer Ian Crawford supposes a much faster space ship, and gives the much smaller figure of "50 million years" (Crawford, "Where Are They?," 41).

9   See ibid., 590: "[T]he Newman-Sagan analysis yielded a value...the same to within a factor of 3."

10 Paul Davies, *Are We Alone?*, 72.

11 Webb, *If the Universe is Teeming with Aliens, Where is Everybody?*, 100.

12 See George W. Swenson, Jr. "Intragalactically Speaking," *Scientific American* (July 2000) 44.

13 See Frank Drake and Dava Sobel, *Is Anyone Out There?* (New York: Delacorte Press, 1992), 43.

14 See Swenson, Jr. "Intragalactically Speaking," 44-47.

15 See H. Paul Shuch "Optical SETI and the Arecibo Myth" in *The Search for Extraterrestrial Intelligence (SETI) in the Optical Spectrum II*, Stuart A. Kingsley, Guillermo A. Lemarchand, eds. Society of Photo-Optical Instrumentation Engineers Proceedings, 2704, May 1996 (electronic reprint). Shuch, a former Executive Director of The SETI League, Inc., and a strong supporter of microwave SETI, questions "the assertion that Arecibo (Earth's largest radiotelescope) would be able to detect its theoretical twin across the Galaxy." Shuch comes up with the much more modest figure of 10,000 LY which is approximately one eighth of the diameter of the galaxy. He maintains that "Cyclops" is capable of inter-Galactic transmission. Cyclops was designed in a 1971 SETI study, but never constructed: "Its phased array of 900 fully steerable 100 meter dishes would have given us truly impressive range....Cyclops is clearly capable of interstellar communications on a trans-Galactic scale, even at the hydrogen line, and constrained to very conservative estimates of Earth transmitter and receiver technologies."

16 One SETI project has been collecting data by using a small antenna on the Arecibo telescope; it has only been running for four years. The collected data was analysed on volunteers' desktop computers

(SETI@home). In March 2003 researchers from the University of California Berkeley got to use the main Arecibo telescope for two or three days to look at the most promising signals (such as repeat signals) of those analysed by SETI@home, as well as at some other likely candidates, such as stars known to possess planets. The group expects to be back about two years later with a new set of candidates to test. See "Alien hunters take a closer look," 12 March 2003 Nature Science Update (websource) and Amir Alexander, "On Last Day at Arecibo, SETI@home Turns Up Distant Planetary System," March 24, 2003 (www.planetary.org).

17 See Andrew J. LePage, "Where Could They Hide," *Scientific American* (July 2000) 40: There is a scheme for classifying how technologically advanced a civilization is that was devised by Nikolia S. Karashev and later extended by Carl Sagan. Type I civilizations could transmit signals with a power equivalent to…about 1016 watts. Type II…about 1027 watts. Type III…1038 watts. For example, based on the Arecibo output, humanity rates as a type 0.7 civilization….SETI programs completely exclude Arecibo-level radio transmissions out to 50 or so light-years. Farther away, they can rule out the most powerful transmitters. Far beyond the Milky Way, SETI fails altogether, because the relative motions of galaxies would shift any signals out of the detection band. These are not trivial results. Before scientist began to look, they actually thought that type II or III civilizations might actually be quite common. This does not appear to be the case…. On the other hand, millions of undetected civilizations only slightly more advanced than our own could fill the Milky Way. A hundred or more type I civilizations could also share the galaxy with us."

18 Human salvation history holds interest even for the angels. See 1 P. 1:12: "The Spirit of Christ which was in them [i.e., the prophets] foretold the sufferings of Christ and the glories that would come after them…. Even angels long to catch a glimpse of these things." See also Crowe, *The ET Life Debate 1750-1900*, 102: "[James] Beattie's…final reply posits extended effects from the redemption. He states that extraterrestrials 'will not suffer for our guilt, nor be rewarded for our obedience. But it is not absurd to imagine, that our fall and recovery may be useful to them as an example; and that the divine grace manifested in our redemption may raise their adoration and gratitude into higher raptures and quicken their ardour to inquire…into the dispensations of infinite wisdom.' Moreover, he suggests that this view is 'not

mere conjecture [but] derives plausibility from many analogies in nature; as well as from holy writ, which represents the mystery of our redemption as an object of curiosity to superior beings, and our repentance as an occasion of their joy.'"

19   The Fermi Paradox becomes more persuasive when placed alongside evidence that planets capable of sustaining life are rare, as Webb does in *If the Universe is Teeming with Aliens, Where is Everybody?*.

Chapter 11—Philosophical Arguments concerning ETI

1   Crowe, *The ET Life Debate 1750-1900*, 4, 5.
2   See Aristotle, *Physics*, Bk. II, chap. 8. It is fair to ask whether Aristotle regarded necessity as a third type of explanation for natural phenomena, alongside chance and goal-directed action. However, here is not the place to embark on an in-depth analysis of his views on the subject.
3   It is commonly assumed that if an outcome is chance or random that this excludes the possibility that it be planned. Both Aristotle and Gould appear to think this way. Without entering into an in-depth discussion of contingency, I note that Aquinas adopts the view that what is chance at one level may be planned at another level. See *ST* I, q. 116, art. 1 and *Compendium Theologium* q. 137.
4   See Lucretius, *The Way Things Are*, trans. Rolfe Humphries (Bloomington: Indiana University Press, 1973), chap. 5, and note 9 (248).
5   Ibid., 164, 165.
6   See Kukla, "SETI: On the Prospects and Pursuitworthiness of the Search for Extraterrestrial Intelligence," 44-46 for an analysis of modern day Lucretian arguments.
7   Edward O. Wilson, *The Diversity of Life* (Cambridge: Harvard University Press, 1992), 345.
8   Lucretius, *The Way Things Are*, 172.
9   See Conway Morris, *Life's Solution*, xiii: "To paraphrase much of this book, life may be a universal principle, but we can still be alone. In other words, once you are on the path it is pretty straightforward, but finding a suitable planet and maybe getting the right recipe for life's origination could be exceedingly difficult: inevitable humans in a lonely Universe. Now if this happens to be the case, that in turn might

be telling us something very interesting indeed. Either we are a cosmic accident without either meaning or purpose, or alternatively..."

10 It would be wrong to say that Paul Davies is a dyed-in-the-wool biological determinist. In one of his earlier books, *Are We Alone?*, he does propose that: "[G]iven the laws of physics and the initial conditions of the universe, the emergence of life and of consciousness can, I assert, be expected. In a re-run the details would be different. You wouldn't have *Homo sapiens*; you wouldn't even have Earth. But somewhere in the cosmos conscious life would emerge (107)." However, in more recent works, such as *The Fifth Miracle*, Davies is more cautious about making assertions, and instead limits himself to teasing out the philosophical consequences of biological determinism, and to discussing problems with this view (e.g., physical laws seem incapable of accounting for the information-rich molecule, DNA).

11 Davies, quoted on the back cover of *Many Worlds*.

12 Davies, *Are We Alone?*, 3.

13 Paul Davies, *Research News & Opportunities in Science and Theology*, 1, 5 (January 2001), 29.

14 Dick provides the historical development of the idea of uniformity in nature in chap. 6 of *Plurality of Worlds*: "Newton, Natural Theology, and the Triumph of the Concept of Other Worlds." Dick notes that Newton himself was not convinced that his laws applied everywhere in the universe, but eventually later thinkers, such as William Whiston, affirmed that the operation of gravity was the same throughout the universe. Kant embraced the view that Newton's laws held throughout the cosmos, and used this to argue that other earthlike planets have formed elsewhere and are populated. Kant "emphasized that in his system matter was formed according to necessary laws, rather than subject to blind chance; he thereby avoided any atheistic implications, because the natural laws are evidence of a supreme plan" (*ibid.*, 167). Kant's position is very much like Davies's, at least as to its main points.

15 *Cosmos and Anthropos A Philosophical Interpretation of the Anthropic Cosmological Principle*, Errol E. Harris (Atlantic Highlands, NJ: Humanities International Press, 1991), 171.

16 Wiker, "Alien Ideas Christianity and the Search for Extraterrestrial Life," in *Crisis*, November 4, 30.

17 *ST* I, q. 47, art. 3.

18 See *ST* II-II, q. 164, art. 1, ad 1 and *Quaestiones Disputatae de Malo*, q. 5, art. 5, regarding the "necessity of the matter." Aquinas doubtlessly got this notion from Aristotle (e.g., *Parts of Animals*, Bk. 4, chap. 2, 677a15-18).

19 Perhaps another example of something resulting from the necessity of the matter is the existence of galaxies that are out of causal connection with ours. While it may be the case that their existence is necessary for the gravitational force of the whole universe, it may also be the case that principal reason for their existence is simply that our galaxy could not have been produced without their also being made at the same time. Whewell argues in this vein, maintaining that the laws ordered by God in view of producing the earth result in the production of other planets and the stars by way of by-product: "The planets and stars are the lumps which have flown from the potter's wheel of the Great Worker....If even these superfluous portions of the material are marked with universal traces of regularity and order, this shows that universal rules are his implements, and that Order is the first and universal Law of the heavenly work" (*The Plurality of Worlds*, 243).

20 St. Albert, *De Caelo et Mundo*, 69.

21 I am not so familiar with Davies's works to affirm that he never considers the final cause when discussing ETI existence, but certainly efficient causality has the center stage in his books *Are We Alone?* and *The Fifth Miracle*.

22 Eugene F. Mallove, *The Quickening Universe* (New York: St. Martin's Press, c1987), 12. See Davies, *Are We Alone?*, 128: "I conclude from all these deliberations that consciousness, far from being a trivial accident, is a fundamental feature of the universe, a natural product of the outworking of the laws of nature to which they are connected in a deep and still mysterious way....[I]f consciousness is a basic phenomenon that is part of the natural outworking of the laws of the universe, then we can expect it to have emerged elsewhere."

23 Ernest Barnes paraphrased by Wilkenson, *Alone in the Universe?*, 116: "First, God had created the Universe for the emergence of consciousness, therefore consciousness would not be confined to just one world." Again, planning can have as its goal something that is specifically meant to be a one-time event or thing.

24 See *ST* I, q. 70, unicus and *Quaestiones Disputatae de Potentia*, q. 3, art. 11, sed contra and corpus. See also *ST* I, q. 73, art. 1, ad 3: "New species, if such appear, preexist in certain active powers even as animals generated from putrefaction are produced from the powers of the stars and of the elements from which they receive their beginning, even if new species of such animals are produced. For some animals belonging to a new species sometimes arise even from the mixing of animals diverse in species, as the mule is generated from the ass and the horse...."

25 I reiterate that Davies's current view may well be other. This view does correspond to that of biological determinists such as Christian De Duve: "Life is either a reproducible, almost commonplace manifestation of matter, given certain conditions, or a miracle" (*Vital Dust*, 292).

26 My suspicion that there is plenty of bacteria out there, but no animals is shared by other authors, including Stephen Webb and Monica M. Grady. At the end of the section entitled "The Prokaryote-Eukaryote Transition is Rare," Webb concludes: "It is at least a plausible resolution of the Fermi paradox that life elsewhere in the universe has stalled at the unicellular stage. We may one day visit planets and find everywhere oceans teeming with strange, microscopic organisms—lots of life, but life at a low grade. Perhaps nowhere did the right sequence of biological and environmental events take place that would make possible the evolution of animal life—and thus with intelligent species with which we can communicate" (*Where is Everybody? Fifty Solutions to the Fermi Paradox and the Problem of Extraterrestrial Life*, 211). Grady expresses the following view on whether we are alone: "The discovery of micro-organisms on Earth that seem to be able to overcome the disadvantages of extreme heat, cold, pressure and radiation encourages the view that there may be life elsewhere. There is an abundance of organic materials and water within the Solar System, and the potential for their presence on planets around other stars. But even if microbial life is widespread within the Solar System or galaxy, there is no guarantee that it has managed to survive and evolve into sentient or intelligent beings" (*Astrobiology*, 91).

27 Aristotle, *Metaphysics* in *The Basic Works of Aristotle*, ed. Richard McKeon, trans. W. D. Ross (New York: Random House, 1968), 1075a16-23. Aristotle would not see the causal disconnection of certain inanimate portions of the universe from one another as being

contrary to the good order of the universe, whereas he would see the disconnection of intelligent material beings as being such.

28 *Physics*, in *The Basic Works of Aristotle*, trans. R. P. Hardie and R. K. Gaye, 199b32-200a10.

29 See *SCG* III, chap. 74.

30 *ST* I, q. 116, art. 1.

31 See *SCG* III, chap. 72. While some reject the notion that chance is involved in the production of intelligent material beings on the grounds that, if this were so, the universe might never have produced such beings, others, such as Arthur Peacocke adopt the stance that God "takes risks" with his creation, and "most of all with created humanity." Peacocke's take on chance in creation is that "it impels us to recognize more emphatically than ever before the constraints which we must regard God as imposing upon himself in creation and to suggest that *God has a 'self-limited' omnipotence and omniscience*....The attribution of 'self-limitation' to God with respect to his omnipotence is meant to indicate that God has so made the world that there are certain areas over which he has chosen to have no control" (*Theology for a Scientific Age* [Minneapolis: Fortress Press, 1993], 121). Peacocke's view is another instance of the fairly common opinion that chance events somehow escape God's knowledge and power—a view which is of course contrary to Catholic teachings on Divine Providence.

32 See Crowe, *The ET Life Debate 1750-1900*, 434: "Pohle's claim...that unbelievers and Christians had reached agreement in favor of pluralism is certainly excessive. As this discussion of the extraterrestrial life debate in German religious writing of the later nineteenth century shows, neither camp had attained a consensus even within itself. Among materialists, Büchner's antipluralist universe was strikingly -different from that of Strauss, Du Prel, and Haeckel. Among Christians, the Lutheran Zöckler was similarly opposed to the antipluralist views of his confessional colleague, Luthardt. Catholics were scarcely less divided.... Once again the pluralist hypothesis has shown its remarkable flexibility and appeal, while those who discussed it revealed the difficulties man has experienced in attaining any sort of evidence—scientific, philosophical, or religious—on which even persons of similar perspectives could concur."

33 Another teleological argument runs: "if there were stars which could not be seen from the Earth, then they must have been created for the benefit of those who could see them" (Wilkenson, *Alone in the Universe?*, 18 paraphrasing arguments given by Christiaan Huygens).

34 Barrow and Tipler, *The Anthropic Cosmological Principle*, 3. Even today, after Barrow and Tippler, some people hold Alvin Plantinga's view that: "It would seem strange if God would have created this entire universe and have creatures in only one small corner who were able to witness it and see what miraculous work he has done" (quoted by Todd Halvorson and Robyn Suriano, "Finding other life wouldn't shake most faiths," *Florida Today*, Online Special Report, 1999). See also Ernan McMullin, *Research News & Opportunities in Science and Theology* (July/August 2001), 46: "Fields like cosmology emphasize the immensity of the time and space scales that we are dealing with and call into question the whole idea of a special Christian dispensation focusing on a single planet..."

35 Whewell gives another argument against the claim that a universe uninhabited by ETIs would represent a colossal waste of planets, using an analogy with time. He first points out that intelligent life has only existed on earth for a fraction of the total time that the planet has existed. He then goes on to argue by analogy: "The intelligent part of creation is thrust into the compass of a few years, in the course of myriads of ages; why not then into the compass of a few miles, in the expanse of systems?" (*The Plurality of Worlds*, 107). In other words, one would have to blame God for wasting time in taking so long to produce intelligent inhabitants on earth, if one was to blame him for wasting space and planets by leaving them uninhabited (see ibid. 104, 105). Note that this argument in a certain way dovetails with the later anthropic argument against wasted space in that just as a universe of a certain size is needed for the production of a single earth, so too a universe of a certain age is needed both for the production of a single earth, and for an intelligent species to evolve. In our universe of motion and development, plainly certain end products are only achieved after long periods of time before which they do not exist, and they appear in places that were not always there, but which had to first develop.

36 Whewell, *The Plurality of Worlds*, 224.

37 Ibid., 223.

254 Christianity and Extraterrestrials?

38 Sir Arthur Eddington, quoted by Annie Dillard in *Pilgrim at Tinker Creek* (New York: Harper's Magazine Press, 1974), 175.

39 Metrodorus of Chios in the fourth century B.C. argues in the opposite sense that Whewell does: "It would be strange if a single ear of corn grew in a large plain or were there only one world in the infinite" (Simplicius quoted by F. M. Cornford, "Innumerable Worlds in Presocratic Philosophy," *Classical Quarterly*, 12 [1934], 1-16:13). It does not affect the argument to substitute "vast universe" for Metrodorus's "infinite."

40 See Ps. 19: "The heavens declare the glory of God, the vault of heaven proclaims his handiwork; day discourses of it to day, night to night hands on the knowledge. No utterance at all, no speech, no sound that anyone can hear; yet their voice goes out through all the earth, and their message to the ends of the world."

41 See *ST* I-II, q. 113, art. 9, ad 2: "the good of the grace of one individual is a greater than the good of nature of the entire universe."

Chapter 12—Fallacious Arguments for ETI Existence

1 See Crowe, *The ET Life Debate 1750-1900*, 552-554: "Recurrent fallacies and linguistic abuses."

2 Kenneth J. Delano, *Many Worlds, One God* (Hicksville, New York: New York Exposition Press, 1977). See chaps. 3 and 6 where one will find an authority cited every page or two.

3 Ibid., 8. Delano's book is rife with personal attack, to cite another instance, "…a great many people still maintain that the human race embodies the ideological and spiritual center of the cosmos. *This conceited opinion* was expressed by the renowed scholar Peter Lombard…Lombard developed the following theological view of man's relation to the universe, 'Just a man is made for the sake of God—that is, that he may serve Him,—so the universe is made for the sake of man—that is, that it may serve him; therefore is man placed at the middle point of the universe; that he may both serve and be served.' *People who still entertain twelfth-century ideas* like those expressed by Peter Lombard will have the greatest difficulty in trying to fit the discovery of ETI into their religious philosophy of life" (ibid., 11). I have italicized the personal attacks.

4 Barry Friedman quoted by Todd Halvorson and Robyn Suriano, "Finding other life wouldn't shake most faiths," *Florida Today*, 1999, Online Special Report.

5 Russell Stannard, "Our Place in the Scheme of Things," *Research News*, Dec. 2000, 22 reprinted from the *Tablet*, 13 May 2000.

6 Davies, *Are We Alone?*, 54, 55.

7 Jastrow, "A Cosmic Perspective on Human Existence," in *God for the 21st Century*, 62.

8 Delano, *Many Worlds, One God*, 11. Delano is quoting Percival Lowell. He does not, however, provide a reference to Lowell's works. Since Delano quotes the statement with approval, I will treat it as if it were his own.

9 Aristotle, *Generation of Animals*, trans. A. L. Peck (Cambridge: Harvard University Press, 1963), 736b27-29.

10 De Duve, *Vital Dust*, 301. See Whewell, *The Plurality of Worlds*, 109-10: "[Man has] also an intellect by which he can speculate about the relations of things, in their most general form.... He can discover truths, to which all things, existing in space and time, must conform. These are conditions of existence to which the creation conforms, that is, to which the Creator conforms; and man, capable of seeing that such conditions are true and necessary, is capable, so far, of understanding some of the conditions of the Creator's workmanship. In this way, the mind of man has some community with the mind of God: and however remote and imperfect this community may be, it must be real. Since, then, man has thus, in his intellect, an element of community with God, it is so far conceivable that he should be, in a special manner, the object of God's care and favour. The human mind, with its wonderful and perhaps illimitable powers, is something of which we can believe God to be 'mindful.'"

11 CCC #704, #705 (footnotes removed). Aquinas, in keeping with what the *Catechism* says, spells out very nicely what human dignity consists in: "Since man is said to be in the image of God according to his intellectual nature, correspondingly he is above all in God's image according as the intellectual nature is chiefly able to imitate God. The intellectual nature chiefly imitates God as to this that God knows and loves himself.—Whence the image of God can be considered in man in three ways. One way, according as man has a natural aptitude for

knowing and loving God; and this aptitude consists in the very nature of the mind which is common to all men. In another way, according as man knows and loves God in act, but nevertheless imperfectly; and this is the image through conformity to grace. In a third way, according as man perfectly knows and loves God in act; and thus the image is ascertained according to the likeness of glory" (*ST* I, q. 93, art. 4).

12 See 2 Cor. 1:18: "And we, with our unveiled faces reflecting like mirrors the brightness of the Lord, all grow brighter and brighter as we are turned into the image that we reflect; this is the work of the Lord who is spirit." See also *CCC* #2809 (footnotes removed): "In making man in his image and likeness, God 'crowned him with glory and honor,' but by sinning, man fell 'short of the glory of God.' From that time on, God was to manifest his holiness by revealing and giving his name, in order to restore man to the image of his Creator." (This paragraph is part of a commentary on the Our Father, whence the reference to God's "name.") We will ultimately be as perfect images of God as we can be only in heaven: "My dear people, we are already the children of God but what we are to be in the future has not yet been revealed; all we know is, that when it is revealed we shall be like him because we shall see him as he really is" (1 Jn. 3:2).

13 St. Athanasius, *On the Incarnation*, quoted by *CCC* #460. See *CCC* #460: "The Word became flesh to make us 'partakers of the divine nature' [2 Pet. 1:4]. 'For this is why the Word became man, and the Son of God became the Son of man: so that man, by entering into communion with the Word and thus receiving divine sonship, might become a son of God' [St. Irenaeus, *Against Heresies*]. 'For the Son of God became man so that we might become God' [St. Athanasius, *On the Incarnation*]. 'The only-begotten Son of God, wanting to make us sharers in his divinity, assumed our nature, so that he, made man, might make men gods' [Thomas Aquinas, *Opuscula*]."

14 See *Romans* in *The Jerusalem Bible*, note q to Rom. 8:30, 281: "Christ, the image of God in the primordial creation, Col 1:15+, cf. Heb. 1:3 has now come, by a new creation, 2 Co 5:17+, to restore to fallen man the splendour of that image which had been darkened by sin, Gn 1:26+; 3:22-24+; Rm 5:12+. He does this by forming man in the still more splendid image of a son of God (Rm 8:29); thus, sound moral judgement is restored to the 'new man', Col 3:10+, and also his claim to glory which he had sacrificed by sin, Rm 3;23+. This glory which

Christ as the image of God possesses by right, 2 Co 4:4, is progressively communicated to the Christian, 2 Co 3:18, until his body is itself clothed in the image of the 'heavenly' man, 1 Co 15:49.

Chapter 13—Would Adjustments to Catholic Teaching Have to be Made if ETI was Discovered?

1   Robert Jastrow, "A Cosmic Perspective on Human Existence," in *God for the 21st Century*, 63.

2   Pierre de Cazre, "Letter to Gassendi" quoted by Crowe, *The Extraterrestrial Life Debate 1750-1900*, 17, 18.

3   See *Dei Verbum* in *Documents of Vatican II*, #12: "Those who search out the intention of the sacred writers must, among other things, have regard for 'literary forms.' For truth is proposed and expressed in a variety of ways, depending on whether a text is history of one kind or another, or whether its form is that of prophecy, poetry, or some other type of speech. The interpreter must investigate what meaning the sacred writer intended to express and actually expressed in particular circumstances as he used contemporary literary forms in accordance with the situation of his own time and culture. For the correct understanding of what the sacred author wanted to assert, due attention must be paid to the customary and characteristic styles of perceiving, speaking and narrating which prevailed at the time of the sacred writer, and to the customs men normally followed at that period in their everyday dealings with one another."

4   See Aristotle, *De Anima*, 431a16. See also C.S. Lewis, *Miracles* (New York: McMillan Publishing Co., 1960), 74, 75: "When we point out that what the Christians mean is not to be identified with their mental pictures, some people say, 'In that case would it not be better to get rid of mental pictures, and of the language which suggests them, altogether?' But this is impossible....No doubt we are unspeakably different from Him; to that extent all man-like images are false. But those images of shapeless mists and irrational forces which, unacknowledged, haunt the mind when we think we are rising to the conception of impersonal and absolute being, must be very much more so. For images, of the one kind or of the other, will come; we cannot jump off our own shadow." See also Mariano Artigas and William R. Shea, *Galileo in Rome: A Chronicle of 500 Days* (Oxford: Oxford University Press,

2003), 43: "The world has not only to be understood, it must also be imagined."

5   See *ST* I, 70, art. 1, ad 3: "[A]ccording to Aristotle, the stars are fixed in their spheres and actually move only with the movement of the spheres. The senses, however, perceive only the movement of the celestial bodies, not that of the spheres. And Moses, having care for ordinary people, as we have already observed, follows what appears to the senses."

6   Scripture doubtlessly signifies something true when it says that God made the firmament. What has to be avoided is to attribute to "firmament" a specific scientific meaning in light of the science of one's day, given how science is subject to revision. As Aquinas points out "firmament" can simply refer to part of the sky where condensation takes place and clouds form (see *ST* I, q. 68, arts. 1-3).

7   See Ps. 93 and Hab. 3:11 which also make reference to the immobility of the earth.

8   *CCC* #400: "The harmony in which they [Adam and Eve] had found themselves, thanks to original justice, is now destroyed: the control of the soul's spiritual faculties over the body is shattered; the union of man and woman becomes subject to tensions, their relations henceforth marked by lust and domination. Harmony with creation is broken: visible creation has become alien and hostile to man. Because of man, creation is now subject 'to its bondage to decay.' [Rom. 8:21] Finally, the consequence explicitly foretold for this disobedience will come true: man will 'return to the ground,' [Gen. 3:19; cf. 2:27] for out of it he was taken. *Death makes its entrance into human history*."

9   See Keith Ward, *Religion and Human Nature* (Oxford: Clarendon Press, 1998), 159: "Death and suffering existed for millennia before humans arrived on the scene, and the first humans were probably ignorant, barbaric, and religiously primitive. The idea of a 'fall' from grace seems to have been replaced by the idea of a hesitant, ambiguous, and only partly successful 'rise' towards moral and rational action." (Keith Ward is an ordained minister in the Church of England.) See also, "Fifth Session, June 17, 1546," in *Council of Trent*, ed. and trans. H. J. Schroeder (St. Louis, MO: B. Herder Book Co., 1941), #1, 21: "If any one does not confess that the first man, Adam, when he had transgressed the commandment of God in Paradise, immediately lost the holiness and justice wherein he had been constituted; and that he

incurred, through the offence of that prevarication, the wrath and indignation of God, and consequently death, with which God had previously threatened him...let him be anathema."

10 Pius XII, *Humani Generis*, #36.

11 Pope John Paul II, in a non-magisterial address, stated that evolution is "more than a hypothesis" ("Theories of Evolution," Address to the Pontifical Academy of Sciences, October 22, 1996, #4, *First Things*, 71 [March 1997], 28).

12 See *CCC* #338: "Nothing exists that does not owe its existence to God the Creator."

13 *ST* I, q. 91, art. 2.

14 See John Paul II, "Address to the Pontifical Academy of Sciences," October 31, 1979 in *L'Obsservatore Romano*, 44 (November 4, 1992), 5.

15 See ibid., #12: "Spiritui Sancto mentem fuisse nos docere quomodo ad coelum eatur, non quomodo coelum gradiatur." This saying is attributed to Cesare Baronius.

16 See Mariano Artigas, "I think the ETI issue was a part of the background of the resistance to admit Galileo's heliocentrism. It was not, however, an explicit issue, at least to the same extent as the interpretation of Scripture was. We have only a few hints [five texts], and only one of them treats explicitly of living beings outside the Earth....[In the latter text] Galileo writes in order to clarify that he does not argue for the existence of living beings on the Moon, showing thus that this was a point that he was anxious to make perfectly clear" (Personal communication).

17 See Pius XII, *Humani Generis* #37, 15 and CCC #404 concerning the unity of descent of the human race (both passages are quoted in the introduction).

18 See *Pastoral Constitution on the Church in the Modern World* in *The Documents of Vatican II*, ed. Walter M. Abbott (New York: Guild Press, 1966, #15, 212: "Man judges rightly that by his intellect he surpasses the material universe, for he shares in the light of the divine mind." It is a constant teaching of the Fathers and Doctors that the faculty of intellect, as well as the human soul are immaterial. See, for example, *ST* I, q. 3, art. 1, ad 2: "[M]an is not said to be to the image of God in virtue of the body, but in virtue of that by which man excels the other animals.... Man, however, excels all animals as to reason and intellect.

Whence man is to the image of God according to intellect and reason, which are incorporeal."

19 Paine, *The Age of Reason*, 52.

20 See *In Libros Posterior Analyticorum Expositio*, ed. Raymond M. Spiazzi, O.P. (Turin: Marietti, 1964), #6: "For through a process of this sort [namely, a process of discovery]…sometimes faith or opinion is engendered on account of the probability of the propositions from which it proceeds: for reason turns entirely toward one side of a contradiction, granted with fear of the other, and to this is ordered Topics or Dialectics. For a dialectical syllogism is from what is probable…."

21 See *SCG* I, chap. 9: "We do not believe those things that are above human reason except when God reveals them. There are nevertheless some reasonings possessing verisimilitude for manifesting truths of this sort conducive to the exercise and solace of the faithful, but not to convince adversaries; for the very insufficiency of these arguments would confirm them in error [rather than lead them to truth], if they would think that we consent to the truth of the faith on account of such weak arguments."

22 See *ST* III, q. 1, arts. 5 and 6.

23 Pius XII, *Divino Afflante Spiritu* (Boston: St. Paul Editions, s.d.), #47. The encyclical came out in 1943.

24 See *CCC* #340, 341: "God wills the *interdependence of creatures*. The sun and the moon, the cedar and the little flower, the eagle and the sparrow: the spectacle of their countless diversities and inequalities tells us that no creature is self-sufficient. Creatures exist only in dependence on each other, to complete each other, in the service of each other. *The beauty of the universe*: The order and harmony of the created world results from the diversity of beings and from the relationships among them."

Chapter 14—Do ETI proponents have an anti-Christian agenda?

1 Jaki, *Cosmos and Creator*, 118.

2 Jill Tarter, "SETI and the Religions of the Universe," in *Many Worlds*, 145.

3 Willem B. Drees, "Bethlehem: Center of the Universe?," in *God for the 21st Century*, 69.

4   See Peters, "Exo-Theology: Speculations on Extraterrestrial Life," 202: "Jack A. Jennings, a Presbyterian campus minister, contends that both UFOs and ETI should become items of theological debate; but, unfortunately, the debate is not being carried on in learned journals. Because the church ignores the topic, we find it being considered in the marketplace."

5   Michael McAteer, "The Truth is Out There," *The Star* (Toronto), Saturday, August 17, 2002, Life Section, K14.

Chapter 15—What Might the Catholic Church Say on the ETI Question?

1   See John Dietzen, "Did God Create Life on Other Planets," *The Tablet* (September 25, 1999), 19: "It is said that UFOs are the second most popular subject on the Internet these days—second only to sex."

2   There are a certain number of Catholic clergy with Vatican ties who are interested in the Christianity-ETI debate, e.g., Msgr. Corrado Balducci (who is quoted on internet sources), along with many of the members of the Vatican Observatory. Archbishop Patrick J. O'Boyle (now deceased) thought it was important that the Church settle the ETI question: "In June 1959 the commission preparing the agenda for the Second Vatican Council wrote to all the bishops of the world, asking them what they'd like to talk about....Archbishop O'Boyle proposed that the council pronounce, 'in light of the doctrines of creation and redemption,' on 'the possibility of intelligent life on other planets'" (George Weigel, *Letters to a Young Catholic* [New York: Basic Books, 2004], 43).

3   Thomas F. O'Meara, "Christian Theology and Extraterrestrial Intelligent Life," 20.

4   See 2 Peter 2:4: "When angels sinned, God did not spare them: he sent them down to the underworld and consigned them to the dark underground caves to be held there till the day of Judgment."

5   See Mt. 18:10: "See that you never despise any of these little ones, for I tell you that their angels in heaven are continually in the presence of my Father in heaven."

6   See Hebrews 2:16: "For it was not the angels that he took to himself; he took to himself descent from Abraham."

7 A note to *Dei Verbum* in the Abbott and Gallagher edition of *The Documents of Vatican II* says that an earlier draft of the constitution said "salutaris," i.e., tending to salvation, but was finally replaced by the broader sounding "for the sake of our salvation" (note 31, 117).

8 *Dei Verbum*, #11 as quoted in *Iesus Dominus*, #8.

9 *CCC* #280. See *CCC* #2174: "Jesus rose from the dead 'on the first day of the week.' Because it is the 'first day,' the day of Christ's Resurrection recalls the first creation. Because it is the 'eighth day' following the sabbath, it symbolizes the new creation ushered in by Christ's Resurrection." See also: *CCC* #315: "In the creation of the world and of man, God gave the first and universal witness to his almighty love and his wisdom, the first proclamation of the 'plan of his loving goodness,' which finds its goal in the new creation in Christ." The latter passage is weaker in that one could take the creation "of the world" to mean "of the earth."

10 *CCC* #668. Note that Aquinas's *Summa Theologiae* is patterned on the notion of "exitus-reditus," i.e., on the notion that creation flows from God to ultimately return to him through Christ who is the Way. One sees this notion in other of Aquinas's works as well. For example, in commenting on Ecclesiates 1:7 which reads: "All the rivers run into the sea, yet the sea doth not overflow; unto the place from whence the rivers come they return, to flow again," Aquinas says: "The mystery of the Incarnation is intimated by this return of the rivers, when it is said 'unto the place from whence the rivers come they return.' But the fruit of the Incarnation is suggested by this second flowing, when the text says 'to flow again.' These rivers are the natural gifts which God showered on his creatures, existence for example, and life, and understanding, and things of this sort....Though these 'rivers' are dispersed throughout creation, in the human person they converge in a certain sense, for man is as it were the horizon and boundary between spiritual and corporeal nature, and being a kind of midpoint between the two natures shares in the gifts of each....and thus when human nature was joined to God through the mystery of the Incarnation, all the rivers of natural goodnessses reversing course returned to their source.... For God himself, who had showered us with natural goods, when he had in a sense reabsorbed all things into himself by assuming human nature, now not as God alone but as the God-man abundantly flooded mankind with his graces" (III *Scriptum super Sententiis*,

prologue, trans. R. James Long in "Aquinas and the Cosmic Christ," in *Medieval Masters*, ed. R. E. Houser [Houston: Center for Thomistic Studies, 1999] 245-6).

11 *CCC* #1066. See *CCC* #772: "It is in the Church that Christ fulfills and reveals his own mystery as the purpose of God's plan: 'to unite all things in him.'"

12 *Dominus Iesus*, #12.

13 John Paul II, *Ecclesia De Eucharistia*, #8.

14 See Ep. 4:10: "The one who rose higher than all the heavens to fill all things is none other than one who descended."

15 See Arthur Peacocke, "The Challenge and Stimulus of the Epic of Evolution to Theology," in *Many Worlds*, 103: "Christians have to ask themselves (and skeptics will certainly ask them), What can the cosmic significance possibly be of the localized, terrestrial event of the existence of the historical Jesus? Does not the mere possibility of extraterrestrial life render nonsensical all the superlative claims made by the Christian church about his significance?" The Catholic Church would answer that Christ and his redemption do have cosmic significance: All of creation is ordered to Christ and to the new creation that he would bring about.

16 Christopher J. Corbally, S.J., "Religious Implications from the Possibility of Ancient Martian Life," Vatican Observatory, 1997, www.aaas.org/spp/dser/cosmos/perspectives/corbally.shtml.

17 See chap. 1, note 23.

18 See *CCC* #769: "'The Church...will receive its perfection only in the glory of heaven,' at the time of Christ's glorious return....Here below she...longs for the full coming of the Kingdom, when she will 'be united in glory with her king.' The Church, and through her the world, will not be perfected in glory without great trials. Only then will all the just...be gathered together in the universal Church in the Father's presence.'" (footnotes removed)

19 Tommaso Campanella (1568-1634) felt a need to clarify that ETIs, if such there be, do not belong to the race of Adam: "If the inhabitants which may be in other stars are men, they did not originate from Adam and are not infected by his sin....Galileo expressly denies that men can exist in other stars..., but affirms that beings of a higher nature can exist there. Their nature is similar to ours, but is not the

same, despite whatever sportfull and jocose things Kepler says...." (quoted by Crowe, *The ET Life Debate 1750-1900*, 12, 13).

20 Davies, *Are We Alone?*, 137-138.

21 *Dei Verbum* #4, quoted in *CCC* #66. See also *CCC* #67: "Christian faith cannot accept 'revelations' that claim to surpass or correct the Revelation of which Christ is the fulfillment, as is the case in certain non-Christian religions and also in certain recent sects which base themselves on such 'revelations.'"

22 See *CCC* #67: "Throughout the ages, there have been so-called 'private' revelations, some of which have been recognized by the authority of the Church. They do not belong, however, to the deposit of faith. It is not their role to improve or complete Christ's definitive Revelation, but to help live more fully by it in a certain period of history....Christian faith cannot accept 'revelations' that claim to surpass or correct the Revelation of which Christ is the fulfillment...."

23 See V. Ascheri and P. Musso, "Cosmic Missionaries?" (P. Musso provided me with this English translation; the original article appeared in *S.E.T.I.—die Suche nach dem Ausserirdischen* [Munich: Beustverlag, 2002] 170-184): "Certainly, we cannot limit God's freedom and it is in principle possible to Him to assume whatever nature He wants. The main objections to this view is not an anthropocentric, but a Christocentric one, that is: the problem is not that human nature is something special in itself, but the fact that Jesus Christ (who assumed it with a fully gratuitous act of freedom) was resuscitated and glorified and became the King of the Universe, the Center of Cosmos and History, *both in His divine and human nature.*"

24 God is master of history. See Aquinas: "The spiritual sense of Scripture is grasped from this that in writing the course of events the writers signify something other (wherein lies the spiritual sense). However, to order things thus in their course, so that from them such a sense can be gathered, belongs only to the one who governs things by his providence, who alone is God. For just as a man can proffer words or fictional likeness in order to signify something, so also God can present the very course of things that are subject to his providence for the purpose of signifying something" (*Quaestiones Quodlibetales* in vol. 2 of *Selecta Opuscula*, ed. A. Michaele de Maria [Castello, Italy: Typographica S. Lapi, 1886], Quodlibet 7, q. 6, art. 16, 433).

Epilogue

1 Paul Davies, *Are We Alone?*, 136.
2 Barrow and Tipler, *The Anthropic Cosmological Principle*, 598.
3 David Wilkinson is a Methodist chaplain who has a Ph.D. in theoretical astrophysics. In this particular passage, the beliefs he expresses coincide with Roman Catholic beliefs.
4 Wilkinson, *Alone in the Universe?*, 146, 147.

Bibliography

Abbott, Walter M., ed. *The Documents of Vatican II*. New York: The American Press, 1966.

Albertus Magnus. *De Caelo et Mundo*. Vol. 5 of *Opera Omnia*. Aedibus Aschendorff: Monasterii Westfalorum, 1971.

Alexander, Amir. "On Last Day at Arecibo, SETI@home Turns Up Distant Planetary System." (March 24, 2003): www.planetary.org.

Anselm. *Cur Deus Homo*. In *St. Anselm: Basic Writings*, translated by S.N. Deane. La Salle, Illinois: The Open Court Publishing Company, 1974.

Aristotle. *Generation of Animals*, translated by A. L. Peck. Cambridge: Harvard University Press, 1963.

------ *Physics*. In *The Basic Works of Aristotle*, edited by Richard McKeon, and translated by R. P. Hardie and R. K. Gaye. New York: Random House, 1968.

------ *Politics*. In *The Basic Works of Aristotle*, edited by Richard McKeon, and translated by Benjamin Jowett. New York: Random House, 1968.

Artigas, Mariano and William R. Shea. *Galileo in Rome: A Chronicle of 500 Days*. Oxford: Oxford University Press, 2003.

Athanasius. *On the Incarnation*, edited and translated by Penelope Lawson. New York: Macmillan, 1981.

Augustine. *The City of God*. New York: The Modern Library, 1950.

------ *Letters*. Vol. 2 of *The Fathers of the Church*, translated by Wilfrid Parson. New York: Fathers of the Church, Inc., 1953.

Barrow, John D., and Frank J. Tipler. *The Anthropic Cosmological Principle*. Oxford: Oxford University Press, 1986.

Basil. *Exegetic Homilies*, translated by Agnes Clare Way. Washington, D.C.: The Catholic University of America Press, 1963.

Bieri, Robert. "Huminoids on Other Planets?" In *Philosophy of Biology*, edited by Michael Ruse. New York: Macmillan, 1989.

Blanchette, Oliva. *The Perfection of the Universe According to Aquinas: A Teleological Cosmology*. University Park, PA: Pennsylvania State University Press, 1992.

Bonaventure. *Sententiarum*. Vol. 4 of *Opera Omnia*, edited by A. C. Peltier. Paris: Ludovicus Vivès, 1865.

------ *Sententiarum*. Vol. 1 of *Opera Theologica Selecta*, edited by Leonardi M. Bello. Florence: Typographia Collegii S. Bonaventurae, 1934.

Bradley, Denis. *Aquinas on the Twofold Human Good*. Washington, D.C.: The Catholic University of America, 1997.

Catechism of the Catholic Church Bloomingdale, Ohio: Apostolate for Family Consecration, 1994

Chrysostom, John. *Homilies on First Corinthians*, vol. 12 of *Nicene and Post-Nicene Fathers*, edited by Philip Schaff. Grand Rapids, MI: Wm. B. Eerdmans Publishing Company, 1988.

Clement of Alexandria. *Stromata*. Vol. 2 of *The Ante-Nicene Fathers*, edited by A. Cleveland Coxe. Wm. B. Eerdmans Publishing Company, 1986.

Clement of Rome. *The Epistle to the Corinthians*. In *The Epistles of St. Clement of Rome and St. Ignatius of Antioch*, translated by James A. Kleist. New York: Newman Press, 1946.

Congregation for the Doctrine of the Faith. *Dominus Iesus*. Manchester, UK: Catholic Truth Society, 2000.

Conway Morris, Simon. *The Crucible of Creation*. Oxford: Oxford University Press, 1998.

------ *Life's Solution: Inevitable Humans in a Lonely Universe*. Cambridge: University of Cambridge Press, 2003.

Corbally, Christopher J. "Religious Implications from the Possibility of Ancient Martian Life." 1997: www.aaas.org/spp/dser/cosmos/perspectives/corbally.shtml.

Coxe, A. Cleveland, ed. "The Divine Liturgy of the Holy Apostle and Evangelist Mark, the Disciple of the Holy Peter." In vol. 7 of *The Ante-Nicene Fathers*. Wm. B. Eerdmans Publishing Company, 1985.

------ *The Clementine Homilies.* In vol. 8 of *Fathers of the Third and Fourth Centuries*, translated by Thomas Smith and James Donaldson. Wm. B. Eerdmans Publishing Company, 1986.

Crawford, Ian. "Where Are They?" *Scientific American* (July 2000): 39-43.

Crick, Francis. *Life Itself: its Origin and Nature.* New York: Simon and Schuster, c1981.

Crowe, Michael J. *The Extraterrestrial Life Debate 1750-1900 The Idea of a Plurality of Worlds from Kant to Lowell.* New York: Cambridge University Press, 1986.

Danielson, Dennis. "Copernicus and the Tale of the Pale Blue Dot." Lecture delivered to the American Scientific Affiliation, 2003: *www.english.ubc.ca/~ddaniels/*.

Darling, David. *Life Everywhere.* New York: Basic Books, 2001.

Davies, Paul. *Are We Alone?* New York: Basic Books, 1995.

------ *The Fifth Miracle.* New York: Simon & Schuster, 1999.

------ *Research News & Opportunities in Science and Theology* (January 2001) 1.5: 29.

Davis, Charles. "The Place of Christ," *Clergy Review*, n.s., 45 (1960): 707-18.

Davis, John Jefferson. "Search for extraterrestrial intelligence and the Christian doctrine of redemption," *Science and Christian Belief* 9.1 (April 1997): 21-34.

De Duve, Christian. *Vital Dust.* New York: Basic Books, 1995.

Delano, Kenneth J. *Many Worlds, One God.* Hicksville, New York: New York Exposition Press, 1977.

Denton, Michael J. *Nature's Destiny: How the Laws of Biology Reveal Purpose in the Universe.* New York: The Free Press, 1998.

Denzinger, Heinrich, ed. *Enchiridion symbolorum: definitionum et declarationum de rebus fidei et morum.* Rome: Herder, 1963.

Dick, Steven J. *Plurality of Worlds.* Cambridge: Cambridge University Press, 1982.

------ *Life on Other Worlds: The 20th-Century Extraterrestrial Life Debate.* Cambridge: Cambridge University Press, 1998.

Dick, Steven, ed. *Many Worlds The New Universe, Extraterrestrial Life & the Theological Implications*. Philadelphia: Templeton Foundation Press, 2000.

Dietzen, John. "Did God Create Life on Other Planets?" *The Tablet* (25 September 1999): 19.

Dillard, Annie. *Pilgrim at Tinker Creek*. New York: Harper's Magazine Press, 1974.

Drake, Frank and Dava Sobel. *Is Anyone Out There?* New York: Delacorte Press, 1992.

Dyson, Freeman J. *Origins of Life*. Cambridge: Cambridge University Press, 1999.

Frazier, Kendrick. "First Contact: The News Event and the Human Response." In *Extraterrestrial Intelligence: The First Encounter*, edited by James L. Christian. Buffalo, New York: 1976.

Galileo. *Two New Sciences*, translated by Stillman Drake. Madison, Wisconsin: The University of Wisconsin Press, 1974.

Garriga, J. and A. Vilenkin. "Testable anthropic predictions for dark energy." *Physical Review* D67 (2003).

George, Marie I. "Aquinas on Intelligent Extra-Terrestrial Life," *The Thomist* 65 (April 2001): 239-258.

Gilberson, Karl and Donald Yerxa. "Interview: Ernan McMullin." *Research News & Opportunities in Science and Theology* (July/August 2001): 45-6.

Giordano Bruno. *On the Infinite Universe and Worlds*, translated by Dorothea Waley Singer. New York: Henry Schuman, 1950.

Gonzalez, Guillermo and Jay W. Richards. *The Privileged Planet*. Washington, DC: Regnery Publishing Company, 2004.

Görgemanns, Herwig and Heinrich Karpp, eds. *Vier Bücher von den Prinzipien*. Darmstadt: Wissenschaftliche Buchgesellschaft, 1976.

Gould, Stephen Jay. *Wonderful Life The Burgess Shale and the Nature of History*. New York: Norton, 1989.

Grady, Monica M. *Astrobiology*. London: The Natural History Museum, 2001.

A Greek-English Lexicon of the New Testament (Grimm's Wilke's *Clavis Novi Testamenti*), translated by Joseph Thayer. New York: Harper & Brothers, 1893.

Halvorson, Todd and Robyn Suriano. "Finding other life wouldn't shake most faiths." *Florida Today* (1999): Online Special Report.

Harris, Errol E. *Cosmos and Anthropos A Philosophical Interpretation of the Anthropic Cosmological Principle*. Atlantic Highlands, NJ: Humanities International Press, 1991.

Herbermann, Charles G., Edward A. Pace, Condé B. Pallen, Thomas J. Shahan, John J. Wynne, eds. Vol. 4 of *The Catholic Encyclopedia*. New York: The Encyclopedia Press, Inc., 1908.

Hippolytus of Rome. *The Refutation of All Heresies*. Vol. 5 of *Fathers of the Third Century*, edited by A. Cleveland Coxe. Grand Rapids, Michigan: Wm. B. Eerdmans Publishing Company, 1965.

Irenaeus. *Against Heresies*. Vol. 1 of *The Ante-Nicene Fathers*, edited by Alexander Roberts and James Donaldson. Wm. B. Eerdmans Publishing Company, 1987.

Jaki, Stanley. *Cosmos and Creator*. Chicago: Regnery Gateway, 1980.

Jakosky, Bruce. *The Search for Life on Other Planets*. Cambridge: Cambridge University Press, 1998.

Jastrow. Robert. "A Cosmic Perspective on Human Existence." In *God for the 21st Century*, edited by Russell Stannard. Philadelphia: Templeton Foundation Press, 2000.

Jerome. *Apology against the Books of Rufinus*. In *Saint Jerome Dogmatic and Polemical Works*, translated by John N. Hritzu. Washington, D.C.: The Catholic University Press, 1965.

------ "Letter 124: To Avitus." In *Letters and Select Works*. Vol. 6 of *Nicene and Post-Nicene Fathers*, edited by Philip Schaff and Henry Wace. Wm. B. Eerdmans Publishing Co., 1986.

John of Damascus. *The Orthodox Faith*. Vol. 37 of *Writings*, translated by Frederic H. Chase. New York: Fathers of the Church, Inc., 1958.

John Paul II. "Address to the Pontifical Academy of Sciences, October 31, 1979." *L'Obsservatore Romano* 44 (November 4, 1992): 5-6.

------ *Evangelium Vitae.* Washington, D.C.: United States Catholic Conference, 1995.

------ *Fides et Ratio.* Washington, D.C.: United States Catholic Conference, 1998.

------ *Redemptoris missio.* Washington, D.C.: United States Catholic Conference, 1990.

------ "Theories of Evolution," Address to the Pontifical Academy of Sciences, October 22, 1996, *First Things* 71 (March 1997): 28-29.

Jones, Alexander, ed. *The Jerusalem Bible.* Garden City, NY: 1966.

Jonkers, E. J., ed. *Acta et Symbola Conciliorum quae saeculo quarto habita sunt.* Leiden: E. J. Brill, 1954.

Kaiser, Christopher B. "Extraterrestrial Life and Extraterrestrial Intelligence." *Reformed Review* 51 (Winter 1997-98): 77-91.

Kukla, André. "SETI: On the Prospects and Pursuitworthiness of the Search for Extraterrestrial Intelligence." *Studies in History and Philosophy of Science* 32.1 (2001): 31-67.

Leo the Great. *St. Leo the Great: Sermons*, translated by Jane Freeland and Agnes Conway. Washington, D.C.: The Catholic University of America Press, 1996.

LePage, Andrew J. "Where Could They Hide?" *Scientific American* (July 2000): 40-41.

Lewis, C.S. *Perelandra.* New York: Macmillan Publishing Co., 1944.

------ *Miracles.* New York: McMillan Publishing Co., 1960.

------ "Religion and Rocketry." In *Fern-Seed and Elephants*, edited by Walter Hooper. London: Fontana, 1975.

Liddell, Henry and Robert Scott, eds. *A Greek-English Lexicon*, translated by Henry Stuart and Roderick Mckenzie. Oxford: Clarendon Press, 1948.

Livre des jours. Paris: Le Cerf, 1975.

Long, R. James. "Aquinas and the Cosmic Christ." In *Medieval Masters*, edited by R. E. Houser. Houston: Center for Thomistic Studies, 1999.

Long, Steven A. "On the Possibility of a Purely Natural End for Man." *The Thomist* 64 (January 2000): 211-37.

Lovejoy, Arthur. *The Great Chain of Being.* Cambridge: Harvard University Press, 1936.

Lovejoy, Owen. "Evolution of Man and Its Implications for General Principles of Evolution of Intelligent Life." In *Life in the Universe*, edited by John Billingham. Cambridge: The MIT Press, 1982.

Lucretius. *The Way Things Are*, translated by Rolfe Humphries. Bloomington: Indiana University Press, 1973.

Mallove, Eugene F. *The Quickening Universe.* New York: St. Martin's Press, c1987.

Malone, Michael. *A Layman's Look At Evolution.* Monrovia, California: Catholic Treasures, 1997.

Mayr, Ernst. *Towards a New Philosophy of Biology.* Cambridge: Harvard University Press, 1988.

McAteer, Michael. "The Truth is Out There." *The Toronto Star*, Life Section (17 August 2002): K14.

McMullin, Ernan. "Life and Intelligence Far from Earth: Formulating Theological Issues." In *Many Worlds*, edited by Steven Dick. Philadelphia: Templeton Foundation Press, 2000.

------ "Persons in the Universe." *Zygon* 15.1 (March 1980): 69-89.

Musso, Paolo and Ascheri, Valeria. "Kosmische Missionare?" In *S.E.T.I.— die Suche nach dem Ausserirdischen*, edited by Tobias D. Wabbel. Munich: Beustverlag, 2002.

Naeye, Robert. "Are We Alone in the Universe? Evidence from a variety of scientific fields indicates that we might be the lonely inhabitants of a vast cosmic ocean." *Astronomy* 24 (July 1996): 36-43.

Namer, Émile. *Giordano Bruno.* Paris: Éditions Seghers, 1966.

Nazianzen, Gregory. *Theological Oration 28: On the Doctrine of God.* In *Faith Gives Fullness to Reasoning*, translated by Lionel Wickham and Frederick Williams. Leiden: E. J. Brill, 1991.

Nebe, Gottfried. "Christ, The Body of Christ and Cosmic Powers in Paul's Letters and the New Testament as a Whole." In *Politics and Theopolitics in the Bible and Postbiblical Literature*, edited by Henning Reventlow, Yair Hoffman and Benjamin Uffenheimer. Sheffield, England: Sheffield Academic Press, 1994.

Origen. *De Principiis*. Vol. 4 of *Fathers of the Third Century*, edited by A. Cleveland Coxe. Grand Rapids, Michigan: Wm. B. Eerdmans Publishing Company, 1985.

O'Meara, Thomas F. "Christian Theology and Extraterrestrial Intelligent Life." *Theological Studies* 60 (1999): 3-30.

Pagan-Aguiar, Peter A. "Human Finality." *The Thomist* 64 (July 2000): 375-99.

Paine, Thomas. *The Age of Reason*. Buffalo, NY: Prometheus Books, 1984.

Paterson, Antoinette Mann. *The Infinite Worlds of Giordano Bruno*. Springfield, Illinois: Charles C. Thomas Publisher, 1970.

Peacocke, Arthur. *Theology for a Scientific Age*. Minneapolis: Fortress Press, 1993.

Peters, Ted. "Exo-Theology: Speculations on Extraterrestrial Life." In *The Gods Have Landed*, edited by James R. Lewis. Albany: State University of New York Press, 1995.

Petit, Charles W. "Icing on the red planet." *US News & World Report* (December 23, 2002) 54.

Pius XII. *Divino Afflante Spiritu*. Boston: The Daughters of St. Paul, c1943.

------ *Humani Generis*. Boston: Daughters of St. Paul, c1950.

Plato. *Timaeus*. In *Timaeus, Critias, Cleitophon, Menexenus, Epistles*, translated by R.G. Bury. Cambridge: Harvard University Press, 1975.

Puccetti, Roland. *Persons: a study of possible moral agents in the universe*. New York: Herder and Herder, 1969.

Purves, Bill, Gordon Orians, Craig Heller, and David Sadava, eds. *Life*. 5th edition. Sunderland, Massachusetts: Sinauer Associates, Inc., 1998.

Renaudot, Eusèbe, ed. *Liturgiarum Orientalium collectio*. England: Gregg International Publishers, 1970.

Schaff, Philip and Henry Wace, eds. "Second Ecumenical Council." In *The Seven Ecumenical Councils*, vol. 14 of Nicene and Post-Nicene Fathers of the Christian Church. Grand Rapids, Michigan: Eerdmans, 1986.

Schroeder, H. J., ed. *Council of Trent*, translated by H. J. Schroeder. St. Louis, MO: B. Herder Book Co., 1941.

Scotus, Duns. *Summa Theologica*, edited by Hieronymus de Montefortino. Rome: Typographia Sallustiana, 1903.

Shuch, H. Paul. "Optical SETI and the Arecibo Myth." *Society of Photo-Optical Instrumentation Engineers Proceedings*, 2704 (May 1996).

Smith, Cynthia. *Shadows of Things to Come: The Theological Implications of Intelligent Life on Other Worlds*. Master Thesis. Georgia State University, 2004.

Stannard, Russell. "Our Place in the Scheme of Things." *Research News*, (December 2000): 22

Stravinskas, Peter. *The Bible and the Mass*. Mount Pocono, Pennsylvania: Newman House Press, 2000.

Suarez, Francisco. *De Angelis*. Vol. 2 edited by D. M. André. Paris: Ludovicum Vivès, 1861.

Swenson Jr., George W. "Intragalactically Speaking." *Scientific American* (July 2000): 44-47

Tanzella-Nitti, G. "Extraterrestre, vita." In vol. 1 of "Dizionario Interdisciplinare di Scienza e Fede," edited by G. Tanzella-Nitti and A. Strumia. Rome: Urbanian University Press and Città Nuova, 2002.

Thomas Aquinas. *Compendium Theologiae*. In vol. 1 of *Opuscula Theologica*, edited by Raymond A. Verardo. Rome: Marietti, 1954.

------ *In Aristotelis Librum De Anima Commentarium*. Italy: Marietti, 1959.

------ *In Duodecim Libros Metaphysicorum Aristotelis Expositio*, edited by Raymond M. Spiazzi. Rome: Marietti, 1950.

------ *In Libros Aristotelis De Caelo et Mundo*, edited by Raymond M. Spiazzi. Turin: Marietti, 1952.

------ *In Libros Posterior Analyticorum Expositio*, edited Raymond M. Spiazzi. Turin: Marietti, 1964.

------ *Quaestio Disputata de Anima*. In vol. 2 of *Quaestiones Disputatae*, edited by P. Bazzi. Turin: Marietti, 1965.

------ *Quaestio Disputata de Spiritualibus Creaturis*. In vol. 2 of *Quaestiones Disputatae*, edited by P. Bazzi. Turin: Marietti, 1965.

------ *Quaestiones Disputatae de Malo.* In vol. 2 of *Quaestiones Disputatae*, edited by P. Bazzi. Turin: Marietti, 1965.

------ *Quaestiones Disputatae de Potentia.* In vol. 2 of *Quaestiones Disputatae*, edited by P. Bazzi. Turin: Marietti, 1965.

------ *Quaestiones Disputatae de Veritate.* Vol. 1 of *Quaestiones Disputatae*, edited by Raymond M. Spiazzi. Turin: Marietti, 1964.

------ *Quaestiones Quodlibetales.* In vol. 2 of *Selecta Opuscula*, edited by A. Michaele de Maria. Castello, Italy: Typographica S. Lapi, 1886.

------ *Scriptum super Sententiis.* Paris: Lethielleux, 1956.

------ *Summa Contra Gentiles*, edited by C. Pera. Turin: Marietti, 1961.

------ *Summa Theologiae*, edited by Instituti Studiorum Medievalium Ottaviensis. Ottawa: Commissio Piana, 1953.

------ *Super Epistolas S. Pauli*, edited by P. Raphaelis Cai. Rome: Marietti, 1953.

Thorne, Kip. *Black Holes and Time Warps.* New York: Norton & Co., 1994.

Tough, Allen. *Crucial Questions about the Future.* Lanham, Maryland: University of America Press, 1991.

Vakoch, D. A. "Roman Catholic views of extraterrestrial intelligence: Anticipating the future by examining the past." In *When SETI succeeds: The impact of high-information contact*, edited by Allen Tough. Bellevue, Washington: Foundation for the Future, 2000.

Vatican Council I in *Dogmatic Canons and Decrees*, translated by Cardinal Manning. Rockford, Illinois: Tan Books and Publishers, Inc., 1977.

Visser, Matt. *Lorentzian Wormholes: from Einstein to Hawking.* New York: American Institute of Physics Press, 1995.

Visser, M., S. Kar, and N. Dadhich, "Traversable wormholes with arbitrarily small energy condition violations." *Physical Review Letters* 90, 201102, (2003).

Ward, Keith. *Religion and Human Nature.* Oxford: Clarendon Press, 1998.

Ward, Peter D., and Donald Brownlee: *Rare Earth Why Complex Life is Uncommon in the Universe.* New York: Copernicus, 2000).

Webb, Stephen. *Where is Everybody? Fifty Solutions to the Fermi Paradox and the Problem of Extraterrestrial Life.* New York: Copernicus Books, 2002.

Webster's New Collegiate Dictionary. Springfield, Massachusetts: G. & C. Merriam Company, 1980.

Weigel, George. *Letters to a Young Catholic.* New York: Basic Books, 2004.

Whewell, William. *Of the Plurality of Worlds*, edited by Michael Ruse. Chicago: The University of Chicago Press, 2001. Reprint of original 1853 edition.

Whitfield, John. "Alien hunters take a closer look." *Nature Science Update* (March 12, 2003): websource.

Wiker, Benjamin D. "Alien Ideas Christianity and the Search for Extraterrestrial Life." *Crisis*, (November 4, 2002): 26-31.

Wilkenson, David. *Alone in the Universe.* Crowborough, East Sussex, Great Britain: Monarch Publications, 1997.

Wilson, Edward O. *The Diversity of Life.* Cambridge: Harvard University Press, 1992.

Name Index

Albert, 61-64, 104-105, 150, 250

Anselm, 91, 229, 232, 267

Aquinas, ix, 4-5, 7, 9, 17, 21, 24-26, 28-29, 31, 33, 35-37, 41, 43, 49, 64, 68, 71, 79-80, 82-86, 91-92, 94-96, 98, 104-106, 111-113, 143, 149-155, 171, 198-207, 209-210, 218-219, 223-225, 229-233, 235, 237, 244, 248, 250, 255-256, 258, 262-264, 268, 270, 272, 275

Aristotle, 55, 62, 64, 79, 104, 143, 152-154, 162, 169, 213, 215, 234, 248, 250-252, 255, 257-258, 267

Athanasius, 67, 220, 229, 256, 267

Augustine, 52, 62, 65, 70, 72-73, 90, 114, 151, 204, 219-220, 237, 267

Barrow, 138-139, 195, 242-243, 245-246, 253, 265, 267

Basil, 28, 67, 220, 267

Brewster, 18

Bonaventure, 67, 214, 221, 236, 268

Bruno, 74-75, 217, 223, 270, 273-274

Clement of Alexandria, 62, 70-71, 222, 268

Clement of Rome, 62, 68, 70, 221, 268

Conway Morris, 129, 134, 146, 239-240, 242-243, 245, 248, 268

Corbally, ix, 189, 228, 263, 268

Cousins, 127

Crowe, ix, 6, 62, 123, 134, 143, 201, 204, 209-210, 213, 216, 230, 240, 244, 247-248, 252, 254, 257, 264, 269

Darling, ix, 85, 123, 125, 129-131, 133, 227, 239-240, 242, 244-245, 269

Davies, 2, 139, 143, 146-149, 151-155, 160, 195, 197, 217, 239, 246, 249-251, 255, 264-265, 269

de Cazre, 168, 257

De Duve, 162, 241, 251, 255, 269

Delano, 3, 159-161, 197, 254-255, 269

Democritus, 61, 64, 66-67, 149
Denton, 85, 226-227, 269
Dick, 2-3, 6, 197, 217-218, 221, 238, 249, 269-270, 273
Drake, 135, 140, 181, 199, 226, 245-246, 270
Drees, 181, 260
Eddington, 157, 254
Epicurus, 61, 64, 66-67, 144, 147, 149
Fermi, 137, 139-142, 245, 248, 251, 276
Filachou, 35, 47, 210, 213
Friedman, 160, 255
Galileo, 84, 171-172, 216-217, 226, 257, 259, 263, 267, 270
Gassendi, 143, 168, 257
Gould, 128-129, 132, 144-145, 147, 241-242, 248, 270
Harris, 148, 249, 271
Hippolytus, 62, 66, 220, 232, 271
Hoyle, 195
Jaki, 3, 180, 197, 200, 242, 260, 271
Jastrow, 1-2, 52-53, 161, 167, 197, 215, 255, 257, 271
Jerome, 62, 65-66, 70, 220, 271
John Chrysostom, 67, 220
John of Damascus, 69-70, 222, 271
John of the Cross, 1
Lewis, 88, 110-111, 113, 198, 202, 228, 236, 257, 272, 274
Lovejoy, 85, 133, 223, 226, 243, 273
Lucretius, 143-144, 146-147, 149, 248, 273
Mallove, 151, 250, 273
Mayr, 130-134, 242-243, 273
McMullin, 123, 127, 199, 224, 240, 253, 270, 273
Melanchthon, 59, 217
Milgram, 106
Miller, 124
Montignez, 18, 54, 210, 216
O'Meara, ix, 184, 187, 219, 261, 274
Origen, 62, 64-68, 70-71, 210, 219-221, 274

Paine, 2-3, 40, 87, 173-176, 179, 182, 197, 210, 228, 260, 274
Pascal, 159, 162
Peacocke, 167, 252, 263, 274
Philastrius, 62, 66, 220
Pius II, 10, 73-74
Plato, 88, 215, 274
Pseudo-Dionysius, 106
Pucetti, 102, 234
Sagan, 139, 141, 247
Sappho, 143
Sawyer, 182
Simpson, 62, 68-71
Stannard, 160, 197, 255, 271, 275
Suarez, 51, 214, 236, 275
Tarter, 181, 260
Tipler, 138-139, 195, 242-243, 245-246, 253, 265, 267
Virgilius, 72-73, 222
Whewell, 53, 156-157, 202, 215, 250, 253-255, 277
Wiker, 149, 249, 277
Wilkins, 60, 218
Wilkinson, 215, 265
Wilson, 145, 248, 277
Zachary, 72-73, 222
Zaninus, 73-74

Scripture Index

Acts 17:24, 11, 201

Col. 1:15, 28
Col. 1:15-20, 75, 93
Col. 1:16, 49
Col. 1:18-20, 33-34, 39-40, 186
Col. 2:10, 188, 205

1 Co. 1: 21, 91
1 Co. 4:15-16, 40
1 Co. 8:5-6, 26-27
1 Co. 11:7-11, 94
1 Co. 11:8, 230
1 Co. 12, 234
2 Co. 1:18, 256

Ep. 1:10, 33, 185, 209
Ep. 1:8-10, 20, 23, 28, 93, 106, 186
Ep. 1:20-22, 93, 185, 187
Ep. 2:15, 211
Ep. 3:9-12, 93, 186
Ep. 4:10, 185-186, 263

Gal. 1:8, 191
Gal. 2:21, 29

Gen. 1:12, 168
Gen. 1:20, 168

Gen. 1:27, 44
Gen. 1:28, 47
Gen. 2:27, 258
Gen. 3:19, 258
Gen. 6:4, 202
Gen. 9:3-4, 47

Hab. 3:11, 258

Heb. 1:2, 1, 69
Heb. 1:14, 49
Heb. 2:8-9, 187
Heb. 2:10-18, 36, 96, 119, 231-232
Heb. 2:11, 36, 210
Heb. 2:14, 37-39, 40, 42, 75, 189, 211
Heb. 2:16, 49, 190
Heb. 2:17, 38, 49, 190
Heb. 4:15, 232
Heb. 9:14, 100
Heb. 10:12, 14-15, 34
Heb. 11:3, 69

Is. 45:12, 18

Jn. 1:18, 98
Jn. 3:5, 22
Jn. 12:32, 34
Jn. 17:5, 18
Jn. 18:37, 99
Jn. 19:11, 230
1 Jn. 3:2, 256
1 Jn. 4:9-10, 19

Jb. 34:24, 213
Jb. 38:7, 202

Jos. 10:13, 169

1 K. 18:20-40, 102

Lk. 1:28, 32
Lk. 1:43, 40
Lk. 1:79, 97
Lk. 2:52, 230

Mk. 7:26-28, 215

Mt. 9:6, 100
Mt. 18:10, 261
Mt. 20:1-16, 54
Mt. 23:10, 39
Mt. 25:31, 48

2 P. 1:4, 256
2 P. 2:4, 261

Ph. 2:6-11, 27, 187
Ph. 2:7, 92, 231
Ph. 3:7, 17

Phm. 10, 211

Ps. 2, 18
Ps. 8, 18, 47, 162, 202
Ps. 19, 157, 254
Ps. 49, 18
Ps. 60, 18
Ps. 89, 69
Ps. 93, 258
Ps. 104, 177
Ps. 139, 42

Qo. 1:15, 56
Qo. 7:30, 22

Rev. 17:14, 116
Rev. 5: 1-3, 7-14, 183

Rom. 1:20-21, 157
Rom. 4:11, 206
Rom. 5: 6, 19
Rom. 5:9, 56
Rom. 5:12, 37, 256
Rom. 5:12-19, 114, 200
Rom. 5:15-19, 38-39
Rom. 5:17, 37, 200
Rom. 5:18, 232
Rom. 8:21, 258
Rom. 8:29, 163
Rom. 8:30, 256
Rom. 11, 215
Rom. 14:9, 93, 185

1 Tim. 4:10, 33
2 Tim. 3:16-17, 59
2 Tim 4:3, 180

Tob. 8:6, 201

Tt. 2:12-13, 222
Tt. 1:14, 211

Subject Index

arguments,
  ad hominem, 160
  by fittingness, 95, 175-176, 211
  probable, 4, 6, 32, 57, 76, 109-110, 116, 119, 174-175, 178, 182, 192, 228, 236, 238
angels,
  achieved beatitude, 24, 29, 50, 51, 58
  relation to man, 48-49
  repair of the fall of, 49, 213, 235-236
Adam, 2, 10-12, 22, 38-40, 50, 55, 73-75, 94, 97, 101, 111-114, 118, 171, 191, 201-202, 211, 223, 231, 233, 258, 263
appeal to authority, 159, 254
appeal to ignorance, 159
anthropocentrism, 55-56, 59, 130, 161-163, 188, 192-193, 264
Antipodes, 72-73, 222
Archaea, 126
arrogance, 55-56, 160, 184, 193, 254
atheism, 143-144, 146-148, 155-156, 249
begging the question, 160-161, 181
Bible, 19-20, 59, 168-169, 172, 201, 205, 216-217, 228, 235, 256, 272, 274-275
Catholic Church, documents of, 4, 8, 10-11, 18, 42-43, 61, 71-75
causality,
  efficient, 30, 50-51, 56, 151-152, 155, 214, 250
  final, 30, 151, 155, 250
chain of being, 87, 179, 223
chance, 128-129, 132, 135, 143-146, 149-155, 248-249, 252
Copernican revolution, 57, 74-75, 168, 216-217
communication,
  problem of, 63, 102-107, 114, 119, 149-150, 178

faster than light, 103, 106, 178
contingency, 127-129, 132, 135, 143-145, 147-148, 154-155, 242, 248
convergence, 84, 129-132, 134-135, 146, 242, 244
design, 143, 146, 148-149, 152, 155, 242
determinism, biological, 146, 152, 154-155, 249, 251
Drake equation, 135, 181, 245
Earth,
  home of man, 11, 44, 209
  property of humans, 47, 55
  rare planet, 134-135, 244-245
  special planet, 44, 53-54, 57-58, 92, 186, 216-217
efficient cause, see causality, efficient and specialness, human
eukaryotes, 128
evolution,
  and Scripture, 170-172
  of higher life forms, 127-134
ETIs,
  anatomy and physiology of, 83-86
  created in glory, 24
  made for supernatural happiness, 20-23
  nature of, 7-9, 12-13, 85-86
  unfallen, 20-23, 40, 42, 52, 57, 75-76, 96, 98, 100-102, 104, 109-114, 117-118, 120, 141, 174-176, 182, 192, 230, 236-237
extreme thermophiles, 126
Fall, 19, 22, 25, 35, 37-39, 50-51, 101, 110-112, 170, 173, 175, 178-180, 191, 193, 237, 247, 258
final cause, 30, 50, 151, 250
geocentrism, 64, 67, 168, 172, 216
God,
  as artist, 88, 157-158
  as master of history, 100, 233, 264
heresy, 41
human being,
  as cosmic accident, 144, 147, 152, 154, 244, 249
  as image of God, 8-9, 44-47, 55, 58, 94, 162-162, 189, 212, 214, 255-257, 259-260
  constraints on anatomy and physiology, 83-88

in the state of grace, 22, 111, 157, 163
human intelligence, 8, 47, 54, 128, 130-131, 134, 162, 178, 200
human nature, 8-9, 11-13, 17, 54, 96, 107, 111-112, 131, 163, 192, 213, 258
human race,
  greatness of, 56, 159, 162
  mediocrity of, 55-56, 162
  unity of, 10-12, 37, 73-74, 115, 191, 259
Humani Generis, 10-11, 21, 184, 200, 202-203, 232, 259, 274
Incarnation,
  benefits of, 26, 97-100
  extraordinary event, 91-92
incarnations,
  likelihood of multiple, 30-33, 92-95, 116-120, 178, 238
  possibility of multiple, 26
incompatibility of the two beliefs, claims as to, 2-3, 40-41, 59, 173-175, 181-182
intelligence,
  immateriality of, 7-9, 46, 131, 259
interactivity argument, 104-109, 118, 149-150, 177-178
Jesus Christ,
  central place in universe, 31, 58, 93, 110, 184-189, 192-193,
  Cosmic, 39, 94, 167, 184-186, 188, 191, 205, 249, 263-264, 271-274
  died to save members of Adam's race, 36-40, 51
  head, 24-25, 28-33, 35, 57, 114, 117, 188, 190, 205-207
  Lord, 24-27, 31, 35, 93-94, 114, 116, 185, 187-189, 204-205, 210
  savior of all, 33-35, 39, 184
Jupiter, 135, 245
Kingdom of God, 25, 50, 190, 204, 263
life, origin of, 5, 124-127, 134, 240, 248
Limbo, 17, 22, 175
materialism, 7-8, 131, 200
Mars, 123-126, 139, 187, 238-239, 244
Mary, Queen over all, 94
Moon, 69, 72, 135, 177, 187, 210, 221-222, 239, 244, 259-260
necessity, 143, 146-148, 150, 153-155, 248
necessity of the matter, 150, 250

particularism, 53-54
personal attack, 160-161, 181, 254
planets, inhabitable, 5, 124, 127, 134-135
plenitude, principle of, 79-83, 89, 190
pluralism, 61-62, 66-71, 143, 155, 252
process philosophy, 148
race, 11, 12
redemption, 17-18, 25-26, 30-31, 35, 51-58, 75, 100, 110-111, 118, 173, 176, 186, 188-190, 193, 204, 209-210, 228, 247-248, 261, 263
redundancy, 63, 79-80, 83, 86-87, 89, 96, 107, 118-119, 151, 155, 176, 228
Scripture,
   interpretation of, 17, 32-33, 39-41, 168-171, 259
   official interpretations of, 17, 40-41, 177
   purpose of, 18, 38, 60, 168-169, 172, 188
   relevance of to ETI debate, 3, 18, 184-188
SETI, 2, 140-142, 147, 240, 243, 246-248, 260, 267, 272, 275-276
silence, argument from Scripture's, 20, 59, 218
space, colonization of, 137-139, 246
special, definition of, 43-44
special creation, 43, 46, 57, 200, 217
specialness, human,
   created to the image of God, 44-47, 58, 189
   details of salvation history tailored to, 96, 100-101, 114, 176
   esteemed or favored by God, 55-56
   natural end of non-rational creation, 47-48, 189
   pinnacle of creation, 19, 44, 46-47, 144, 152
   role as efficient cause, 50-52, 56, 190
special providence, 43, 46, 57, 212-213
species,
   biological, 10-13, 74, 86-87
   philosophical, 10, 12, 84, 86, 201, 225
stars, animate, 7, 59, 218
stock, 10, 12, 36-37, 94, 97, 176
teleology, argument for extraterrestrial existence, 155-158, 253
theism, 143, 146-149, 152, 155, 172, 200

tradition, 17, 33, 60-62, 64, 70-72, 74-75, 97, 106, 111, 178, 185, 188, 189-190, 218
UFOs, 2, 5, 7, 195, 198, 261
unique, definition of, 33
uniqueness
  as a perfection, 87-89
  argument against ETIs based upon, 89-90, 95, 118, 175-176
universe,
size of, 156
unity of, 63, 104-105, 119, 149

978-0-595-35827-4
0-595-35827-6

Made in the USA
Lexington, KY
25 July 2015